BEFORE THE FLOOD

BEFORE THE FLOOD

A Gaza Family Memoir

*Across Three Generations of Colonial Invasion,
Occupation, and War in Palestine*

RAMZY BAROUD

FOREWORD BY **ILAN PAPPÉ**

SEVEN STORIES PRESS
NEW YORK • OAKLAND • LONDON

Seven Stories Press
140 Watts Street
New York, NY 10013
www.sevenstories.com

College professors and high school and middle school teachers may order free examination copies of Seven Stories Press titles. Visit https://www.sevenstories.com/pg/resources-academics or email academic@sevenstories.com.

Library of Congress Cataloging-in-Publication Data is on file.

ISBN: 978-1-64421-528-9 (paperback)
ISBN: 978-1-64421-529-6 (ebook)

Printed in the USA.

9 8 7 6 5 4 3 2 1

To my sister,
Dr. Soma Mohammed Mohammed Baroud.

*I write your name in full, because that is how it
appeared on the white body bag that held your
remains soon after the bomb was dropped.*

Contents

Acknowledgments

This book would not have been possible without the contributions of many family members, relatives, and colleagues in Gaza, most of whom communicated their stories, memories, and ideas while being chased by Israeli bombs from one refugee encampment to another.

To my family, whose love, support, and patience keep me strong, thank you for always being there for me.

My sister, Dr. Soma Baroud, and her husband, Professor Hamdi Baroud, were both assassinated when Israel targeted Gaza's medical staff and educators. They were both critical to my understanding of the current events in Gaza. Their legacies and memories will inspire my future writings as well.

Ibrahim, Wafa, and Mohammed al-Badrasawi were critical to the book's narrative. Even after Ibrahim lost his daughter, two of his brothers, and a grandson, he remained committed to telling his family's story.

Asia al-Masouabi lost her husband and son during the current genocide and had lost other close family members during Israel's previous massacres of Palestinian people. Yet she continued to tell the story of loss, horror, and resilience experienced and displayed by her family and all Palestinians throughout the current war.

Nasser al-Badrasawi was killed by Israeli bombing while still in the process of conducting interviews. He helped shape the book's narrative in its early stages and later became part of the story. I am forever indebted to his valiant spirit.

Israel killed A.A., a Gazan researcher and a young academic who helped gather interviews for the book from several generations of displaced Palestinian people, along with his family in the Nuseirat Massacre on June 8, 2024. He was an example of Palestinian intellectual resistance at its finest. His undying spirit resonates throughout this book.

Although the book was written during a time that was—and continues to be—extraordinarily traumatic and demanding for writers, academics, and journalists concerned with the situation in Palestine, many have generously contributed their time to ensure the utmost quality of this work.

Romana Rubeo, an Italian journalist and intellectual who helped manage the research process for this book from the first chapter to the very last, has been essential to the production of the volume. Without her immense contributions, it would not have seen the light.

Professors Ilan Pappé, Blake Alcott, Jeremy Salt, Sunnivie Brydun, Daud Abdallah, Brahim Aoude, Liana Petranek, and Salman Abu Sitta: I thank all of you profusely for your help, as well as for your proud legacies and ongoing work to better the world's understanding of the just struggle of the Palestinian people.

Ben Boulton's perfectionist editing style has helped convey the book's intricate history in the clearest way possible.

Thank you also to those who have supported and inspired me throughout the years, whether to undertake this crucial project or carry on with my work in academia and journalism. Roger Waters, the late John Pilger, Noam Chomsky, Claude Zurbach, Dr. Sami Al-Arian, Nurah Tape, Samaa Abu Sharar, Robert Inlakesh, John Harvey, Sylvia DeMelo, Professor Ghada Karmi, Rachel Blevins, Scott Horton, Natalie Morris, Peter Lavelle, Paul Salvatori, Malcolm Hugues, Louis Brehony, Bruno Rufini, Michel Tellone, Cynthia Franklin, the Center for Islam and Global Affairs (CIGA) at Istanbul Sabahattin Zaim University, the European Centre for Palestine Studies at the University of Exeter, the Gaza youth of "We Are Not Numbers," the team at the "Palestine Deep Dive," *YES! Magazine*, and many more. I am grateful to all of you for your love, support, and assistance throughout the years.

Greg Ruggiero and the staff at Seven Stories Press, thank you for your critical work and for always giving Palestine and other just struggles the space they deserve in your publications.

And last but definitely not least, thank you to the people of Gaza, as without you, there would be no story of patience, faith, and heroism worth telling.

Foreword

BY ILAN PAPPÉ

Too often numbers numb us. What does it mean that 750,000 Palestinians were uprooted by force in 1948? Do we understand it better if we replace this by saying "half of Palestine's population" was expelled? Would people in other countries be able to imagine what the expulsion of half a population within a period of less of nine months looks like?

Are people able to comprehend a genocide just by referring to numbers? Is this the result of repeating the unbelievable number of 50,000 Palestinians slaughtered in less than a year, or even worse, the much higher estimate of around 200,000, which some believe to be the actual death toll? Is general reference to the killings of babies and old people enough to comprehend the crime against humanity we have witnessed in Gaza throughout 2024 and the first half of 2025? And does it mean that people who read news, within this context, cannot relate to the "mere" 1,000 Palestinians killed in the West Bank during the same period?

These numbers do not convey the level of dehumanization suffered by Palestinians in 1948 and ever since. Nor does the focus on the number of people killed over the years tell the full story of the daily abuse faced by Palestinians wherever they have been during the last seventy-six years: banishment, harassment, imprisonment without trial, demolition of houses, destruction of fields, business, educational institutions. The list is long and what it ultimately represents is the total violation of Palestinian's basic civil and human rights. In any case, such abstractions, even in the hands of the best wordsmiths, cannot begin to express what it has meant to be Palestinian in the last seventy-seven years.

It is crucial to overcome this numbness, because if it prevails, then one subscribes to the Israeli narrative that every Palestinian action is terrorism and that the attack on October 7, 2023 was the worst kind of terrorism, even barbarism. In fact, without overcoming this kind of detachment, the essence of and justification for Palestinian resistance in all its forms can never be fully appreciated.

This mental barrier, in combination with other factors, has made the Palestinian cause a contentious issue when it should never have been one. It must be challenged, as it already is by those with a modicum of decency, who view the Palestinian cause as one the most important issues of justice of our times. These people have already humanized the Palestinian experience and victimhood. This book aims to galvanize many more for the crucial alliance that will eventually help liberate Palestine.

There is no better way to do this than through the story of a family told by a family member who is also an author, an analyst, a scholar, and a committed human being. We are fortunate that Ramzy Baroud embodies all of these qualities.

He tells us the story of the Palestinian countryside and its evolution over centuries until it was destroyed and scorched during the Nakba, a countryside that, until the arrival of Zionism, was thriving in places such as Beit Daras. This village, located about thirty kilometers from Gaza City, was described by a British delegation in 1882—the year Zionism arrived—as a flourishing village surrounded by "gardens and olive groves," with a pond adjacent to it. This was the so-called "desert" and "empty land" or the "land without people," described by Zionist propaganda—a narrative that, unfortunately, some still subscribe to today.

Like the other 350 villages that Israel destroyed during the Nakba, Beit Daras enjoyed accelerated development during and after World War II and could have followed a trajectory of modernity, prosperity, and independence. Instead, the people of Beit Daras found themselves in the densely populated mega refugee camp that Israel created in 1948, now known as the Gaza Strip. The Strip did not exist before 1948; it was created because Israel could not drive hundreds of thousands of Palestinians over the Egyptian border, so it "gave up" a small part of historical Palestine to function as a massive refugee camp.

The family arrived at the al-Shati refugee camp, a camp within the camp of the Gaza Strip. By giving these refugees a name, a place of birth, and a family history, Baroud humanizes the numbers mentioned at the beginning of this foreword. But he does more than that. By narrating the daily acts of resilience and resistance, the humanity of the Palestinians shines through the blanket of deception and defamation that Israeli propaganda uses to obscure the reality in Gaza and Palestine. After reading this book, it becomes difficult to accept the Western portrayal of the people of Gaza as terrorists or faceless refugees.

Baroud offers us two powerful contributions. The first is

a reminder that not one, but three generations of his family have endured a relentless and ruthless attempt to displace and destroy them. Each generation, in its own time, exhibited epic resistance and resilience in the face of a settler-colonial state predicated on what the late scholar Patrick Wolfe framed as the "logic of elimination of the native," which is at the heart of any settler-colonial project. The second contribution is an original and fascinating explanation of the longevity and intensity of this resilience and resistance in Gaza in particular. This steadfastness is a long-term historical structure—what French historians referred as *longue durée*—an attitude that has become part of the DNA of the people of Gaza. This is where we learn that the emergence of Palestinian resistance, and particularly their inventive tunnel system, is the product of long-term historical experience. In this way, Baroud dismantles the Israeli narrative that resistance in Gaza is merely a proxy for Iranian policy in the region.

On reading about the horrors each generation has had to endure, you may feel emotionally depleted. Yet, at the same time, such a story instils hope that the immense sacrifices made by Palestinians over the years have not been in vain. They will eventually be rewarded with freedom and liberation, allowing for the rebuilding of the pre-Nakba Beit Daras, Gaza, and Palestine—a village, a region, and a country where Jews, Muslims, and Christians once genuinely coexisted. It was a Palestine that was part of the Arab world, enmeshed for centuries with the Islamic civilization surrounding it, one that can still become a beacon for the Middle East as a whole.

The Long History of Resistance

"One cannot give oneself courage if one does not have it." This line comes from Alessandro Manzoni's novel, *The Betrothed.*[1] It was uttered by Don Abbondio, a priest in the historical novel who courageously accepts his own cowardice.

Indeed, courage is not given. Like sacrifice, faith, camaraderie, community, resilience, even love itself, courage is an organic process that is innately formulated, often by circumstances beyond our reach. Collectively, such complex social structures could take many generations in the making, a process of which we are hardly cognizant.

Some traditional historians—who continue to subscribe to the methods of *histoire événementielle*, or event history—tend to ignore the remarkable effect of historical phenomena that often, over the course of many years or even centuries, impact our collective behavior. In his foreword to this book, Ilan Pappé references *longue durée*, the long-term consequences of history, a concept crafted by the founders and disciples of the French Annales School.[2]

Credible history can only be seen in its totality, not merely as the total events of history, recent or old, but as the sum of feelings; the culmination of ideas; the evolution of collective consciousness, identities, and relationships; and the subtle changes occurring in societies over the course of time. Palestinians are the perfect example of history being shaped by ideas, not guns; memories, not politics, collective hope, or international relations. The Palestinian people will eventually win their freedom because they have invested in a long-term trajectory of ideas, memories, and communal aspirations, which often translate to spirituality, a deep, immovable faith that grows stronger, even during times of genocide.

In my 2020 interview with the former United Nations Special Rapporteur, Professor Richard Falk, he summarized the struggle in Palestine as a war between those with arms against those with legitimacy. He said that in the context of national liberation movements, there are two kinds of war: the actual war, as in soldiers carrying guns, and the war for legitimacy. The one who wins the latter will ultimately prevail.[3]

Was it the knowledge of such an irreversible historical truth that led the Israeli historian Benny Morris to express his growing sense of pessimism about his country's future? "The Palestinians look at everything from a broad, long-term perspective," he said in an interview with the newspaper *Haaretz* in 2019. "They see that at the moment, there are five-six-seven million Jews here, surrounded by hundreds of millions of Arabs. They have no reason to give in, because the Jewish state can't last. They are bound to win. In another thirty to fifty years, they will overcome us, come what may."[4]

Morris is right: Palestinians will not give up. There can never be a situation where societies indefinitely survive and thrive based on a permanent system of racial apartheid, violence, and exclusion. The very history of Palestine—which I highlight in this book using people's history and personalized narratives—is a testament to such a truth. If the oppressed, the Indigenous of the land, are not fully vanquished, they will rise, resist, fight, and win back their freedom, thus eventually winning the legitimacy war. Morris is right again when he indicates that Palestinian people collectively "look at everything from a broad, long-term perspective." Agreeing with his argument may seem odd: societies are often fragmented by class struggles and competing socioeconomic agendas instead of unified by solidarity and a cohesive long-term collective vision. This is where *longue durée* becomes relevant in the Palestinian case. Even if Palestinians have not made a common agreement to wait for the invaders to leave, or for Palestine to once again become a place of social, racial, and religious coexistence, they are driven, even if subconsciously, by the same energy that compelled their ancestors to push back against the invaders. Characters in this book fulfill the historical role that was assigned to them by circumstances beyond their control. They are reanimating the past, just as their descendants will shape the future.

While many Western politicians today characterize Palestinian people as "terrorists," blaming victims for resisting their own oppression, Palestinian society continues to evolve based on entirely independent dynamics. For example, the culture of *Muqawama*—Resistance—is deeply ingrained in Palestine. It is a culture as old as time. Innate. Intuitive. Intergenerational. It precedes the birth of Israel by thousands of years. Batis put it to the test when he led Gaza in legendary battles against the Macedonian invasion fomented by Alexander the Great in 332 BC. Batis may seem to be a footnote in this book, but, in fact, if read carefully, you will discover that he is the central character. He is the Zaher al-Umar al-Zaydani, the Izz al-Din al-Qassam, the Ghassan Kanafani, and Ehab al-Badrasawi, around whom this story is centered. The deep-rooted historical continuum between the Palestinian past, present, and future is the very essence of this book.

Before the Flood speaks of many things and many people, but ultimately it is about a branch of my family that has chosen to write—with their blood—a chapter in the unending Palestinian saga, demonstrating that history is not moved just by short-term events, but by countless factors. While in-the-moment events are important, *longue durée* provides a more profound understanding of our collective trajectory. *Longue durée* is concerned with historical shifts and changes that are situated within the realm of notions, ideas, collective perceptions, identities, and feelings, like courage and self-sacrifice for the sake of the group. These are the kinds of feelings that "one cannot give oneself . . . if one does not have."

The anti-fascist intellectual Antonio Gramsci spoke about the importance of culture as a driver of history and meaning. "Culture isn't having a well-stocked warehouse of news but is the ability that our mind has to understand life, the place we hold there, our relationship with other people. Those who are aware of themselves and of everything, who feel the relationship with all other beings."[5] For a writer, these relationships fall under the concept of positionality, as in the relationship between the intellectual and their position, and how their position relates to the subject matter. This useful tool has given historians, especially those from the Global South, the power to navigate the painful terrain of our own victimization and long histories of oppression.

In this and all of my previous books, I have attempted to slowly liberate the Palestinian narrative from the convenient histories imposed on my people. It is not an easy task, but an unavoidable one. This book is my latest, and hopefully best, attempt at freeing Palestine from the confines of superimposed language, historical events, recurring dates, dehumanizing statistics, and outright deception. Here, I try to place the Palestinian narrative in entirely different intellectual and historical frameworks, where only truly representative Palestinian voices are centered. I try to prove that the seemingly weak and dispensable peasants, laborers, and workers—the *fellahin*—are the most influential actors in the story of Palestine, past and present, and that while AI, drones, fighter jets, and bunker-buster bombs may impact short-term events, courage, faith, and communal love will determine long-term history.

As you continue reading this, I hope that you will understand why Palestinians are not history's passive victims, but, over the course of generations, its masters—the ones who shape it and the future as well.

Many characters began their relationship with this narrative as storytellers or researchers, but soon became victims of the Israelis' genocide, thus becoming the story. When one of those storytellers was killed, another seamlessly continued where they left off—a wife telling the story of her husband, the son of his father, the sister of her brother. Without prior coordination, they shaped the narrative with no gaps or interruptions. This achievement is not my own. It is theirs.

As I continued to write, my position went beyond storyteller into something else entirely, at times gory and frightening, deeply emotional and raw. When the genocidal war started on October 7, 2023, whole branches of my family perished in large numbers. Scores of my cousins, their wives, husbands, and children, died under the rubble of their homes in the most horrific and unimaginable ways. Some were burned alive. Others were shot by snipers. A few were executed while taking refuge at hospitals or standing in line in UN feeding centers, hoping to fetch a loaf of bread.

The images on this book's cover attempt to honor some of the faces of those lost in the genocide. But no single cover could ever contain all the innocent lives that were extinguished. Even if such a space existed, entire families have been obliterated—burned away with their photo albums. And yet, their beautiful faces, their warmth, and their stories remain etched in our hearts forever.

The photographs chosen here are intimately tied to the lives portrayed in this book—including Ehab, the central character, and members of his immediate al-Badrasawi family, who were killed in harrowing succession, one after the other, before his own death and continuing still. Among them is my sister Soma, the beloved doctor of Khan Younis. Her murder is not only a tragedy—it is a rupture that runs through the very center of my family's story, marking even the chapters yet unwritten, for generations to come.

As I turned to my final task of writing the introduction, I wanted to situate the book in what I believe to be the proper historical context. I have always argued that it was not the Balfour Declaration of 1917 that injected my people into the world's historical discourse; it was not Israel that made us relevant by ethnically cleansing the Palestinians in 1948. But I struggled to define the single most critical event in our history, if any existed, that could serve as the starting point of our historical trajectory. This is when my sister Soma, one of Gaza's most beloved medical doctors, was assassinated by the Israeli army on October 9, 2024, while on her way back from Al-Nasser Hospital in Khan

Yunis. I say assassinated because she was the 166th doctor and 987th medical worker to be deliberately killed by Israel up to that date, part of the Israeli plan to annex our land and dismantle all aspects of Palestinian life and societal continuity.

After days of mourning, it dawned on me that Soma, in her beauty, cleverness, wisdom, patience, and, yes, courage and sacrifice, had always represented the single moment that demarcated the history of our people. Soma, or the representation of all the Somas of our history—including the history yet to be written—gives us meaning, inspires us, and grants us hope and courage.

Benny Morris, a devout Zionist himself, is right to observe that "Palestinians look at everything from a broad, long-term perspective." Indeed, we do, even if, at times, we are not aware of it. Perhaps this lack of constant awareness allows us to continue for generations on the long collective journey to defend our historical home and freedom.

Prelude

A swift decision. A loud boom.
Ehab was gone. This time, forever.

This was not the first time Ehab al-Badrasawi had disappeared. In the past, he always came back. When his mother was still alive, he would depart by saying "pray for me" before stepping outside. She knew exactly what this meant, and learned to pray quietly and say little else. She hardly argued with anyone, only when visited by her "companion." Only then, she was expressive, loud, angry, and at times unstoppable.

But it was not her fault, as her "companion" deserved the blame. After he departed from her body, she returned to her usual state—outwardly docile and kind, but often feeling dejected and abused. She prayed and cried for everyone, keeping out of others' way.

Her name was Madallah Abdulnabi—the extension of God, the servant of the Prophet—and she came from the village of Beit Daras. Among the people of the village, her family long had the good reputation for having plenty of *baraka*—blessing power, a divine gift—and was held in high esteem dating back before Zionist militias ethnically cleansed the region, forcing the community into Shati Refugee Camp* in the late 1940s. Even in the camp, when everyone was mostly interested in mere survival, the reputation persisted, and Madallah—later "Umm Ibrahim"—inherited the "gift" of transcending to another sphere of existence. Yes, she communicated with the "others"—those we must not speak about openly or frequently, only in whispers, gestures, and codes—and sometimes seemed to acquire the power to heal in the process.

But the girl was not crazy, as family members before her also had similar abilities to see things beyond our earthly awareness. What Israelis call their War of Independence, Palestinians call the Nakba—the catastrophe.[6] When the Nakba took place, she went mute for months. She was deeply sensitive and spiritual and, many years later, despite her husband's abuse, she remained committed to him but, more importantly, to her five sons and six daughters, whom she was connected to in ways that many cannot comprehend, let alone relate to. A few days before the Black Sunday** when an Israeli killed her second youngest son Wael, her body was tormented by unfathomable pain. She had begged him and the others to stay home. They disobeyed, promising not to venture far. Wael was shot in the throat as he stood on a corner by his home.

Madallah suffered this torment again years later when her daughter Sumiya died after drinking, at the behest of her moth-

---

* Al-Shati, also known as Shati or Beach camp, is a Palestinian refugee camp located in the northern Gaza Strip along the Mediterranean Sea coastline in Gaza City. It was formally established as a refugee camp in 1950 to host about 23,000 Palestinians who were expelled from their villages and towns across Palestine.

** On May 20, 1990, a group of Palestinian workers from Gaza were waiting to board an Israeli bus to go to work. An Israeli soldier checked their IDs and forced them to kneel on the ground before opening fire, killing seven. Palestinians subsequently referred to this as "Black Sunday."

er-in-law, some concoction to help her conceive. Whatever lurked in her guts that night, it was not the natural process of conception. She was taken to the Shifa Hospital and pronounced dead just before dawn.

Madallah endured much misery in her life, from her birth in 1938 to her death in a refugee camp sixty-eight years later. But the most painful of all sufferings was that of the imprisonment, torture, and loss of her children. When life became overbearing, she hid in a room and spoke to or through them, "the others"—no one really knew for sure. At times she sobbed bitterly, her children eavesdropping outside in bewilderment, the older ones concerned, the younger ones snickering at the spectacle taking place in the mysterious room with unpainted walls and a low ceiling covered in half-broken gray tiles.

Maybe it was a good thing Madallah died long before Ehab ascended to Paradise. But it was never meant to be this way, as there was a different paradise, an earthly one, where the family had once belonged and dreamed of returning to.

Chapter One

Swallowtail

We all have partners and companions whom we do not see. The weaker companions may remain hidden from view, while the strong are more assertive and domineering. Madallah's companion appeared when she was just a child: she was at the well with other girls from the village when suddenly the surface of the water seemed to take on an unblemished milky color, like freshly harvested cotton, a daisy petal, or a summer cloud. She was the only one who witnessed this stunning event, and for some reason, knew to keep it to herself, so she said nothing to the other young girls, who were giggling as they chatted. One of the girls spotted an Umm Suleiman*—a ladybug—on the well's gray stone wall, inspiring her and the others to break into the collective song with which they always greeted this fascinating creature.

Umm Suleiman
Your husband is sick

---

* In Arabic, the prefix "Umm" means "mother of," most commonly used when women acquire the name of their firstborn boys, with "Umm Ahmed," for example, meaning "the mother of Ahmed." In some instances, however, it can be a nickname (e.g., "Umm Suleiman") or a gesture of respect (e.g., "Umm al-Ma'rik" or "Mother of all Battles").

He went to the clinic
They operated on him . . .

The happy song, gaining momentum with every verse, seemed to disappear into the background as Madallah stared carefully into the water.

Petrified, she wanted to run as fast as she could back to her mudbrick home on the outskirts of Beit Daras. But her dusty bare feet were frozen in place. Yes, it was fear, but something else controlled her little body and innocent thoughts. She was mesmerized by the milk-colored water, which seemed to move back and forth without being touched, creating gentle waves in the ground. Deep in her heart, she felt that something about her had changed forever. She remained silent as she walked home, perching a *jarrah*—the family's trusty black clay jar—on her head. Having completed their daily chore of fetching water, the girls entered the village one by one and dispersed back to their homes. Madallah entered her home, put down her load, and threw herself into her mother's arms.

Alarmed by the inexplicable sobbing of her daughter, Mahasin asked in a shaky voice if anyone had hurt her.

When the girl did not say a word, her mother insisted, rephrasing questions while checking her daughter's body from head to toe. Despite being unharmed, Madallah continued to weep, producing the sounds their neighbor Safiya made when her baby boy mysteriously died just a few months after birth. The Jewish doctor, Tsemeh, could not save him, no matter how hard he tried.

Madallah was making the same sound but without uttering a word, as if the pain was bellowing from her guts. As the neighbor women gathered, an old lady began crushing a clove of garlic, mixing it with olive oil, turmeric, and some other ingredients to produce the magic recipe she prescribed for every ailment, ranging from a bad cold and female infertility to bringing down a high fever in a newborn baby.

Only Madallah's father's return from the field for lunch and the *dhuhur* noon prayer* saved her from the frantic neighbors and the old woman's revolting recipes. "Leave her alone," Mohammed shouted, grabbing his daughter's hand and entering the only room in the house before closing the door and locking it from the inside with the extended wooden latch he had made himself.

The room, formed entirely from air-dried mud, was made of two types of material. When a harsh winter compromised the integrity of the walls, Mohammed reinforced them with mortar and stones, giving the room, with its low-hanging ceiling, the appearance of a permanently unfinished structure.

The whole Abdulnabi family household seemed to be a work in progress. When Mohammed and Mahasin first married, their home was a single room made of mudbrick, the outcome of a few days of hard work by Mohammed, his friends, and neighbors—all *fellahin*** just like him. When they knew that Mohammed—the kind neighbor who had memorized the Quran as a child—was getting married, they insisted on postponing everything to help him. He was blessed, and anybody associating with people of his spiritual status would be granted Allah's infinite mercies and blessings.

The house eventually had a *hakoura*—a low wall of crushed

---

* *Dhuhur* is one of the five obligatory daily prayers in Islam, and the second prayer of the day. It is performed after the sun has passed its midday zenith.
** *Fellahin* is an Arabic word that refers to the rural peasants or farmers. The term is used across the Arab world. In the Palestinian case, it is affiliated with the refugees expelled from their homeland in 1948, later to serve as the bulk of Palestine's working-class population.

rocks and dried mud—constructed just outside the room.* A small barn was added to store lentils, wheat, barley, olive oil, and other crops the *fellahin* would preserve for their families after selling the bulk of their harvest at the markets in Yafa or Isdud.

Every harvest seemed to introduce new blessings to Mohammed and his family, which continued growing. Although three daughters died a few months or even years after birth, three boys and Madallah survived. Mohammed and Mahasin decided she was special not just because she was the only girl to survive but because they felt the spirit of the other three girls, whose graves were now little mounds of dirt that washed away with the first heavy rain, were contained in Madallah.

Mohammed and Mahasin overindulged their daughter so much that she earned the nickname *Mdalalih*, "the spoiled one." She owned two dresses, one for everyday life and another for special occasions. Unlike her brothers, she had a pair of sandals that were only brought out from a wooden box filled with other treasures when the occasion called for them. She also had a hairbrush of her own: a wooden comb that Mohammed bought for her during one of his frequent visits to the Yafa market.

Madallah had never been to Yafa herself, but she knew how important it was to the village and her family's prosperity. Stories from the market were always intriguing, including tales about wild white boars and hyaenas on the road, bazaars filled with food of a thousand aromas, harmonious music composed of dreamy sounds of Arab artists from faraway places emanating from magical boxes, and shops that sold anything imaginable.

Despite the paradise that was Yafa, the father's recent encoun-

---

* In some homes, the *hakoura* is a small garden that is often attached to the house itself.

ters with soldiers made his visits less pleasant and less frequent. The soldiers, in Bermuda pants, khaki berets, and long rifles, were always angry, demeaning, and often drunk. Once, they forced Mohammed and many other Palestinian Arabs to lie on their faces for hours before dragging them, one after the other, to be searched and questioned about the rebels, especially those striking English and Zionist convoys from the countryside. It was particularly frightening when the soldiers' dogs sniffed Mohammed for gunpowder on a day when many Palestinian men were detained. Mohammed himself was briefly detained before being released after he convinced the soldiers that his dagger was for work and would never be used to hurt anybody.

That day, he returned home late and distraught. To make matters worse, the soldiers had stolen the money he brought to purchase seasonal supplies for his family. It was the first time that Madallah saw her father cry. It was not his lost money—just a few precious *junayhs**—that made him shed tears, he explained to his confused and scared wife, but rather his bruised *karameh*.

Karameh

"Dignity"—*karameh*—was a term Madallah had repeatedly heard, even before this stressful day. She would often hear *fellahin* speaking about Zionists stealing Palestinian land and *karameh*. In the course of rowdy village meetings, she would hear shouts about the English trampling on the Palestinian *karameh*, along with calls for wealthy Palestinians from the cities and the countryside landowners to protect it.

---

* *Junayh*, also spelled *gineh*, is the Palestinian currency used during the British Mandate in Palestine, from 1927 until 1948, replacing the Ottoman Lira. It was divided to 1,000 mils.

Once, while joining her father to a council meeting in Beit Daras, she heard the *mukhtar** thunderously declare: "In the name of Allah, it seems that the only ones with an iota of *karameh* in the whole of Palestine are the *fellahin*." All the men, in tandem, nodded their heads vigorously while repeating, "Ah, *wallah*, you are right, *Mukhtar*."

Madallah never understood much of what was said at the meeting.** Other words were repeated without context or explanation: "Zionists," "Jews," "English," "soldiers," "commissions," "land purchases," "Arab traitors," "martyrs," and "massacres." But she gleaned enough to gather that her little life in Beit Daras was being threatened by a force more powerful than her father's strength and the boundless love and kindness of her mother, and more expansive than the harshest of winters or the social influence of the *mukhtar* himself.

Around this time, Madallah began having strange dreams. Until then, her dreams were mostly confined to the village, including the ancient fortress, the old *khan* (a small inn), and the underground tunnels with strange symbols all over their walls.*** Back then, even her scarier dreams had been hardly frightening, and she was reassured when her mother told her that when she woke up, she just needed to say "I seek refuge with Allah from the accursed devil"[7] three times, safe in the knowledge that if a devil were indeed involved, it would quickly vanish. But the new dreams were different, featuring men she

* The head of the local government of a town or village in Palestine and the Levant. The term is also used to refer to a clan leader.
** In Palestine, the term *diwan* refers both to the council of the members of the same large family or a clan, and to the actual place they hold their meetings.
*** The ancient and relatively modern ruins scattered in and around Beit Daras included a one-kilometer-long tunnel ornately decorated with the art and script of an ancient Canaanite civilization, which Beit Daras children played in.

had never seen before, who spoke in strange tongues, wore khaki clothes, and brandished long rifles.

In the scariest dream, one of the caves outside the village, where she often used to play hide-and-seek with the village's girls and boys, overflowed with blood that pulled some children under by the power of its menacing current. Her parents were separated from her, and she was left alone, sobbing as the numerous colors of the village coalesced into a single hue of red.

Then, she saw him, or it, manifesting entirely in pure white. Whatever it was stood there. Unafraid. Although she felt it was a person or being, she saw no eyes nor a face. As it stared at her, she slowly walked towards it before waking with a shriek that disturbed the whole house and presumably the neighbors. That night, not even the typical cursing of the devil* helped alleviate her fears, even after her parents took turns patiently repeating the tried-and-true formula in her left ear. Her father even read the Quran's Yassin chapter in full, then Al-Rahman, and then many short *surahs* again and again, to no avail.

The dreams continued, confined to the intangible world, as the news grew grim. The *fellahin* felt increasingly abandoned. The sound of bullets whizzing from behind the walls of the Jewish settlement of Tabiyya** near the village could be heard with greater frequency. Dr. Tsemeh could no longer visit, despite the villagers needing him more than ever.

The *mukhtar* declared: "Our Jewish neighbors are ready to make their move," before asking: "Their move to do what? And why? And if this 'move' is ever made, when would it happen?

---

* The word for devil in Arabic is *shaytan*.
** Bir Tibiyya, whose spelling and pronunciation often varies, was a Jewish colony northeast of Beit Daras that gained a strategic value in the decisive battles that determined the fate of the Palestinian village.

And again, towards what end?" Madallah could barely understand the questions or conjure reasonable replies or answers. Yet, everything appeared to converge on the same violent dreams with flowing rivers of blood, strange-looking soldiers with guns, and, increasingly, a white figure. Standing. Staring. Unafraid.

The day she returned from the well, Madallah and her father were in the room a long time. From outside, Mahasin could only hear murmurs of Quranic recitation mixed with the repetition of peculiar words that made little sense to her and her simple daily existence. Behind the mudbrick walls, Madallah said nothing. Only Mohammed seemed to speak, and for hours. Just before the Maghreb prayer, the two emerged. Mohammed looked exhausted, but Madallah had a calm look on her face, an appearance of a serenity she had not experienced in a long time. Mohammed solemnly said, "the girl has a companion," before walking away and leaving the house altogether. Mahasin fell to her knees, pressing Madallah close to her heart. She cried, murmuring: "O Lord of the House, protect this house ... O Lord of the House, protect this house." When she finally let go, the girl turned to her mother and asked without hesitation or apprehension, "Yamma,* would you like me to fetch you more water from the well?"

Beit Daras

Beit Daras was an ordinary village, like any other in Palestine's southern terrain. Part of the Gaza district—about thirty-five kilometers northeast of Gaza City and fifty meters above sea

---

* *Yamma* is a Palestinian colloquial term for "Mom" or "Mother."

level—Beit Daras's population had grown consistently since it was established. However, few records reference its demographics before the sixteenth century. According to these early records, 319 people lived in Beit Daras as early as 1596.[8]

The Ottomans conquered Palestine in 1516–17 after they defeated the Mamluks, who had governed the entirety of the Levant region, including Palestine, for more than 260 years, starting in the mid-thirteenth century. Mamluk rule in that region started after their sultans defeated the Ayyubids, who defeated the Crusaders, who had conquered much of the Islamic world over many years, beginning in the late eleventh century.

It would be unfair to claim Palestine viewed all of its occupiers in the same way. While the Christian Crusaders pillaged, stole, burned villages, and crushed populations, Muslim "liberators" or "conquerors" (depending on one's perception) often used cruel strategies to triumph in brutal wars, but offered partial compensation by ensuring social stability as a praxis of governance. Ultimately, they all disappeared, leaving behind only faint traces of their presence and activity. In Beit Daras, the Crusaders left a fortress. The Mamluks built an inn for weary travelers journeying between northern Levant cities, including Damascus and Gaza, or onto Cairo—the Mamluk power base for over two centuries. The village's location made it strategically advantageous for facilitating communication between points north and south of the Mamluk Empire. Beit Daras soon had its own post office, where all letters were gathered before being taken to Cairo on saddled horses with tight security.

This is how the Egyptian quarter in the southern part of the village was formed. It was the natural outcome of centuries of uninterrupted movement between Palestine and Egypt. It began with the few Mamluk officers who remained in the village after triumphant Ottoman armies vanquished their empire. This was hardly the end of the Egyptians, who returned in 1831 as soldiers in the army of Ibrahim Pasha, which conquered much of the Levant and large swathes of Arabia, including the Hejaz. When the rebellious Ibrahim, acting on orders from his father, Mohammed Ali Pasha, was eventually routed by the armies of Constantinople and their allies, he left behind disgruntled soldiers, traitors, and those whose wounds were too deep to carry them through the arduous journey in the Sinai Desert.

They, too, remained in Beit Daras, forming small clusters of families with no roots and no large clans to vouch for and protect them when the pages of history once again turned. Over time, some small families merged into larger ones through intermarriage, land ownership, and everyday struggles against new invaders. Resistance always unified Palestinians, and the village's history offers abundant evidence to support this time-honored truth.

It seems the villagers of Beit Daras, like the populations of hundreds of other Palestinian villages and towns, and indeed Palestine itself, had been fated to exist against the backdrop of relentless foreign military stratagems, sometimes nearby, and sometimes thousands of miles away. But the village's population grew, often reflecting prosperity and intercommunal harmony, resulting in more land ownership.[9]

The village's name has always been a source of debate among village inhabitants, including its survivors. Beneficiaries of both formal and more worldly education have resolved that the word could come from *darasa*, which could allude to study or the pressing of wheat and olives, with the latter being more likely. Traditionalists, meanwhile, argue it is named after the Prophet

Idris,* insisting he lived in the village for an indefinite time, long ago. This subject was endlessly discussed at the *mukhtar's* evening council meetings, along with the low or high yields of cereal and fruits expected in any given season, the need to schedule a collective visit to an ill villager, and why Abu Aliyan's cows or Umm Fathi's chickens never stayed within their allocated barns, *hakouras,* and lots.

The few village conflicts were usually linked to animals misbehaving or, more precisely, to owners failing to respect long-held traditions of the village regarding grazing or water rights. Before conflicts devolved into physical quarrels, involving clubs but rarely daggers, the *mukhtars* of each large family or clan** met with other clan representatives in the village *mukhtar's* house, implicitly acknowledging that the *mukhtar's* moral authority superseded everyone else.

This is how a mighty clan, such as Abu Shamaleh, got along with al-Makadmeh, Baroud, and 'Abed. True, it was also due to those from smaller clans, such as Sa'ad, Salameh, Wadi, Mansour, Haddad, Haj Ahmed, Zuhud, and others, recognizing that they belonged to a different social order and acceding to their place in this unwritten hierarchy.

Jockeying for a better social standing and more significant share in land ownership was one of the primary motivators behind marriage, along with the occasional love story. Those who aspired to higher social ranking had to work exceptionally hard to earn the right to marry girls from larger clans. This is how part of the Sa'ad family, for example, became members

---

* Prophet Idris (Enoch) is regarded as either the second or third Prophet in Islam, known as Idris (from the Arabic verb *darasa,* taught) because he preached the magnanimity of God and the excellence of Islam.
** *Hamouleh* is the Arabic word for large family or clan.

of the Baroud clan, and it is also how al-Badrasawi, a once-dis-owned branch of the Barouds, formed their own collective, becoming one of the most reputable families. Not only did the al-Badrasawis have a larger share of the village's 709 houses, mostly made of hardened mud mixed with crushed stones, but they also collectively owned large tracts of land. Education was also a factor, as the literate were better able to defend their land rights when, wielding contracts,* they could prove their ownership of their land. This was especially important when dealing with more educated, and sometimes crafty, city dwellers.

The Abdulnabi family did not belong to any of these groups and lived physically and figuratively on the outskirts of the village. Their one-room house, with a small barn and low-walled *hakoura*, near the edge of the village's southeastern border, was only separated from the three Suwafir villages by thick olive orchards. They also had no social status from land ownership or affiliation with larger clans. Some villagers suspected the Abdulnabis were descended from past travelers, particularly Egyptians, who tried to invade before peacefully settling in the village instead. Despite this, the family was respected and even revered for something entirely unrelated to money, the Ottoman's certified land contracts, or blood association with large clans. They belonged to the bloodline of the Prophet himself.

Ahl Al Bayt

No family can demonstrate, beyond doubt, its direct connection to the Prophet or his immediate descendants, though this

---

* *Tabu* is the old term used in the Levant region to certify the ownership of the land. It was prevalent during the Ottoman period.

does not deter many from making such claims, often for personal gain. But the Abdulnabi household were not usurpers. They sought no financial leverage, power, or even status within the humble social order of Beit Daras simply because they happened to be members of the *ashraf*—the "honorable ones." In fact, they hardly ever boasted about their lineage, partially because they did not need to, as the people of the village simply knew and always had. What mattered was that the acquired *baraka* was equally distributed between all family members, who passed the blessings onto everyone else, whether in Beit Daras or nearby villages and towns. But no one was as blessed as Mohammed, the embodiment of the true man of God.

There were two mosques in the village, the Great Mosque and the Sheikh Abu Yassin Mosque, the former frequented by the *mukhtar* and all other less influential *mukhtars*. Since Islam, at least theoretically, preaches that no social hierarchy matters in the eyes of God as from birth, all are sinless and equal, Mohammed never approved of affluent residents receiving preferential treatment at the main mosque. Hardly ever critical of anyone, honoring the maxim that "Allah knows best," he nonetheless insisted that obedience to the word of God was a line that could not be crossed, arguing that no Imam should lead prayers if they have not memorized the Quran.* When his concerns were not taken seriously by the elders, he relegated himself to the smaller mosque at the eastern end of the village where he led all prayers, including *Fajr*, waking up at dawn to wash and hurry through the village's dark streets to join the other faithful in their daily quest for spiritual salvation.

---

* *Hafez* (f. *ḥafeẓa*), literally means "protector." Muslims use the term to refer to someone who has memorized the Quran in its entirety.

Returning home briefly, he took his knapsack full of yesterday's bread, homemade feta cheese, and pressed olives, and rushed to the field, working until it was time for the next prayer. He did this several times a day, without fail. When measles struck the village, killing many children and newborns, Mohammed fell ill. So as not to lose any of the required prayers, he continued to conduct his daily rituals while lying on his back, using the movement of his eyelashes to indicate the required act of prostration and bowing, and his index finger to express the required declarations* following the second, and then fourth, *rakat.***

Even when work injuries—an unruly animal, a snake bite, a falling rock, or sheer exhaustion from laborious work—physically impaired him, Mohammed hardly ever stopped moving his lips, constantly muttering distinct or inaudible religious expressions. He seemed to have a personal prayer*** for everything because supplications were functional to his everyday life. When he woke up in the small hours of the morning, he blessed his children, gently kissing their heads one after the other while praying for their safety, health, and, most importantly, continued strong faith. He duly kissed his wife Mahasin's right hand as he stepped outside to determine the nature of the prayer that followed. Though the "supplication of the traveler" is often uttered before a long journey, he applied it to the shortest of distances, consumed with worry about the fate of his family after speaking the following, and leaving.

---

* *Sujud* refers to the act of prostration. *Ruku* refers to the bowing position during prayer. *Shahadatain* refers to the two testimonies or declarations that are central to the Islamic faith: "There is no God but Allah" and "Mohammed is the messenger of Allah."
** A *Rak'a* is a single iteration of prescribed movements and supplications performed by Muslims as part of the obligatory prayer known as *salah*. Each daily prayer has a different number of *rakats* per prayer.
*** *Du'a* is a personal prayer, a supplication to, and direct communication with, God.

*O Allah, we ask You on this our journey for goodness and piety,
and for works that are pleasing to You. O Allah, lighten this journey
for us and make its distance easy for us. O Allah, You are our Companion on the road and the One in Whose care we leave our family.
O Allah, I seek refuge in You from this journey's hardships, and from
the wicked sights in store and from finding our family and property
in misfortune upon returning.*

Anxiety that comes from love is the hardest to endure.
Mohammed Abdulnabi often cried when he prayed. Though his
wife, ever reassuring and kind, shared his fears, they approached
the matter from two perspectives. Her fears were fully justified
by the harsh everyday reality and unpromising future: grinding
poverty under the British occupation, distrust of their armed
neighbors in Tabiyya, low crop yields, dwindling family savings
(decreasing from an already low point), the caving dirt wall of
the house's only bedroom, and, unknown to Mohammed, her
ailing health.

His apprehension was the kind that originates deep inside,
producing small and numerous palpitations of the heart that
are not connected to a hidden ailment but rather anticipate a
dreadful fate, looming and irreversible. These fears were partly
confirmed when Madallah met her *jinn** on that ominous afternoon by the village well. Mohammed feared the girl was too
young to endure it, and her uninvited companion could be a
manifestation of something evil that could lead her to insanity
or death. These were the thoughts that occupied Mohammed
as he tried to argue with the uninvited creature, to compel it
to leave in the name of God, the Prophet, and the People of the

---

* *Jinn* (or *Djinn*) are supernatural creatures in Islamic belief and Arabic folklore, often
described as spirits.

House. But the unwelcome guest refused, insisting it meant no harm. Its voice, though emanating from Madallah's lips, seemed to be that of a little boy trapped deep in a well: "I am here to help her," it stubbornly repeated, time and time again, to Mohammed's bewilderment.

Help her? But in what way? And why? As gentle and soft as Mohammed was in his treatment of everyone, he was eventually forced to use the verses meant to exact punishment on stubborn ethereal beings that refuse to depart the bodies of their victims. But even the harshest of spells made no difference and simply caused the "companion" pain, resulting in groaning, crying, and his repeating that he was not a devil but rather a protector and friend. Mohammed eventually relented in his efforts to free the girl when, seeing the tears of the boy being shed from the eyes of his daughter, he could not bear it. He stopped his incantations and walked away.

For days, he tried new ways to coax the boy to leave. Yet, as he saw that the presence of her new companion did not harm his daughter's well-being, he was slowly reassured that maybe things would sort themselves out. For once, he thought with relief that his intuitions may have been wrong.

Swallowtail

The waters of the Beit Daras Valley were fed by numerous streams that flowed gently in the spring and furiously in the winter, running between the village's orchards and arable lands in the east. Children were told to keep away from the valley when the water was "angry." In pleasant months, the valley was reduced to patches of small and large pools, with a faint stream of clean water that ebbed and flowed, depending on how much of the streams had been depleted by the *fellahin* beforehand and whether an unexpected rainstorm had visited southern Palestine and replenished the water. A meeting place for those seeking joy or solace, the valley united the village's children with tender forest creatures, including butterflies and miniature brown hares, especially when the village's only elementary school classes finished, just before the *Asr* prayer, signaling to the children that a life of innocent hedonism was now permitted.[10]

For the kids, adventure was a daily occurrence. Hopscotch and jump rope were popular among the girls, while the boys never seemed to tire of climbing the walls of the many old archeological ruins, especially the mysterious Khirbet Oudeh and Khirbet Ghyadah. The caves, the old fortress, and the valley presented yet more options to the inquisitive boys, whose occasional quarrels among themselves were outnumbered by their skirmishes with boys from nearby villages.

When they dared to venture into the village, the boys of Batani, Qastina, Sawafir, and even Hamameh and Jules invariably hurled the insult "Badrasawis have large heads" at their counterparts, obliging their parents to reassure their offspring that this "large head" stigma originated in the unfortunate tendency to mistake bravery for hard skulls. If this proved insufficient and the boys remained unconvinced, the kids of Beit Daras traveled to the valley water to check their heads in their reflection; on seeing the water perturbed, their fear and anxiety increased.

But nothing was as frightening as seeing the still body of Mohammed Abdulnabi covered with swarms of swallowtail butterflies, floating aimlessly on one side of the valley's waters.

Chapter Two

Rebels of the Valley

If the band of fighters had successfully crossed the orchards between Jenin and Nablus and then headed to the Red Valley,* modern Palestinian history would have been very different. But they did not.

The Qassamite bands[11] consisted of hundreds of fighters already dispatched to towns and villages throughout the Palestinian countryside. However, the British and their collaborators were more interested in the core leadership, especially Mohammed Izz al-Din al-Qassam, a Syrian preacher whose radical speeches and constant calls for jihad first captivated audiences in Haifa, then Yafa, Jenin, Nablus, and even Al-Quds itself.

The period leading to the fateful day on November 20, 1935, seemed unpromising for the nascent revolution, beginning with a passionate plea by al-Qassam at the iconic Al-Istiqlal Mosque[12] in Haifa. As his body shook and his hands trembled,

---

* The Red Valley (Wadi al-Ahmar), a valley in the northern Jordan Valley, gets its name from its distinctive reddish soil. This rugged terrain holds historical significance as a hiding place and base of operations for Arab resistance leader Izz al-Din al-Qassam and his followers in the 1930s. The area's inaccessibility made it an ideal location for their guerrilla activities against British Mandate forces.

he said in a shaking voice, holding back tears, "I have taught you the matters of your religion. I have taught you the affairs of your homeland. Haven't I spread the message? O Allah, be my witness. To the jihad, O Muslims. To the jihad."[13]

As soon as the prayer ended and the faithful gathered to say their last goodbye, al-Qassam stepped outside, walked slowly to a car awaiting him at the street corner, and drove off to an unknown destination. Some say the revered stranger, having arrived in Haifa under equally mysterious circumstances, departed the Palestinian city for the last time under the cover of night, whether on October 26 or 27, 1935. His jihad, however, did not last long.

He left because the British were fed up and ready to permanently detain or even assassinate him. Whenever they arrested him in the past, Haifa's downtrodden—port workers, peasants pushed off their land by unfair colonial policies, and the like—forced the city to shut down with general strikes that even the elites did not dare to defy. Every time, he returned to the Istiqlal Mosque, preaching against injustice and advocating jihad. In his final sermons, he no longer appeared before his audience as a fiery preacher but as a commander of war.

He had no other option but to declare jihad. The Arab elites had failed him, including King Faisal of Syria,[14] who reneged on his promise to send weapons, and Hajj Amin al-Husseini, the Mufti of Palestine, who persisted in the illusion that negotiations and peaceful resistance would resolve Palestine's growing predicaments.[15] Al-Qassam's repeated appeals to the Mufti—desperately trying to alert him that the British policy of flooding Palestine with Jewish immigrants was part of a larger colonial scheme to ethnically cleanse the region of Palestinian Arabs—were ignored. Even the renowned power of his tongue could

not persuade wealthy Palestinians or the self-serving *effendis**
of the cities to sacrifice their false prestige, empty titles, and
fleeting wealth.

But some aid did arrive, including from the brave Jordanian
prince, Rashed al-Khuzai, who sent money and arms,[16] along
with a pledge to fight alongside his men if they were not preoc-
cupied with their battle against British-imposed rulers in east
Jordan. By then, the Al-Qassamite band had already acquired
enough weapons to launch a decisive revolution that would not
just end Zionist infiltration of Palestine, but British colonialism
itself.

Everything that al-Qassam aspired to achieve in life came
down to reaching the Red Valley. Though a relatively short distance away, the naturally fortified mountains between Nablus
and the Jordan Ghor were, in fact, impossible to reach. Before
beginning their journey, the leadership of the Mujahideen's
small army divided into two groups, with the first heading
north, in the hope of ultimately making it back to Haifa and
Nazareth. Along the way, they were given the critical mission of
damaging railroads and cutting off the British telephone lines.
The second band wanted to move south, from the Jenin countryside to Nablus, before veering east to reach the Red Valley.
This was, however, a dangerous plan, as the route was filled
with spies, and the British seemed to be everywhere.

Al-Qassam was not the first to see the valley as the only salvation of his new rebellion. The ancient road there—long known
as the "Road of the Mataba'on"[17]—had been used by traders and

---

* Though the term *effendi* was used as an official title for bureaucrats in the Ottoman Empire, with time, and until this day, it is employed to convey a sense of authority or nobility.
Though the use of the term is no longer widespread in Palestine, it is often used in Egypt
and to some extent in Syria.

warriors since the time of the Phoenicians and extends as far as the Jericho mountains.* The road's name changed over time, eventually becoming known as the "*Salatieh,*" an acknowledgement of its traversing many miles and crossing a river, reaching to the Jordanian city of As-Salt and its natural defenses of mountains and valleys.

Many had previously sought the help of these hazardous but protective roads. Before the British imposed their Mandate on the Palestinians and the other populations of the eastern Mediterranean,** many Palestinians, known as "those who were being followed," escaped to the Red Valley. Not all dared to defy the authorities. In Ottoman times, the valley was the main escape route for those who refused to be conscripted to fight faraway wars, as only a few of those dragged away by Ottoman soldiers to feed the war machine thousands of miles away ever returned.

Abu Kbari of Beita,*** eventually followed by Salah Abu Sliqa, Hamdieh, and others, continued this path of defiance after the British army came, captured Palestine, and sent thousands of its men to fight in distant wars. He had too much self-respect to die for the British crown that brought his fellow Palestinians nothing but pain, blood, and grief. These rebels held firm for years before being ambushed in the late 1920s in the Za'tara hills, when Abu Kbari and others were killed, and others

---

* Jericho is one of the earliest continuously inhabited settlements in the world, dating from about 9000 BCE. Ancient Jericho/Tell es-Sultan is located northwest of present-day Jericho in the Jordan Valley in Palestine, and is a UNESCO World Heritage Site.

** The Mandate for Palestine was a League of Nations mandate for British administration of the territories of Palestine and Transjordan, which were both conceded by the Ottoman Empire following the end of World War I in 1918. In 1920, at the San Remo Conference, the Mandate was assigned to Britain after France's concession, subsequently being in force from September 1923 to May 1948.

*** Beita is a Palestinian town in the Nablus Governorate in the northern West Bank, which lies thirteen kilometers southeast of Nablus City.

wounded and sentenced. The *fellahin* sang many songs of defiance in honor of these men. "My whole life, O God, I will never wear their khaki uniform, even if they kill me as they did Abu Kbari. My whole life, O God, I will never hang my head (in obedience), wear their small uniform even if they sentence me as they did Abu Sliqa."[18]

Al-Qassam, however, did not want to reach the valley to escape. Instead, he sought a safe command center where he could launch his long-anticipated rebellion, organizing small bands in many villages. His trusted companion, Farhan al-Sa'adi, later one of the leaders of the *fellahin* rebellion of 1936, went in a different direction than al-Qassam. He steered his horse towards Ya'bad, near Jenin, in the hope of changing his course east a short distance later.

When al-Qassam and his men ran out of water, they were forced to seek help at Khirbet Sheikh Zaid.* By then, the British and their collaborators had reached Jenin. Beleaguered, al-Qassam sought shelter at the home of an old acquaintance, a friend of the rebellion, before disappearing into the forest of Ya'bad, where the rebellion ended. As hundreds of well-trained enemy fighters descended on the small forest from all directions, there was no escape, no Red Valley, no revolution. "Die as martyrs!" yelled the preacher, taking position behind a large rock,[19] followed by his remaining nine men all yelling "Allahu Akbar!" in tandem, as the sound of guns rang out from all directions, lighting the darkness with the blaze of fire. "Allahu Akbar!" was repeatedly heard—each time more quietly—as the voices faded away one after the other. The night slowly turned dark once more, the silence only interrupted by the unfamiliar sounds of

---

* Khirbet Sheikh Zaid is an area near the village of Ya'bad.

foreign tongues and the reluctant whispers of Arab policemen who, for the sake of a few British pounds, had killed their liberators.

Jableh

When al-Qassam arrived in Haifa in the 1920s, his ideas about Muslim liberation had matured, both through study and numerous encounters, mostly outside Palestine. His first trip out of beautiful Jableh, on the northern Syrian coastal line between Beniyas and Latakia, was to Cairo. There, he obtained two strands of knowledge: Al-Azhar taught him the principles of *fiqh, shariah,* and *usul al-din,** while the city taught him to hate the foreign men with military uniforms and guns. At just fourteen years old, he drew on his Egyptian experience to develop his own ideas about Islamic liberation theology, centered on Islam as a unifier of a great *ummah*** that had lost its unity and political cohesion.

To reach Cairo, the young sheikh joined a fishing boat from Arwad Island to Alexandria, traveling from there to the busiest of all Arab capitals.[20] He was joined by his brother, a cousin, and several young scholars, some eager for knowledge and others only driven by a sense of adventure. Al-Qassam spent a decade of his life at that historic institute of learning. Unlike today's

---

* *Fiqh* is Arabic for Islamic jurisprudence. Shariah is the system of Islamic law, driven mostly from the Quran but also the Hadith, the teachings of Prophet Mohammed. *Usul al-Din* refers to the fundamental principles, or the foundations of the faith in Islam. They include the oneness of God, justice, and prophethood.
** *Ummah* refers to the global Muslim community, which is united by the belief in the oneness of God, justice under God, and the acceptance of Prophet Mohammed as the final messenger.

Al-Azhar, the university then relied on the system of *halakat,**
wherein students gathered around scholars of their choosing in
corners of the vast mosque. In a *halakhah,* students come and
go as they please as long as they can pass rigorous exams super-
vised by the oldest and supposedly wisest scholars.

Egypt was then occupied by the British,** not long after
Napoleon had failed in his expedition to subdue the rebellious
Ottoman province and the Levant, including Palestine. The
British were not different from their French cousins, and the
still young and now learned scholar returned home.

In Jableh, al-Qassam's knowledge was initially of little value
to the small town's minority of *effendis,* who owned most of the
land and dominated the *fellahin* majority.[21] The rulers hated him
and his ideas about justice and equality so much that they almost
exiled him north to Izmir before he chose Istanbul instead.[22]

He only stayed in the capital of the Ottoman Caliphate for a
short time, as he felt there was little Islamic knowledge for him
there. Subsequently he returned to Jableh, this time avoiding
the domineering *effendis* and their selfish interests. He taught
children in the morning, teenagers in the afternoon, and adult
men at night. His eloquence and ability to connect with a
wide range of people eventually earned him the status of the
khatib—preacher—at the Al-Mansouri Mosque in the center of
the town.

Al-Qassam saw the Prophet as a revolutionary and his
teachings as a guide to combating oppression and injustice.
The captivating preacher did not see People of the House as

---

* An Arabic term that refers to a circle or gathering, often associated with religious or
educational settings.
** Egypt was occupied by the British from 1882, after the Anglo–Egyptian War, until 1956,
after the Suez Crisis, when the last British troops withdrew under the Anglo-Egyptian
agreement of 1954.

a source of blessings whose names should only be repeated at religious ceremonies, but rather as part of a legacy that must be emulated through action. The small mosque rapidly gained the largest congregation in Jableh and its environs, with worshipers flocking from near and far. Al-Qassam spoke of the word of God, the *sunnah* of the Prophet and Islam, in accessible, relatable language, often returning to the concept of jihad.

"There is no faith to those who accept their lowliness, *istakana*, submission, to injustice and those who became addicted to the slavery of man," he preached.[23] Those who experienced nothing but oppression and felt constant inferiority to outsiders, *effendis*, and oppressive landlords looked at him with adulation.

Yet al-Qassam's jihad did not start in Syria but in Libya, where his attempt to launch a holy war against colonialism did not last long. The Italians besieged the Libyan coast in 1911, sparking calls for jihad that echoed from Tripoli to Damascus to Istanbul, inspiring Al-Qassam— and the hundreds of volunteers he led— to set sail from Syrian coastal towns to Alexandria.[24] However, the ship that the High Seat in Istanbul had promised for the mission to Libya never arrived, and forty days later, the young fighters used the money donated to their failed expedition to increase literacy among the people of Jableh.[25]

The French invasion of Latakia in 1918 instigated calls for jihad to be extended to Syria itself. "It is not important that we win," al-Qassam declared as he carried arms against the new invaders, who burned everything in their way in their attempt to establish a foothold in the Levant. "All that matters is that we use ourselves as an example for the *ummah* and future generations."[26] Al-Qassam sold his humble dwelling to buy arms, moving his wife and children to a safer town, away from the dangerous coast.

The fight was doomed. The French responded to every rebel attack by burning villages and massacring inhabitants, including the almost 170 villagers executed by a French firing squad in the town of Hifeh in response to al-Qassam's attack on French barracks in the region.[27] After the French issued an executive order against al-Qassam and many of his followers, he was forced to flee to Palestine—first to Akka and then to Haifa, where he finally settled.

He could have traveled to Haifa along the Hijaz railway that ran inland, parallel to the Mediterranean coast, extending from Damascus in the north to the Hijaz in the south. At points, extensions of the railroads branched out to cover a wider area, including in Yafa, in central Palestine, and Lod, where the railway connected with the line that ran from Jerusalem to Cairo via Gaza City. But this would surely be a dangerous journey for a man on the run, as the French presence was pervasive, and the British were not known for being much kinder to wanted men. So he took different routes, sometimes using a horse carriage, to get to Beirut and then Sidon before traveling to Akka by boat. Months later, he left for Haifa, a bustling place populated by newcomers, the unemployed, traitors, and revolutionaries. This coastal Palestinian town, the embodiment of the injustice suffered by the people of the Levant, was where Al-Qassam's rebellion was meant to begin.

The preacher's path to the city's collective heart began in small steps, first as a teacher in a women's school, then in an Islamic school for boys, before he opened his own school to educate the illiterate. When Al-Istiqlal Mosque was established in 1925, he was the first preacher and committed his first sermon to explaining how the British were the origin of the trouble and ailment of his people. Warning about Jewish migration, he explained it was part of a Zionist plan to colonize Palestine, hatched and carried out from the start by the British themselves.[28] He was not wrong.

In the ten years he spent as the mosque's imam, he confronted three enemies: British colonialists, Zionist settlers, and Arab feudalists who had, for years, benefited from their relationships with both of the aforementioned. But Al-Qassam was hardly alone in confronting adversaries, as his constituency included former factory and port workers whose livelihoods had been destroyed by the Histadrut's scheming,[29] peasants driven off their farms in the countryside,[30] and rebels who had grasped, even back then, that colonialism was a disease that could only be cured with fire. "Who amongst you believe in God and the day after, must own one of these," al-Qassam once announced from the pulpit. "One of these" was a gun, which he had obtained, along with many other weapons purchased and held secretly for years in anticipation of a fateful day ahead.

"Die as Martyrs"

The plan to establish a band of Qassami fighters was an old one. But Haifa, now under joint British-Zionist control, was the most opportune place for the band to take shape as the foundation for a much bigger future rebellion. Everything was done in great secrecy: personal conversations turned into home visits, then into small groups consisting of three to five members that rigorously trained in mountain terrains. New recruits were urged to return to their villages to organize meetings between Al-Qassam and the local *mukhtars*, who would either be asked to join the rebellion or, if weak-willed, would be kept away.

The Al-Buraq Uprising of 1929 provided one of the best recruiting opportunities,* with the ensuing bloodshed leaving no doubt that the British and Zionists were allies who schemed and killed together. Those Palestinians who had once questioned the wisdom of armed revolutions began to change their minds when they saw the heaps of bodies of men, women, and children being buried *en masse.*

The veil of secrecy lifted, Al-Qassam, previously seen only as a teacher and preacher, emerged as a military commander. Amid rising violence between soldier, settler, and *fellahin*, he felt the revolution had reached its boiling point. Although he was correct, he did not live long enough to oversee it or lead it to fruition. When al-Qassam left Al-Istiqlal Mosque for the last time, on the night of October 26 or 27, 1935, he was certain this would not be his last journey. He believed that upon reaching the Red Valley, all the pieces would come together, and the revolution of Palestine would spark the liberation of an entire *ummah.*

Alas, the Red Valley was nowhere to be found. But when al-Qassam urged his nine warriors to "die as martyrs," the echoes of his voice somehow reached the valley of Beit Daras.

---

* On August 15, 1929, a group of Zionists, led by Betar members, demonstrated at al-Buraq Wall (The Western Wall). In a clear provocation of the Palestinian population, they raised the Zionist flag and sang the Zionist anthem, producing a riot and week of violence that killed 113 Jews and 116 Arabs, and wounded more than 200. This followed years of rising Jewish immigration to Palestine and a Mandate decision to increase the number of Jewish worshippers allowed to access the Buraq Wall.

Chapter Three

Nakba

Mohammed was not telling the truth. The dagger, concealed very carefully inside his *sirwal*,* was not the type the *fellahin* used for harvest, which usually had a narrow blade with a curved edge. Instead, it had a sharp ending point and two sharp edges. The knife had been handed to him at a gathering near Yafa. He was nervous as he took it, gazed at it for a moment, flipped it from one side to the other, and then hastily hid it in a small, secret pocket tucked around the elastic waistband of the *sirwal*, which was where he usually, with the same kind of nervous care, hid his precious money. Though the strange and drunken men in the khaki uniforms had confiscated his money, they let him retain his weapon, unaware that he was now officially a Qassamite rebel.

This was sometime in the mid-1940s, years after the end of the Great Revolt. Al-Qassam was long dead, but his presence was still felt throughout Palestine. Movement leaders, or at least those who claimed to be, saw the three-year effort as a failure that had achieved none of the rebellion's main demands, namely

---

* *Sirwal* are large baggy trousers with an elastic waistband and drawstring.

Arab independence and an end to Jewish immigration and the sinister purchasing of Palestinian land,[31] undertaken with the goal of expelling the local population and establishing a "national home" for Jewish settlers.[32] They now saw the British government White Paper as the only fleeting positive of the Revolt, which permitted land transfers in certain areas and restricted them in others.[33] Zionist migration did slow, but this was only for a short time, and it failed to offset the dismal Palestinian Arab reality on the ground, which included burgeoning unemployment, mass arrests, summary executions, and military raids.[34]

For the *fellahin*, however, there was a silver lining, as the revolution enabled them, for the first time, to realize their collective power and wrestle their destiny from the hands of urban leaders and corrupt, self-seeking elites. The prominent Husseini and the Nashashibi families were back in the picture, some still believing that more commissions would liberate the Palestinians. Others were willing to do whatever it took, including direct collaboration with the enemy, to maintain their status and wealth.

But the revolution, now decentralized, was felt in every town and every village, its influence extending from urban centers to the countryside. Al-Qassam's disciples, starting with Farhan Saadi,* ensured that the martyred sheikh's legacy and words were honored and spread far and wide, especially in the countryside.

This is how Mohammed Abdulnabi found his place in life. He was in the vanguard of a revolution meant to end in an isolated, dark orchard in Ya'bad that instead persisted for years, and indeed decades.

---

* Farhan Saadi was a Palestinian rebel commander in the Great Revolt.

Collaborators

Each village had a *mukhtar*, a rebel, and a Zionist spy, or at least someone willing to collaborate in exchange for some form of personal gain—usually money or a promise of protection. Toward the end of the Rebellion in 1939, some of the *mukhtars* collaborated in the hope of being spared the fate awaiting those who fought back.[35] Time proved them wrong, with their fate sometimes being as bad or worse. Those who refused at least died with honor, their blood mixing with the soil of their land in a development that mattered greatly to the *fellahin*. "Die as martyrs!" al-Qassam shouted as his nine fighters fell one after the other, alongside the thousands of others who gave their lives in the 1936 rebellion.[36] Many more were killed during the Nakba.

Creating full-fledged collaborators requires ample time and careful planning. In the four years before the Nakba, the Zionist military intelligence, Shai, worked tirelessly to keep count of all the villages in Palestine, from the farthest north to the farthest south, obtaining detailed information about their inhabitants, *mukhtars*, fighters, and, more importantly, recruiting potential collaborators.[37] These "village files"* built a powerful infrastructure of information and surveillance. Over time, Zionists cultivated informants who kept watchful eye on the intentions of the *mukhtars*, the movement of rebels, and any evidence of weapons, particularly firearms and ammunition.

Many Zionist gangs were active in the vicinity of Beit Daras, including the Haganah militias, which maintained a base in

---

* Military intelligence documents that gathered data on every Arab village in Mandatory Palestine.

Tabiyya. Although the Zionists' elite fighting force—the Pal-mach—did not begin its ominous activities until 1941, it quickly became the main force in acquiring and colonizing as much land as possible. Even then, very little was obtained and constructed. "Selling your land to the Jews is *forbidden*,"* Mohammed once declared at the mosque, following an impassioned sermon about the lurking Zionists, the scheming British, the collab-orating landowners, and other things he learned during his secret meetings in Yafa. His name was quickly added to the list of agitators.

The truth is that the people of Beit Daras never sold their lands and did not concede an inch to the Zionists. Mohammed had taught his fellow villagers that selling land not only betrayed the community and Palestine but also betrayed God. He was becoming dangerous in the eyes of the Zionists and their British allies, and alarm bells must have sounded when the young Badrassawi preacher declared at the village's Sheikh Abu Yassin mosque: "It is jihad, victory, or martyrdom," the sig-nature closing statement of the great sheikh himself.

However, the Zionists' collaborators were not the only ones who understood the significance of Beit Daras. The rebels, too, had been eyeing the village and decided it could not be lost. If Beit Daras fell, they calculated, the less defensible three Sawafir villages would surely follow, with the two villages of Batani East and Batani West, along with Qastina and Al-Msmeieh, being fully encircled if they were cut off from Beit Daras. A siege would isolate this cluster of villages from the towns of Al-Ma-jdal and Isdud, the region's major economic hubs. Barqa in the north and Adas in the south would also have no chance, as they

---

* *Haram* is an Arabic word that refers to something that is forbidden or prohibited in Islam.

were mere extensions of the larger villages situated strategically around the more central, prosperous, and influential Beit Daras.

For years following 1939, the armed rebellion moved southward. After the killing of al-Qassam Sheikh Farhan al-Sa'adi, the disciple and new Al-Qassamite leader had more time to strategize than his predecessor. If only al-Qassam and his nine men could have reached the Red Valley. But that did not matter now, when Palestine's valleys, orchards, and caves were brimming with fighters old and young, who sold their humble worldly possessions—including their wives' gold and their share of harvests—to purchase rifles.

This was how Mohammed expanded his arsenal that had once consisted of one lonely dagger. He sold everything he owned of value at the Yafa flea market* and bought a Turkish rifle with a leather handle, possibly sold by an Ottoman soldier before Palestine was conceded to the British. Yafa had become a hotbed. It had been simmering for years, especially since the rebellion redrew the lines, with the *fellahin* and the workers on one side and everyone else on the other.

Yafa was a miniature Palestine, where oppressive colonial policies, Zionist intransigence, riots, and rebellions roiled in the same cauldron. After al-Qassam was martyred and mosques were placed under the authority of the British in the late 1930s, the people rioted. When the Great Revolt started, Yafa was on the frontline, not merely joining the initial strike but electing a national committee that was solely responsible for maintaining the strike for as long as it took to defeat the settler colonialism imposed by the British and Zionists.

---

* The Yafa flea market was founded in the early 1900s during Ottoman rule.

It turned out that the end of the Great Revolt was not the end of the war, but the beginning of a different kind of war—between one nation fighting to survive and another determined to be born on its ruins. Palestine was then unfairly divided and torn, with the new settlers getting the most territory and arable land, most of the coastal line, and more. The indigenous Palestinian communities were left with scraps of a homeland they had identified with since time immemorial. For Palestinians, the "Partition Plan"* was an egregious injustice.

The war had begun. The intricate work of the informers was applied in earnest to ensure that the Palestinian rebels, part of every town and village, were duly purged. It took a single bullet to cut short the life of piety and rebellion of Mohammed Abdulnabi. Following a brief visit home, he had returned to his land to pray and refill his knapsack with yesterday's bread and feta cheese when a loud boom was heard. "So this is what martyrdom feels like?" The soft nudging of small waves from the flowing waters of the Beit Daras Valley brought Mohammed's body back to Beit Daras, covered with the kind of butterflies Madallah never tired of chasing while her father patiently plowed his field, barefoot and alone. "Die as martyrs!" al-Qassam yelled at his fighters. They all did, and so did Mohammed Abdulnabi, the blessed man, the servant of the people and the Prophet.

---

* The UNGA adopted the United Nations "Partition Plan" on November 29, 1947 when it passed UNGAR181 (II), which called for Historical Palestine to be divided into two states—one Jewish and one Arab state—and for Jerusalem to be placed under an international trusteeship.

A Kiss

As Madallah gazed at her father's body lying in the middle of the *hakoura*, everything seemed to go silent, though only for a brief moment. The screams of her mother as she tore her hair in a fit of inconsolable grief and rage; the weeping old woman with the revolting recipe; her crying, bewildered brothers; the men that came running from all directions; the *mukhtar* declaring that the Zionists had crossed the last line; and more. In her head, they were all muted. When the cacophony gushed back all at once, the girl could no longer talk.

It was not that Madallah tried to talk and failed. She simply had no desire to speak, displaying only a frozen look on a face that suddenly grew much older. Her eyes were neither lively nor lifeless. They were in a suspended state of their own, as if they were still processing information that could not be deciphered. This gentle and loving father, who seemed to be kindly staring at her with open eyes, was no longer there. "His spirit has returned to Paradise," declared the elders. But what use was that Paradise when the only person in the world who had understood her, stood by her, protected her in words and deeds, was no longer with her now, on this very earth, on this very day when evil had descended from all gates of hell? What good is Paradise up there if her earthly paradise down here is shattered, never to be whole again?

"Kiss your father, kiss your father," the crowd shouted as they pushed her and her terrified brothers forward towards the blood-stained face. They did so, trembling, except for Madallah, who kissed his forehead calmly. She wanted to whisper into Mohammed's left ear all the protection spells he had taught her before he embarked on his final journey. But she didn't. It would have sufficed if she had only said a word or two: *"Allah ma'ak yaba"*—"God be with you, O father." But the words didn't come out. If only Mohammed could have joined the villagers as they defended Beit Daras in its final, most decisive battles. But he couldn't. If only al-Qassam could have reached the Red Valley. But it was a distance away. "Die as martyrs!" he yelled. Hundreds of Badrasawis have.

Bread and Bullets

Hussein Ageel, the *mukhtar* of Beit Daras, lay on a small mattress at his home, which was surprisingly neither the largest nor the most opulent of the village's humble dwellings. Though the blood mainly gushed from his head, he looked as if he was bleeding from every part of his body. The Zionists' shell, along with several others, struck the center of the village where the *mukhtar's* house was located, killing three men and one woman in the first of several attacks.

The *mukhtar*, who spoke with a loud voice and was liked by many, was dead. In his last speech at the council, he referred to the dignity of the *fellahin* more than once. On this day, women wept for him, with even the hardened *fellahin* men shedding tears. But the resistance continued. The Beit Daras fighters, with a total of nine rifles, some purchased from Yafa and others from Al-Majdal, successfully repelled the initial Zionist attack that originated in neighboring Tabiyya. This was the first Beit Daras battle. It took place on March 16, 1948, one of several dates etched into the collective memory of the village survivors.

In this first round, many Zionist militias were forced to retreat by the peasants-turned-warriors who fought with everything they could find, including daggers and clubs. Women mostly stayed at the back of the lines, caring for the children or the wounded, except for Latifa Abu Shanab, who refused marriage in order to dedicate herself to the jihad, initially by providing water to the fighters. Every time a battle started, she could be seen running to the frontlines with her *jarrah*, unafraid of whistling bullets often aimed at her. She even went as far as Ghaiyada, the closest village to Tabiyya from the direction of Beit Daras. As the war grew more difficult, she took up a rifle without waiting for permission and began shooting at invaders.[38]

A few days later, the Zionist militia, Haganah, bombarded Beit Daras from several directions, killing at least nine civilians.* Skirmishes continued before culminating in an attempted invasion on April 16. The air was warm but pleasant, and the poppies blooming, when the earth began shaking as four enemy tanks rumbled into Beit Daras. Madallah's mother held tightly to all four of her children as she repeated *Ayat Al-Kursi*—the 255th verse of the Quran**—in exceptional haste, urging them to do likewise. The tanks left following their exploratory mission, leaving the dirt roads gouged open and the whole village smelling like freshly plowed land ready for seeding.

A decisive battle took place two weeks later, on May 1. David Ben Gurion's army saw this as the first and final battle to conquer the Palestinian village and claim a strategic position. Instead, many of his men perished. It began at dawn with Zionist militias mercilessly shelling Beit Daras. Under the cover of mortars, a large number of enemy soldiers commandeered the village's elementary school, using it as a base and new line of defense. Beit Daras held on for hours, fighters marking their

---

* The first bombing was on March 27–28, 1948.
** In *Ayat al-Kursi* (the Throne Verse)—the 255th verse of the Quran—God introduces himself to mankind.

positions by occasionally shouting "Allahu Akbar!" When the shouts became sporadic and infrequent, the battle seemed to be nearing its end, the soldiers in the schools apparently ready to mount their final attack. Then, suddenly, chants of "Allahu Akbar!" grew louder as a surge of Palestinian comrades armed with rifles and *kuffiyehs* began arriving from Isdud, Hamameh, the three Suwafirs, and the two Batanis. With the help of the remaining Beit Daras fighters, they pushed the enemy back, besieging the soldiers in the school.

Beit Daras only suffered the loss of eight combatants and around twenty wounded. The enemy's losses were more than they could bear. If it were not for the British, who arrived just before the Palestinian fighters entered the school, the fight on the entire southern front could have been altered. The British claimed that they were intervening to end the bloodshed and restore peace. However, the peace of Beit Daras had been shattered when the colonies were built with the sole aim of expelling communities from their ancestral homeland. Why didn't the British come to shield Beit Daras when it was being attacked, shelled, and invaded?

The battle of May 21* was the last to be fought by the villagers before Arab armies—mostly made up of underequipped, disorganized volunteers—belatedly arrived without a plan.**

In the last battle, no one came to the rescue, as the other

---

* The date of the decisive battle, which emptied Beit Daras completely of its inhabitants, is not easy to pinpoint, partly because Beit Daras was not defeated in a single battle, and also because the fight to regain the village extended to the war's closing stages. Israeli historian Benny Morris claims May 10 as the date, which is inconsistent with Ben-Gurion's own diaries. Meanwhile, Palestinians who cite May 21 are not acknowledged by Israeli sources, including Morris.

** Contingents of four (Egypt, Iraq, Transjordan, and Syria) of the seven Arab League countries belatedly joined the Palestinian fight against the Zionists, supported by the Arab Liberation Army and volunteer corps from Saudi Arabia, Lebanon and Yemen and, later, six companies of Sudanese regulars and a Sudanese battalion.

villages were attacked too. The Haganah, supported by other Zionist militias, launched a war against the entire southern front. As the enemy closed off the village from all directions, there were no supply lines or brave warriors chanting *"Allahu Akbar!"*

"I bear witness that there is no deity but Allah, and I bear witness that Muhammad is the Messenger of Allah," is what Muslims are urged to repeat when it seems death may be imminent. Many such declarations were heard on that day.

"Die as martyrs!" a loud voice summoned. As Palestinian fighters continued to battle, Latifa joined in, firing many shots and striking her targets. Where did she learn to fight this way? Nobody saw when she was shot or captured, and she was never seen again.

Hundreds of women and children rushed to the southern road where sunflowers were in full bloom, all running in one direction, away from Tabiyya and the bloodbath unfolding in Beit Daras. The whole village was besieged, with snipers firing from hilltops and bushes with the intention of mass execution. Some children asked about their fathers, but not Madallah and her brothers, who knew exactly where their father was. "In Paradise there are rivers of honey and milk, and whatever fruits your heart desires are lowered in front of you on a tree branch," Mahasin told her children soon after their father's murder. "Paradise looks very similar to Beit Daras, except that there, no one could ever hurt you," she further elaborated. But down here, especially now, no paradise was to be found.

Rat-tat-tat! Gunfire originating from a spot on a high mound mowed down women and children as they fled. Those who managed to avoid the stream of bullets were struck by the more precise aim of the snipers, the shadowy figures in the distance who only emerged to confirm their kills before returning to their positions. *Crack, crack, crack!* The shots continued to pop, one after the other.

"Yama, run! Yama, run! Yama..." The cries and shrieks of women and children filled the air during the methodical massacre in Beit Daras. Some estimates say 265 Palestinians were killed.[39] Others say more, as many of the wounded who managed to flee would die on the roads. Days before the massacre, as if answering the questions of her children before they were even asked, Madallah's mother had told her: "When children die, they become birds of heaven." But Madallah had no questions. The horror and trauma kept her silent for months.

Madallah's mother coughed incessantly, mixing the repeated hacks with occasional loud sobs of mourning for a paradise lost. The exhausted woman, fleeing with her children from the killing fields in southern Beit Daras, began coughing blood. At first, she tried to hide it from the already terrified children. But as the hours and days passed, it appeared on her scarf, sleeves, and all over her *thobe*, her most special dress, known among the women in Beit Daras as *jannah wa nar*—paradise and hell.

The men of Beit Daras mostly wore the traditional Palestinian garb—a *dimayeh*, either checkered or lined. The colors of this traditional attire were largely fixed: two lines of light blue and white, with a less accentuated line of yellow in between. The women had more options, as their traditional *thobes* came in a variety of colors, especially those that distinguish the southern regions of Palestine from other parts. True, the blue *thobe* was becoming fashionable among the women of the village; however, *jannah wa nar*, a mix of floral patterns dominated by purple, light green, and blue, with small yellow flowers scattered in perfect harmony, along with other, less vivid shades of red and dark blue, remained the mark of women's fashion in Beit Daras.

The woman had obtained that dress for her wedding and only wore it on special occasions, especially during the *samers*, the intimate family gatherings which often followed the main public weddings earlier in the day. Men would stand on the one side, and women on the other, and they would perform the traditional *dabka* dance. The men's movement could follow many styles, and the leader of the troupe, often the most flamboyant, would improvise depending on the occasion and the energy of the crowd. The women, however, would sway back and forth, and, unlike the men, would stomp their feet gently on the ground. "*Yahweida hweida lak, yahweida hwieda hwedia li*"—"I prefer your hellfire to the paradise of my family"—they would sing collectively, and move, in two clusters of groups, all holding hands in opposite directions, from one side to the other.

But her "paradise and hell" was now covered with her own blood, changing the scheme of colors of her *thobe* altogether, red dominating all others. But this frail, fatigued, and ill woman was still the only possible path to salvation for her boys and Madallah.

Though Madallah lost her voice as the family journeyed south in a desperate search for safety, small growls began to emerge, not from her throat but from her belly. These were not growls of hunger, although she was, like the others, starving. It was instead a voice, although not her own. Unlike previous "visitations," her mother didn't urge her to quiet down, didn't read any verses in her ears, didn't even look in her direction, and instead kept moving forward while coughing as her children held onto different parts of her *thobe*, torn everywhere and covered with dirt, dust, blood, and tears. It was not as if she knew the road to Gaza well; indeed, she had never been there. She simply followed the crowd, an endless stream of dusty bodies rushing in utter desperation towards some unclear point on the horizon.

A nation that had lived and prospered in southern Palestine for millennia had just been destroyed.

Chapter Four

The Badrasawis

Though not the only survivor, all that mattered to him in that moment was the survival of his family. In fact, for the rest of his life, Abdallah al-Badrasawi could not comprehend how they managed to escape the killing fields of Beit Daras: the journey, the ensuing starvation, the soldiers dotting the hilltops of southern Palestine, and much more. "It was the hand of God that shielded us," he would say every time the story of the great escape was brought up, as it often was.

Every time, a new detail would emerge. The two little sisters shot holding hands. The burned corpses under the fig tree. The old man who lost his family and then his mind—laughing hysterically, pulling his hair, cursing the day he was born. The dead woman lying exposed on the road to Julus, who had run in the opposite direction looking for her missing child until the Zionist Haganah militia caught her and did "unspeakable things."[40] Abdallah's mother used to say many of these types of stories were buried because "they needed to be forgotten." Acknowledging their occurrence would drive a man crazy, Abdallah's father commented in the mudbrick room in a Gaza refugee camp, telling everyone to busy themselves with more useful things than dwelling in the past.

But dwell they did. How could they not, when their present reality was equally distressing? When every new day was a mere reminder of the one before and of the shameful past, leading up to the single event that changed the course of the family's life forever?

The al-Badrasawis arrived in Gaza sometime in mid-June 1948, having taken similar routes as other displaced Palestinian families, only staying in Hamameh a few days longer. Ibrahim, Abdallah's father, had a story about that village, years before the Nakba, which he preferred remain untold. He had been accused of killing a man in Beit Daras, a charge he vehemently claimed was untrue, or at least exaggerated, holding that if he had killed anyone, it was not premeditated and, therefore, not murder. It started with an ordinary fight between youths over some trivial matter that escalated from fisticuffs to clubs. Everyone seemed to be swinging his weapon, striking at random. Ibrahim swore that he was nowhere near the young man who received the lethal blow. But members of the rival clan told the *mukhtar* it was Ibrahim, and no one else, who killed the boy.

It could have been much worse. Ibrahim was part of the powerful Baroud clan, and exacting revenge on a member could lead to a civil war between the major families of Beit Daras. "We are already fighting a great menace, the English and the Zionists," the *mukhtar* began, in a speech at the end of several days of charged testimonies and angry calls for revenge. "We cannot lose our finest youth because of a fight between brothers which ended in a tragedy," he pleaded. Some nodded with enthusiasm, others begrudgingly.

Following repeated consultations between the two clans, the *mukhtar* resolved that the Baroud family would publicly disown Ibrahim, who would be exiled to a village of his choosing.

Under the agreement, the rival clan would forfeit their "debt of blood" and receive a piece of land, two calves, and a few sheep in return. At the end, men from both sides stood and hugged in the *mukthar*'s presence, in the very courtyard where the victim had lain, fatally wounded, a few years earlier. The women of the victim's clan sobbed, emitting a collective and sudden scream that, in the words of those who claimed to have heard it, "made the stones cry." The Baroud women abstained from ululating out of respect for the other family. Ibrahim, now publicly renounced, shamed, and alone, took a few of his belongings and made his way to Hamameh.

There he married Miriam al-Qassas, and they had two children, Abdallah and Jameelah. Their son, Saeed, and two girls, Haleemah and Sa'ada, were born in Beit Daras when the family returned to their original home, having been allowed to return when the rival clan retracted their demand that Ibrahim be permanently exiled. Ibrahim never reclaimed his family name and had no last name in Hamameh, where he was known as "Badrasawi"—"the man from Beit Daras." When allowed to return, even the Beit Daras villagers called him "al-Badrasawi," a family name forever affiliated with Ibrahim's branch of the Baroud family.

When Ibrahim and his wife took their children and fled Beit Daras for the last time, it was engulfed in smoke, gunfire, explosions, and the screams of dying villagers. At first he thought Hamameh would be safer for a short stay. He trusted, like most Palestinians, that they would all soon return home. But, a few days later, Hamameh and all the villages around Beit Daras fell, one after the other, to advancing Zionist militias. Since Yafa, one of the closest major cities, had already fallen, the only rational path was to flee south to Gaza, where the Egyptian army remained strong and most of the survivors of the ongoing onslaught were gathering.[41]

After a few days' journey, the family arrived at Shujaiyeh. The old Gaza neighborhood overflowed with desperate refugees seeking food and shelter. The need was far too great, and only one organization came to the aid of the refugees.[42] The Quakers were pitching tents in different parts of Gaza, in areas allocated by the Egyptian army, which administered the southern coastal region at the time. The empty areas by the beach were ideal for such a task. True, they were arid, with no running water or infrastructure of any kind, but they were largely uninhabited. In northern Gaza, the new encampments, with Quaker-supplied tents, quickly became synonymous with the surrounding beach, and the Shati refugee camp was born.[43]

The al-Badrasawi family eventually settled there in a small tent, initially with just a few used blankets and no mattresses. Soon, many of the oldest and youngest in the tent camp began to perish, the former too frail and exhausted to endure more torment, the latter succumbing to malnourishment, diarrhea, measles, and other ailments and diseases. Others, per the wisdom of the time, died from broken hearts after being separated from their land and often their families. But Ibrahim's family survived.

Those who survived were either the most able-bodied and resourceful or belonged to large clans that remained together, whenever possible. A makeshift graveyard was dug at the Shati beach within days of the first displaced families arriving. Unfamiliar with the land's topography, the refugees didn't yet comprehend the habits of the Mediterranean, its changing moods and rising tides. In one single nighttime storm, hundreds of dead bodies were swept away at once, swallowed by an angry sea. A new graveyard was erected elsewhere at a higher elevation, and quickly grew.

But Ibrahim and men like him learned, with time, to befriend the sea, which became the main source of income for thousands of families. He learned to fish, but his porous little boat, which he had fashioned himself from discarded wooden planks, proved too risky. Stronger and more capable men had lost their lives fishing from better-built boats. So Ibrahim taught himself to make fish hooks, selling them to other fishermen in the area, and eventually as far as Nuseirat and even Khan Younis. This skill was a valuable addition to other expertise he had acquired while in Hamameh, particularly the weaving of baskets, a best-selling item at Yafa flea market.

Abdallah, ten years old when he accompanied his father in his Nakba journey, also joined him in his refugee camp business a few months later. The work, never easy, was always life-saving. The numerous cuts to his hands from working with old, rusty knives and sharp objects carved more than physical scars, charting a life of suffering that concluded with his death in the same Shati refugee camp many years later.

"House of Hair"

The evolution of life in the refugee camp can be traced back through the types of shelters that the refugees created for themselves immediately after the Nakba, or that were provided for them over time.

When the al-Badrasawi family arrived at Shati, they lived in old British military barracks, which were surrounded by trenches that had been dug out years earlier when the British military was stationed in Gaza.[44] The family later pitched a small tent that Palestinian Bedouins called a "house of hair." Theirs was not the most sophisticated structure, especially compared to the quality of tents made by the well-rooted Bedouin tribes of Gaza[45] who had mastered the craft of weaving animal hair into sturdy shelters. The "house of hair" was not only convenient in terms of mobility but was also adaptable in the face of intense heat and rainwater. In the summer it provided shade and allowed cool breezes to enter the simple dwelling, and in the rainy season it contracted, preventing water from pooling on top or seeping inside.

The Al-Badrasawis didn't know how to weave goat or camel hair, or even sheep wool, to make homes. By the time they left their home back in Beit Daras, it had more stone than mudbrick. In the words of Mariam, the house had more than enough space for a horseman to run wild. Ibrahim's fishing business enabled him to raise enough money to purchase a woven animal hide, which he used to assemble the family's first tent a short distance from the beach. Less fortunate families lived in ditches or slept in the open; and others bartered endless hours of their labor in the services of Gaza's aristocratic families or Bedouin tribes in exchange for temporary shelter and meager food.[46]

The Quakers introduced modern tents when they began demarcating the borders of the eight refugee encampments across Gaza. They were not necessarily better or more durable than the "houses of hair" but did come with an occasional piece of bread, a can of cheese, or even a warm meal. Under the Quakers, the camps became, relatively speaking, "proper" refugee camps. They were never intended to be permanent—the displaced communities truly believed that their tribulations were fleeting moments in history and that their rights would soon be restored, starting with their triumphant return to their villages.

This collective feeling was buoyed by the Right of Return, an international decision cherished by Palestinian refugees to this day.[47] The clearly worded language of this 1948 United Nations resolution, resolving that "refugees wishing to return to their homes and live at peace with their neighbors should be permitted to do so at the earliest practicable date," encouraged the refugees to keep the keys to their homes. It was also why they treasured the deeds to their land and all relevant papers that attested to the fact that these 200,000 refugees in Gaza belonged somewhere else, that they came from villages with names and homes with *hakouras*, with traceable histories, memories, and more importantly, identities of their own, as old as time itself.[48] The al-Badrasawis and the rest of the displaced families also believed, or perhaps wanted to believe, that the "house of hair" or Quaker tent, flimsily erected over arid land surrounded by an angry sea, would not be their enduring legacy.

Speaking to his father, Abdallah often expressed his deep concern that the road to Beit Daras might be lost forever, to which Ibrahim would reply, with unmistakable certainty, that no one can ever miss the road to Paradise, and that the gentle hand of God, which had protected them from snipers on their way to Shati, would guide them back to their homes.

Ibrahim didn't live long enough to be guided by the hand of God. He died sometime between the Quaker tents and the mud-brick rooms of the United Nations Relief and Works Agency (UNRWA). "He is in a better place now," his sobbing wife told the crying children, trying to console them as their father's body was prepared for his ascension to the same place above, now all too familiar to the refugees. He was buried in the new graveyard, far away from the sea, in accordance with the Shati elder wisdom that the soul only ascends when it receives a proper burial.

Although a young teen, Abdallah was immediately declared *rajul al-bait*—man of the house—and proudly embraced his new responsibilities for a whole family of refugees.

Ibrahim's sudden death called for a new division of labor within the household since, before this earth-shattering event, he had been the main breadwinner, and Abdallah merely his ever-obedient assistant. The family had no money, and barely enough food for a few days. All Ibrahim left behind was the skill of making fish hooks and other fishing-related items he had devised as he gained more experience. Abdallah and Saeed resorted to their father's business, but only for a short while, before embarking on careers as fishermen.

It was a daunting task, but it had to be done, and they were helped by those with more experience who were kind enough to lend a hand. They fixed and repainted their father's small fishing boat, and patched the fishing net worn out by neglect and gnawing rats. The girls, who had joined the class of Sit Fathia to learn the Arabic alphabet and basic math, had to abruptly leave the tent school in the camp's Bloc A to instead learn how to make fishing supplies.[49] Even after Ibrahim's death, the family was determined to survive.

Mariam, however, did not. The ailment that caused her death soon after her husband's demise was diagnosed by other camp women as resulting from *waja al-qalb*, the "pain of the heart" that seemed to kill many back then, mostly men grieving for their lost land and *karameh*, and women for their husbands, children, and honor. Though Mariam cried endlessly for Hamameh, Beit Daras, and all her beloved who perished there, her heart gave in when her husband Ibrahim died. She was buried next to him. Neither had a tombstone, just a few words scribbled in the dirt, the letters vanishing quickly in the first gust of wind: Ibrahim Mahmoud al-Badrasawi and Mariam Ahmed al-Qassas. Places of birth: Beit Daras. Hamameh. Nothing else.

Shati became an official refugee camp in 1951, as the encampment had grown to a population of 23,000 Palestinians. It was registered with the UN, meaning refugee inhabitants, bearing a name and card, were now entitled to stand in long lines to receive monthly rations of food, mainly rice, flour, and sugar. The food was never enough, with some immediately selling their rations to buy clothes or medicine, and others consuming them within the span of a few days, leaving themselves hungry until the next month. But UNRWA's greatest contribution was replacing the tents with mudbrick shelters.

The process of tearing down tents and replacing them with more stable structures started in mid-1950s but didn't reach Shati until a year later. The size of each family's allocated space varied depending on the number of family members, with a large family receiving a dwelling of sixteen square meters (around 172 square feet). Most homes consisted of a single mudbrick room with little ventilation, and roofs made of mixed material, including dry vegetation such as straw, with zinc and, later, asbestos sheets.

The al-Badrasawi family adapted to their new life, and their chances of survival seemed to improve. There was an UNRWA clinic nearby, although it was known to prescribe the same aspirin pills for every ailment. When the sick were not saved by the miracle of aspirin, their deaths were blamed on mysterious forces beyond UNRWA's control. The camp's two latrines, or more precisely holes in the ground, were separated by gender, set a distance apart to protect women's privacy. A long, sometimes agonizing wait was better than no sanitation system at all.

But the introduction of these apparently permanent structures was not universally welcomed, leading to two questions
that seemed conspiratorial at the time but would later seem
entirely justified. First, if the world was pressuring the new
state of Israel to allow displaced Palestinian families back to
their villages, why was the UN replacing tents with mudbrick
houses? And second, if the Arabs, and particularly the Egyptian
government, intended to restore the refugees to their homeland, why were they collaborating with the United Nations to
resettle them elsewhere?

Just Like Nasser

While the al-Badrasawi children were not consumed by any of
these questions, Abdallah and, to some extent, Saeed, would
occasionally opine about the general situation by repeating
what they heard from other fishermen at the beach. For
example, they knew that Jamal Abdul Nasser and his Free Officers had taken over Egypt after overthrowing the King.* They
were excited by this because their father had often praised
Egyptians, and Nasser in particular, for his Fallujah heroics.[50]

Those who better understood the political upheaval in Egypt
were more concerned. Two years after the 1952 Revolution,
Nasser and the British government signed a treaty that would
end the British military presence in the country.[51] The British
were hated by most Egyptians, who, having experienced humiliation, servitude, and outright atrocities at the hands of their
British colonial masters, were not predisposed to allow them
a phased, slow withdrawal. The Nakba deepened the wounds,

* Jamal Abdul Nasser toppled the Egyptian monarchy in a coup on July 23, 1952.

increasing popular demands for the invaders to leave immediately. The Muslim Brotherhood rejected some of the treaty's terms, openly challenging the authority of Nasser and his Free Officers.[52] The ensuing struggle defined Egyptian politics, wars, and revolutions for subsequent decades, and indeed up to the present day. However, years into Nasser's revolution, Palestinians saw little to reassure them the Arabs were about to defeat Israel, which continued to attack refugee encampments, not only in Gaza but wherever refugees pitched their tents or built their mudbrick homes.[53]

Abdallah al-Badrasawi didn't meet Jamal Abdul Nasser when, accompanied by a large military convoy, he visited Gaza in March 1955, but he remembered the sense of joy that permeated the area at the time and the large crowds cheering in unison when Nasser promised their safety, return, and liberation.[54]

Nasser's visit was followed by the formation of several battalions under the command of the Egyptian army, which largely consisted of Egyptian officers and Palestinian soldiers.[55] But even before the national guards were established by a presidential order, Palestinians were already fighting, and indeed had been for years, often in small groups known as the *fedayeen*. These Gazan freedom fighters would, over time, become legends that would inspire future armed rebellions. Now, however, they were army-like units with specific missions, namely protecting Gaza against Israeli military raids and, when the time was right, crossing the border into Palestine, freeing the captive homeland, and restoring the refugees to their rightful place.[56] Alas, the *fedayeen* never crossed into Palestine, at least not as a conquering army. Those who did cross the "border" carried out attacks that resembled daring *fedayeen* operations in the late 1940s and early '50s. Otherwise, the new fighting units, with little training and limited munitions, found themselves embroiled in a war they would not endure.

In late 1956, a major war broke out, pitting the British, French, and Israeli armies against Egypt, which withdrew from Sinai, leaving the national guards of Gaza with no option but to surrender.[57] Those who didn't surrender, like the Khan Younis garrison in southern Gaza, fought to the bitter end. The Khan Younis battle and subsequent massacre became a painful but proud chapter in Gaza's history.[58] By November 1956, Israel controlled Gaza and much of Sinai. Though the British and French forces withdrew later that year, the Israelis remained until the following March, attempting to ensure that neither Gaza nor Sinai would be used to attack their newly founded state. When they finally left, Gaza's makeshift graveyards had grown in every direction.[59]

Nasser remained a hero to Abdallah al-Badrasawi. Even when the relationship between Gaza's political elites and Cairo became difficult following the war, Abdallah tried to imitate Nasser's speech and public conduct, listening carefully to Nasser's speeches on the radio and repeating whatever lines he retained to the fishermen at the beach, who would clap in amusement, some mockingly and others genuinely impressed. Abdallah challenged those who dared doubt that Nasser would one day liberate Palestine with evidence from Nasser's own radio speeches, as if the fiery lines were irrefutable evidence: "Brothers, it is impossible that history should repeat itself. Today, we do not repeat what happened in the past. We are eradicating the traces of the past."[60] The fishermen cheered "Nasser, Nasser, Nasser!" for Abdallah, who paused, smiled, and moved his right hand in an upward and then downward motion, just like Nasser.

Abdallah received little formal education, attending Miss Fathia's classes only briefly due to his work at sea, leaving at dawn and returning, depleted, in the evening after selling his catch, if any. When Miss Fathia converted her Ihsan School to the Ihsan Kindergarten after UNRWA set up a school project in the camp, Abdallah joined other pupils, staying long enough to learn how to read and write. His more scholarly brother, Saeed, who had fewer responsibilities due to physical infirmities that lingered from childhood to old age, continued in the UNRWA school system. Sa'ada, the youngest of the girls, did the same, while Jameela and Halima settled on barely knowing how to draw their names in the wet sand near their father's old boat.

Life nonetheless improved for the family. Abdallah, largely oblivious to the politics of his era but also impressed by Nasser's persona, wanted to be a fighter.[61] Saeed settled on the quest of becoming a teacher, as did Sa'ada. The others looked after the home, facilitating the survival of a family of children who had been orphaned at the worst possible time.

Like Love

If Abdallah ever loved Madallah, it was sometime between the immediate aftermath of the 1956 war, when they first met, and the 1967 Naksa—meaning "setback" or "defeat"—when Israel conquered what remained of Palestine.* Madallah was known in the area as the once-mute girl who only spoke to the *jinn*, an unflattering designation for a girl who had already missed the "marriage train," as she was repeatedly reminded by her distraught and anxious mother, Mahasin. Already twenty-one years old, with little physical beauty, and haunted by a reputation concerning her association with ethereal beings who spoke with

---

* What Palestinians call "The Naksa," Israelis call "The Six-Day War."

terrifying voices, she accepted her fate, confiding to her only friend in the camp that she intended to dedicate her life to God and study the Holy Quran. Alas, she could neither read nor write.

Abdallah freed her from that commitment when he met her at the beach just before sunset. She was hoping that he would lower the price on his new catch of fish. It was not love at first sight. He only noticed her eyes, seeing that they, just like his own, epitomized sorrow. Her style of haggling wasn't aggressive like the others: she simply said that her family had not tasted meat or fish in a long time, and that she only had a small amount of money, hardly enough to meet the asked price. He didn't argue, took the money, gave her the fish she asked for, and added two small sardines, handing her the bag with a gentle and awkward smile. It was not difficult to find out who the girl was, as the fishermen, and indeed the whole neighborhood, had known about her "blessed family" for years. Though her father never joined the refugees in their Nakba journey, his reputation as a man of God transcended time and distance.

Speaking in a whisper as if revealing a big secret, though the story was widely known, one of the fishermen addressed himself to Abdallah and others, who sat listening attentively: "They say that when the man died, his coffin levitated over the shoulders of the other men carrying him to the graveyard. The only way to bring down the coffin was to desecrate it somehow." According to him, the only way to do this was for one of the mourners to put out their cigarette on the side of the coffin, finally compelling the soaring spirit to settle down until the end of the funeral prayer.*

But Abdallah didn't need any convincing that the girl pos-

---

* Ṣalāt al-Janāzah is the Arabic term for Islamic funeral prayer.

sessed a beauty of a different kind. Madallah's eyes alone told him that, beneath her rough and tired exterior, she was loving, loyal, hardworking, and patient. Abdallah could sense this just by looking at her face, as she stood with old, mismatched slippers in a patched dress, tightly gripping a small amount of change.

After this encounter, a small delegation made its way to Madallah's house, consisting of a chatty old neighborhood woman, her husband, who said little throughout proceedings, and Abdallah and his siblings. Madallah's mother asked for no dowry, not even a single gift for her daughter: "Since my husband's death, all I have been seeking is *sutra* for Madallah," she muttered in a hardly audible voice, looking at the dirt ground in front of her. In those days, everyone wanted *sutra*, the coveted hope of securing one's daughters, protecting them against dishonor and solitude.

Still, Abdallah gathered most of his savings to furnish an additional small space granted to him by UNRWA, building another mudbrick room, furnished with a new mattress, an old wooden closet, an attached mirror, and a straw rug, which contained two new dresses for his bride. He even bought her a golden bracelet, whose authenticity was never questioned or verified. Their honeymoon was a day without work for Abdallah. The following day, she was back at work, offering her cleaning services to Gaza's aristocrats, who paid little and shouted derogatory comments about her looks, her hygiene, and the cursed day Gaza became infested with refugees.

In the beginning, Abdallah was kind to Madallah. But his kindness faded over time, as another side began to appear, especially after she failed to deliver on the unspoken promise to have children. It mattered little to Abdallah or the gossipy women of Shati that the cause of such delay might be the young man himself. Madallah was two years older than Abdallah; this unusual occurrence was all the evidence needed by some to demonstrate her infertility. No specialist was consulted on the matter, partly because there were none in the area; in any case, it did not matter if there was one in the big city, as they would be unaffordable.

Madallah's mother would not be there to support her during the difficult time. After years of living with an untreated illness, one day she choked a little, froze for a minute, tipped over to her right side, and was gone. The once-mute girl with strange habits was now barren and alone. But there was a limit to the abuse she could endure without protesting or fighting back.

She would sit for days in that room, once a wedding nest and now a dark space for her equally dark thoughts. Abdallah would return, quickly wash, do what he needed to do to fulfill what he saw as his manly duty and go to bed, still reeking of fish and the sea. With time, he began to give up some of this routine, seeing no point in prolonging the illusion that his wife was capable of getting pregnant and giving birth.

His resentment turned to verbal abuse. But even if she would allow herself to be physically harmed, a force larger than her would not permit this. A single slap to her face changed the dynamic of their relationship, a change that prevailed until his unceremonious death in the same refugee camp years later. Her eyes seemed to turn red, as if anger was not emanating from her throat or guts but her very soul, as she roared in an unfamiliar voice: "The hand that will touch Madallah will be broken." Even as he ran outside, carrying his shoes in one hand and his pajama shirt in the other, he could still hear the voice, growing deeper and stronger: "The hand that will touch Madallah will be broken." After this, she was not physically abused by her husband again for years, until after the war.

After five years, she eventually gave birth to Ibrahim, softening the family dynamic. Time and the hardships of life taught Abdallah and Madallah to care for each other, with Ibrahim's arrival renewing a sense of love, or something like love, that they had once, however fleetingly, shared. Ibrahim had dark skin like Madallah, and small, slightly twisted ears like his grandfather, whose namesake lived in the family for generations. Madallah dedicated every waking minute to her son, granting him all the love she could give, and all the love she never received. She knitted his clothes and seemed to be constantly feeding him, although her breasts sometimes ran dry due to her own malnourishment. A friend advised: "Women who cry too often produce little milk." But there was little Madallah could do to stop the tears from falling, even when breastfeeding. The birth of their daughter Sud was less exciting for the couple, not because of her gender but because poverty was exceptionally grinding in the years leading up to the war.

Liberation Postponed

Abdallah eventually joined the military, although the Palestine Liberation Army (PLA) was hardly an army in the sense of answering to a centralized political leadership that possessed a forward strategy or war plan. Like most decisions pertaining to Palestine and the Palestinians before the war of 1967 and Naksa, the new Palestinian army and the Palestine Liberation Organization (PLO) were not actually led by Palestinians.

Abdallah didn't comprehend much of this and, even if he had, would not have cared. His political discourse consisted mainly of simple maxims, such as "all Arabs are brothers" and "Nasser knows best." In 1964, when men were being sought to populate the PLA's Gaza brigades, he was one of the first to stand in line. The Ain Jalut Brigades took shape quickly after the recruiting process began, with some men, like Abdallah, joining to fight, and others joining to stave off starvation.

The PLO was wholly incorporated into Egypt's political domain. Its leader, Ahmad al-Shuqayri, was a follower of Nasser. He had been chosen as the first leader of the PLO in 1964 because he was the best fit for a job that had no space for independent minds. Throughout his life, he sought to achieve political balance with the ultimate aim of serving his own interests. Born in what is now Lebanon when it was part of the Ottoman Empire, his mother was Turkish and his father Palestinian. He worked as a lawyer under the British in Palestine, joined the Syrian delegation at the UN, was prominent in the newly formed Arab League, and was even, at one point, the Saudi ambassador to the UN.[62]

But al-Shuqayri alone cannot be blamed for this lack of a truly independent Palestinian leadership. Nasser was too powerful—some say even too loved—to be disobeyed. Any Palestinian leadership was expected to "rubber stamp" decisions made on its behalf elsewhere. For example, though the decision to establish the PLA was held to have been made in May 1964 by Palestinian national figures who had congregated in East Jerusalem as part of the Palestinian National Conference, the decision was actually made a few months later by the Egypt-dominated Arab League.[63]

In full formation, the new army had eight brigades—12,000 soldiers with light weapons, mortars, and rocket launchers, who traveled in personnel carriers and tanks.[64] Yet they never fought as a single military unit, only as auxiliary forces led by other Arab armies, whether in Gaza (under Egyptian command), Iraq, Syria, and later Jordan.

Each of the initial brigades bore the name of a victorious but historically distant battle: the Ain Jalut of Gaza was named after a historic battle in which the Mamluk army defeated the arrogant, and until then invincible, Mongols in the thirteenth century; Qadisiya of Iraq was named after a seventh-century battle, when a Muslim army humbled the Persians; and Hittin after a twelfth-century battle, when the conquering army of Salah al-Din al-Ayyubi vanquished the Crusaders.

These brigades fought without a Palestinian version of Sayf al-Din Qutuz, Sa'd ibn Abi Waqqas, or Salah al-Din, not because none existed but rather because Palestinian bravery and bloodshed could not be acknowledged. Beyond the Palestinian-inspired insignias, colors, and slogans, these splintered Palestinian armies were actually someone else's fighting forces, to be utilized throughout the years, at best to strengthen the supposed bond between various Arab capitals and Jerusalem, and, at worst, to fight internal Arab wars.

History does not say anything about Abdallah al-Badrasawi, and little about the thousands of other Palestinians who, in joining the PLA, hoped, but failed, to liberate Palestine. Nor does it say much about the tens of thousands of Arabs, mostly *fellahin* and laborers, who were conscripted or volunteered to fight against layers of Western colonialism that had plagued their world for generations. Some scholars of the war, dubbed Naksa by the Arabs and the "Six-Day War" by Israel, dedicate much time to blaming Egypt for the conflict. These scholars say Nasser had shut down the Strait of Tiran, thus forcing Israel to initiate a preemptive "war of self-defense." These scholars have

not read the last letters written by Egyptian and Palestinian soldiers, which littered the Sinai Desert along with thousands of
lifeless bodies in June 1967. If they did, maybe they would have
realized that the Arabs were fighting a just war.

Abdallah, however, was not in Sinai on June 5, when the war
began. He was stationed somewhere west of Gaza City, keeping
an eye on the coast in case of a surprise Israeli attack. He took his
few bullets, allocated to each soldier, out of his pocket, and loaded
them carefully into his rifle, trying to mask his fears by reciting a
verse from the Quran, one he frequently repeated whenever on
guard duty for his PLA unit: "If Allah should aid you, no one can
overcome you; but if He should forsake you, who is there that
can aid you after Him? And upon Allah let the believers rely."[65]

His last note to his family was written in obvious haste. It
was addressed to his brother and not Madallah, who could not
read. "Dear Brother Saeed," he began, in what was supposed
to be an ordinary letter that read more like a last will, "Shall
I not return, please look after my wife, children, and our own
dear sisters. Life has been unkind to them, but this victory shall
change everything. If I die, I die as a martyr. If I live, all of us
shall return to our home in Beit Daras." The letter, replete with
spelling errors and grammatical mistakes, was eventually delivered, but Abdallah neither lived nor died and instead simply
disappeared. Those who served with him in the Gaza branch of
the PLA were killed, went missing themselves, or later informed
Abdallah's family that they knew nothing of his whereabouts
after the devastating bombing of the camp.

The war was over before it began, as Israel, using Western
intelligence and weapons, decimated Egyptian air defenses
while the planes were still on the tarmac. Without air support,
Sinai became a killing field for tens of thousands of fleeing

Egyptian soldiers and PLA youth attacked from the air, ground, and sea. The brave young man who pushed in to activate the camp's only anti-air defense didn't alter what seemed like an imminent and crushing defeat. Abdallah was, along with most of his comrades, blown up, destroying the hope that the war would reverse Palestinian misfortunes that began in Beit Daras and 500 other villages two decades earlier.

One year later, Abdallah finally returned. Though he had only been gone a year, he seemed much older. On that fateful day in June, a bullet irreversibly damaged his spinal cord, and a shell that had exploded close to him left blood pouring from wounds all over his neck and body. When the Israelis found him still alive, they did not take him to a hospital but instead to an interrogation.

He was conscious but also unaware. The whole experience seemed to be a hazy episode produced by a failing memory. He simply could not grasp the events that had transpired so quickly after the initial explosion, and did not realize for days that a bullet, which would accompany him for the rest of his life, had penetrated his back. First, so much pain; then no pain at all, followed by short bouts of excruciating pain that made him faint time and again; and then back to the state of utter numbness. He remembered officers dressed in clean uniforms who kept repeating the same questions, threats, words: "What do you know? Where are the others? It is all over... If you refuse to collaborate, there will be more of *this*..." "This" was torture, which Abdallah began to feel as the initial shock to his body faded away, fingers inside one of his wounds pressing harder and harder.

But Abdallah al-Badrasawi had nothing to say, even to save his own life, receive medical attention, or take a sip of water. Images of his father's old boat, his first fishing expedition, the road to Julus, his mother's kindly face, little Ibrahim with his twisted ears, Madallah—alternately silent, subdued, and angry—and many more flashed in his mind. The voice of Nasser promising liberation and verses from the Quran promising Paradise to the righteous kept replaying in his head like a broken record. The flashing images and the recurring voices intersected with the unfamiliar Arabic of a well-dressed officer, who sometimes laughed and on other occasions spat in his face for "making things too difficult" for him and the other interrogators.

Abdallah didn't know what to make of any of this and indeed knew only one thing with bitter certainty: the war was lost, and the road back to Beit Daras and Paradise was—at least for him and his generation—also lost forever.

Chapter Five

Ibrahim

When Abdallah arrived in Shati a year after his initial disappearance, he was a changed man, though the source of the dramatic change in his personality was never truly understood. His impairments, which were self-evident, were a form of amusement for some of the camp's children. Upon emerging from a year of torture and imprisonment, Abdallah seemed to walk in slow motion, his right foot advancing slowly to become parallel to the left foot, before both feet and his whole body froze for a moment, as if deliberating the next move. The left foot would then, at the same speed, repeat the same motion. Abdallah had to be aware of these movements at all times, as they were no longer intuitive. If he lost focus, he'd freeze for a long time or even collapse to the ground.

The experience was humiliating for the family, especially when coupled with the speech impediment that, at times, made it impossible for him to communicate. When he stood to swear at the unruly children, the easiest expressions were still too difficult to convey: "Youuuuuuu, soooooooooons offff a bbbbb..." was almost never uttered in full, provoking more bursts of laughter, and a collective attempt by the children to mimic Abdallah's funny way of speaking and even funnier way of moving.

Only the grown-ups understood why Abdallah, once a PLA freedom fighter, had become this way, and would yell at the children, sometimes reprimanding them or shaking their heads, lamenting, "There is no power and no strength except with God,"[66] before adding, "If injuring him was not enough, they tortured him as well."

Their understanding of his condition was hardly scientific, and it was clear his ailment could only be managed by the better-equipped Egyptian medical facilities. But his family had no income, no savings, and barely enough to eat. The only realistic option was for Ibrahim, now eight years old, and then his brothers, Tala't and Nasser, to generate some kind of income themselves.

Although Abdallah and Madallah's boys remained in school for several years before joining the growing child workforce, they were not interested in education at UNRWA's impoverished schools solely for the sake of learning. Staying in school meant possessing the precious *kart al-t'umeh*, a card that entitled them to a meal, however old or stale, from one of UNRWA's centers. This daily meal took care of lunch. If dinner was an option, they would be satisfied with cheaply produced but filling meals such as the famous *damseh*—lentil soup—or *mallaha*. The latter's name comes from the word *maleh*, meaning salt, and consists of old, dry bread softened and then crushed in boiling water before being mixed with a large amount of salt. The excessive amount of salt was intended to dull the taste buds, helping the children ignore the fact that they were eating old, often moldy bread."

Ibrahim, however, was different from the other children.

He wanted a better life for his family. Seeing his father in that pitiful state made him angry at everyone and everything, but he excelled at managing his anger, especially as the kids in the neighborhood granted him the honorary title *il-walid*—the father. Even Ibrahim's youngest sisters called him "Dad," as he was the one looking after the rest. Before ultimately finding employment inside Israel, Ibrahim would work at the Gaza beach cleaning fishing boats, or, at the Gaza Valley, digging dirt and hauling rocks. These backbreaking tasks often translated to an occasional fish dinner, or, better yet, a few Israeli pounds, the new currency Israel brought along with its soldiers, tanks, and the military government, which managed the occupation of Gaza and the rest of the newly occupied Palestinian areas.[67]

Fedayeen and Bulldozers

The challenges Israel encountered in Gaza far exceeded those experienced in the rest of occupied Palestine. The Gaza population was humiliated, enraged, starved, and hardened by life. The Nakba generation was not too old to overlook the original injustice, which led to their dispossession of a lost, but not forgotten, homeland, while the new generation had internalized all the suffering of the past and the present to become a fighting force of its own, equally angry and determined.

While the Israelis at some level understood this, it did not translate to practice. They continued to entertain the illusion that, by restructuring the demographics of the refugee camps as part of their establishment of a new military order in Gaza, they would be able to break the will of two generations. The Israeli military governor of Gaza wanted to annex the refugee camps into larger towns, with the intention of downgrading the significance of the camps as a source of resistance. He failed, and this failure continues to be a never-ending nightmare for the Israeli occupation.

The integration process, which required major population transfers and equally massive destruction of streets, homes, and whole neighborhoods, began slowly, for it required the pacification of the local resistance—remnants of the PLA, the old *fedayeen*, and the new fighters, who joined the resistance following the defeat of the Naksa. Public executions of fighters and anyone who was suspected of aiding them, or refused to disclose their whereabouts were held in broad daylight and with great fanfare. Israeli military jeeps would speed through Palestinian crowds, usually in open-air markets, come to a sudden stop, drag a blindfolded young man—sometimes a teenage boy—from one of the vehicles, place him in the center of a crowd, shoot him dead, and then retreat as quickly as they arrived.

Though the intention was to instill fear, a different response was often generated, with the body of the new martyr being folded in a Palestinian flag, adorned with olive branches, and buried amid national songs and Quranic recitations jointly harmonized by the grieving refugees: "Oh, mother of the martyr, ululate, for we are all your children," the mourners would sing, as the parents and family of the new martyr were led by a large crowd to the burial place, and then back home to hold the customary three-day funeral.

Through these events, many of the camp's youth joined the ever-growing resistance movement. When the Israeli occupiers became aware of this, soldiers began hauling the bleeding corpses of executed fighters away without giving them proper burial. They were never seen again, and many theories percolated about what became of them, with the most prominent and credible holding that their final resting place was one of Israel's mushrooming "Cemeteries of Numbers."*

Still, the resistance in Gaza continued, alerting the Israeli military authorities to the fact that the greatest challenge was not individual fighters, or small groups of *fedayeen*, but rather the refugee population itself. When Israeli efforts to resettle a large number of refugee communities outside occupied Palestine failed, Ariel Sharon** spearheaded a different strategy, namely breaking up refugee communities within Gaza.[68]

Sharon, the general officer who led the Southern Command at the time, was already known to Palestinians for his cruelty and his tried-and-true methods of subduing what Israel called *al-mukharibeen*—"troublemakers." He resolved that if the refugees of Gaza were to be crushed, army tanks needed to be able to reach every corner of each refugee camp. It was between the years 1970 and 1971 that Sharon acquired his title, "the Bulldozer," as he ordered the destruction of entire residential areas.[69] Tens of thousands became homeless or were forcibly removed to Egyptian Al-Arish in northern Sinai, which also fell under Israeli military occupation.[70] Those who were thrown into the desert were mostly the families of those accused of resisting the occupying army.

The al-Badrasawi family was spared the fate of those who disappeared in the sands of the Sinai. Instead, the family—a

---

* The "Cemetery of Numbers" is a collection of covert burial sites with stone enclosures and no proper markers, each grave identified solely by a metal plate with a number, giving the cemetery its name. Human rights organizations have verified that these graves date back to the founding of Israel and that many have been buried in them since the onset of armed Palestinian resistance in June 1967.

** Ariel Sharon was an Israeli general, and later Israeli cabinet member and prime minister, sent to Gaza to implement the "pacification" plan.

disabled veteran, a broken woman and her otherworldly companion, Ibrahim, and his growing number of siblings—lost
their home to Sharon's grand strategy of bulldozing the will of
the Palestinian people. Forced to live in a tent and rely on the
good will of relatives and friends, a new generation of Badrasawis were forced to relive the experience of their predecessors
in a new Nakba.

It took the family two full years to return to Shati, now a
different camp from the one they were forced to leave behind
in the early 1970s. Though some of the streets were paved and
were broader than before, the homes grew more crowded to
accommodate the growing population. Aware of Israel's intentions, the local Gaza City municipality refused to incorporate
Shati under its jurisdiction. Bureij, Nuseirat, and the Maghazi
camps did the same. The Israeli plan succeeded elsewhere, but
only nominally.

Even if Israel had managed to incorporate Shati into the Gaza
City boundaries, it would have made little difference to the refugees' collective thinking, not least because they never stopped
seeing themselves as exiled people whose roots lay somewhere
else entirely. The rebellious leaderships of the local Gaza coun-
cils paid the price for their intransigence, eventually replaced
with collaborating and handpicked village league "leadership."[71]

It was impossible for Ibrahim to remain at school. The family
could not afford to buy school supplies, let alone feed itself or
manage the worsening pain of Abdallah, whose movement was
becoming more difficult with the passage of time. His speech
became even more unintelligible. At thirteen, Ibrahim al-Badrasawi became a full-time worker. At fourteen, he was joined
by his brother Tal'at and, a year later, by Nasser. The three
children would wake up at dawn and walk with hundreds of

laborers in an early morning ritual to the local taxi stand at the outskirts of Shati. There they would catch another ride in overcrowded trucks, small buses, or old, beat-up Fiats to the newly established Eretz military checkpoint. There, they would gather in large numbers, hoping that they would be picked by the *m'alim*—a general term they used for their new Israeli masters, who arrived in trucks or even buses looking for cheap Arab laborers to work in construction, farming, food services, and a myriad of other low-paid jobs.

Due to their youth and lack of experience, the three Badrasawi boys found themselves working on Israeli farms, the same old farms once owned by their *fellahin* grandparents, where they hauled dirt, dug holes, plucked fruits, and cleaned up after animals. When Madallah learned that the Jewish bosses whipped her children to keep them moving and prevent them from being distracted by the kind of silly things that distract most children, she insisted they must not return to work, even if it meant the family starved to death. The marks on little Nasser's body were too much for her to bear, despite Ibrahim's assurances this was fine since all other children were also whipped by their Israeli bosses. When Abdallah insisted, in a fit of barely intelligible anger, that the children must return to work, she stopped arguing, returning to her familiar habit of talking to those who understood her pain better than her own husband.

By then, the family had replaced its rented house with another home allocated by UNRWA, although this time it was smaller than the first. The children, despite the ongoing abuse, were making, relative to Gaza's standards, good money, and in doing so resolved the family's dilemma. They must remain at work. Survival, at times, trumps humiliation, and Madallah's incurable pain of the heart. Ibrahim and his brothers stayed at work with the understanding that they would be seeking alternative jobs as soon as they gained more experience. A few years later, Nasser, though the youngest, proved to be the most skilled worker. As he learned construction, he eventually created a position for his brother, Tal'at. The two worked in the field for the rest of their lives, or, more accurately, until the start of the 1987 uprising. Ibrahim, on the other hand, joined an Israeli criminal gang. There he learned how to lie, steal, and ultimately exact revenge.

Girl from the Sea

While Dalal al-Mughrabi and Ibrahim al-Badrasawi chose different paths in life, it could also be argued that life's complicated circumstances made their choices for them. Unbeknownst to both of them, their lives intersected many times, first when their families were driven from Palestine in the Nakba, and again on March 11, 1978.

On that day, Ibrahim stole a large number of diamonds from an Israeli gang. To the Israelis it was an act of betrayal, but in his mind he was correcting a historical injustice. He was not a criminal himself, or at least he refused to see himself as one. Sami Cohen, on the other hand, was a bad person, and an unrepentant one at that.

For months, Ibrahim manned a fruit stand that belonged to the gang. The stand was a decoy, and though he had limited formal education, Ibrahim was too sharp to miss the obvious signs that his new job was a cover for something more sinister. The clues included mysterious bags changing hands daily, men and women communicating via nods and codes, and expensive cars constantly parking at the meeting place on the opposite side of the road. Still, he paid little attention to these strange repeated spectacles, both because life in Shati was too difficult for him to ask questions that could cost him his job in Israel, and because he felt fortunate to be among the fortunate Palestinian laborers allowed to access Israel through Eretz.[72]

The years following the start of the Israeli occupation were particularly difficult for Palestinians in both Gaza and West Bank. Though life was not easy under the Egyptian and Jordanian administrations, many Palestinians had government jobs, which fostered education, in turn generating a certain degree of respectability in a society still reeling from the dishonor of the Nakba. All such jobs, and the social prestige they wrought, evaporated a matter of days after the war, replaced by even greater dishonor. Israel's alternative job creation in the early phase of its military occupation consisted of collaborating with the army and Shin Bet or joining the newly created Israeli-run Arab police force.[73] Palestinians considered both to be treason.

The Israeli job market then opened, with Palestinians welcomed only as unskilled, cheap laborers, regardless of their education. They were duly exploited, denied social security and pensions, and enjoyed no additional perks whatsoever. But the few liras the jobs provided were enough to keep them coming back, day after day. Ibrahim and his brothers were initially part of this collective human misery, the direct outcome of the dual oppression of the Nakba and Naksa. The clever Gazan boy wanted more than just a few liras, not for himself but for his family, whose life, even in good times, always teetered on the edge of hunger.

When, later in life, Ibrahim narrated the story of his fortunes or misfortunes, he started with Farid al-Atrash, a Syrian Druze singer, whose fame and deep, baritone voice broke down all of the region's economic, political, and social divides. He knew all of her melodies by heart, and sang them beautifully as well, or at least he did before smoking ruined his harmonious voice and took away its youthful charm. He would fill his long hours of idleness at work, unnecessarily restacking the oranges while vocalizing, loudly and without the slightest embarrassment, the hymns of Farid al-Atrash: "Life is beautiful, if we only understand it. Life is a song, and we are its rhythms." This is how Sami Cohen, an Arab Jew who also loved Farid's work, found Arabic entertainment, the missing piece in his criminal circle.*

For Ibrahim, the pieces of the puzzle of the actual identity of the supposed fruitmongers fell into place. The gang was made up of highly trained diamond thieves. Between big operations, they would lie low, busying themselves by smuggling drugs, mostly cocaine, and selling it in large quantities to other gangs, or in small quantities to highly influential Israelis, including government and military officials. Their den included a makeshift operations room, where an odd-looking doctor would appear once in a while to extract small cocaine packages from body-packing** teenage Israeli girls.

Ibrahim had no reason to care about any of this. He had seen too many army executions in Shati and elsewhere in Gaza to be disturbed by the blood of young Israeli drug runners. Indeed, as a refugee from Gaza, whose life was a perpetual episode of violence, poverty, and humiliation, all that mattered to him was that his daily salary had, overnight, increased nearly thirtyfold, and even more after lucrative heists. In the day, he would sell

---

* "Arab Jews" is a term referring to Jews who originated in the Arab world.
** A "cocaine body-package" refers to a method of smuggling in which individuals internally conceal drug-filled packets—typically in the stomach or other body cavities—to transport them undetected across borders.

fruits, mostly Jaffa oranges, at the decoy fruit stand, and, at night, would serve drinks, wash bloody clothes, and sing Farid al-Atrash songs. Quite often, the long-winded and repetitive notes sent everyone, including gang members, their influential clients, and the occasional prostitute, to sleep.

During the weekend, he would return to Shati with a treasure trove of thousands of liras, which changed his family's life entirely and, as a result of the deteriorating health and mental absence of the actual patriarch of the al-Badrasawi household, cemented Ibrahim's position as the "father." Ibrahim's generosity also attracted new friends and widened the once small social circle of the family. Once a disowned branch of the Baroud clan, the family became the center of attention. Feasts centered around the special Beit Daras *maftoul** nestled under the succulent meat of young calves replaced the daily obligatory portion of *foul*—fava beans and falafel, never mind the canned, sometimes-expired UNRWA meat. Guests of the al-Badrasawi family would return home with the kind of mementos rarely available in Gaza—imported yellow cheese, colored boxes of Dutch candies, and, for the chosen few, boxes of brand-name cigarettes.

The money was good, and while Gaza subsisted in poverty and neglect, Ibrahim's father was finally able to go to Egypt for better healthcare. While his condition never improved, the frequent journeys to Egypt did at least give him a sense of freedom. As the benefactor of the family, Ibrahim grew a mustache, smoked in public, and discussed politics with undeserved confidence. Like most of Gaza's street intellectuals of the time,

---

* Also called "Palestinian couscous," *maftoul* is a Palestinian dish with couscous, aromatic spices, meat, and chickpeas.

his rhetoric mostly focused on the usual subjects of the betrayal
of the Arabs and the latest conquests and bravery of the resistance.

All this suddenly changed, once again, when he heard the
wife of his "Jewish friend" Sami speaking in a phone conversation about an Arab worker fired from whatever low-paying work
he was doing. "Arabs are like dogs," she said in Hebrew while
gnawing on a piece of gum, speaking as if repeating ancient,
unquestionable wisdom. "It is always sad when you lose a dog,
but you also know that you can easily replace him." Whether
this was the decisive moment that turned Ibrahim against his
employers or if he had planned his own heist all along matters
little. On March 11, 1978, he stole for the first time, with a simple
rationale: "Stealing from those who have already stolen from
you is not *haram*"—forbidden by Islamic law. Though the least
religious of his siblings, he was satisfied with his own *fatwa*.*

The truth is, Ibrahim didn't even know exactly what he was
stealing until hours after the crime. If he did, he would most
likely have reconsidered his decision or postponed his plans
until something of lesser value presented itself.

Following the robbery, he rushed home to Shati. As the old
Gaza bus rattled and fumed on its way to Eretz, Ibrahim dis-
creetly opened one of the two small bags he had snatched from
a wooden box at the gang's den. It was an easy heist anyway,
as the thieves were all snoring, loudly and inharmoniously, following a night filled with drugs, alcohol, and Farid al-Atrash.
The actual difficulty was crossing Israeli military checkpoints
and arriving safely at Shati. Exasperated by the tension and
excitement of the event, Ibrahim's hands were shaking when

---

* A ruling on Islamic law given by a recognized authority.

he peered inside one of the two bags, which were not filled with cash or drugs but what seemed like diamonds. For a first-time robber, this was not a good thing.

Two pieces of news made Ibrahim's robbery even more disturbing: first, the gang's original heist quickly became news in Tel Aviv; second, the city and most of the Israeli coastal region were on lockdown because of a young Palestinian girl by the name of Dalal al-Mughrabi.[74]

Dalal was not a thief. She was a twenty-year-old Palestinian-Lebanese fighter who had joined the Palestine Liberation Organization at the age of fourteen, when Ibrahim al-Badrasawi was being whipped by his Israeli masters on a southern fruit farm. Along with her sister, she underwent military training at the age of fifteen. Two years later, she joined the Student Battalion and participated in fighting against the Israeli army at the southern Lebanese border. In late 1977 she was assigned to lead a mission deep inside Israel.

Dalal and Ibrahim had much in common. Her father was a refugee from Yafa, the economic backbone of Beit Daras and most of southern Palestine before the Nakba. They were both offspring of Nakba survivors. She was born in the Sabra refugee camp,[75] while he was born and raised in Shati. Despite their exiles, and distance, they had both experienced Israeli violence—raids, bombardments, and massacres. Their rage, however, was expressed in different ways. He stole diamonds, while she led a group of Palestinian and Arab fighters on a daring mission to take hostages, enter the Israeli parliament, and demand the release of Palestinian prisoners.[76] Another aspect the two had in common is that both of their plans ultimately failed: the inflatable rubber boats, which transported Dalal and her comrades to the Israeli coast, lost their way due to high wind; Ibrahim's robbery, which he hoped would bring him enough money to spare his family a life of degradation, made him the second most wanted villain, not only in the eyes of the Israeli police, but criminal gangs as well. The most wanted Palestinian, of course, was Dalal herself.

Their paths had in fact crossed, at least in Ibrahim's mind. His haggard bus made its way back to Gaza along the highway between Haifa and Tel Aviv, where Dalal's bus, which she and others had hijacked as soon as their boats reached the beach, had zoomed by on its way to the Israeli Knesset. While Ibrahim's vehicle hauled disheveled Gaza workers after a long day of manual labor, Dalal's carried Palestinian fighters in military uniform along with terrified Israeli passengers. As Ibrahim sank into his chair, following the realization that he had acquired the kind of loot that could result in his death or life in prison, Dalal was giving a speech to screaming Israelis about what compelled her and the other fighters to carry out such an operation. Then she began to sing: "My homeland, my homeland, my homeland, I give you my love, I give you my heart." The others joined in: "Palestine, land of ancestors, to you we shall all return."[77] They continued to harmonize about Palestine, the land of the ancestors, to which the refugees must someday return. Ibrahim, however, riding an old bus with rusty metal seats, had nothing to sing about.

Following several successful attempts to break through makeshift Israeli military checkpoints erected hastily along the coastal highway, Dalal and most of the other fighters were eventually killed in an exchange of fire with a unit commanded by an Israeli Lieutenant General, Ehud Barak, who would later become Prime Minister. Many of the hostages were also killed, as the army, Dalal was told, doesn't negotiate with terrorists.

The unfamiliar episode of a Palestinian female commander attacking Israel from the sea was epitomized in a single photograph bringing Ehud Barak and Dalal al-Mughrabi together. In the photo, both wear military uniforms. She is dead and he pulls her body upward as if to confirm the kill before enthusiastic Israeli journalists. He looks triumphant, an Israeli Uzi slung over his back,* while her signature curly hair finally touches the ground of Palestine. She wanted to die in her homeland, and she did. The Israelis called her a "terrorist"; Palestinians immortalized her as the "Bride of Yafa."

When Ibrahim's bus finally arrived on the Israeli side of Eretz, Israeli soldiers surrounded it and ordered all the laborers, including the driver, to step outside and lie face down on the ground. Though only seventeen years old, Ibrahim was skilled in the Palestinian art of survival and started swearing at the soldiers and collaborating Arab policemen. He began hurling all kinds of insults, faking a gouging motion and acting drunk. "This dirty Arab is wasted, sir," a soldier reported to his officer. "Just leave him alone," the officer answered, a look of disgust on his face, possibly imagining this "dirty Arab" vomiting on his newly pressed army uniform.

As soon as Ibrahim arrived at Shati, he rushed to hide his cursed treasure in the hope that time would present him with an opportunity to turn two bags of diamonds into the kind of wealth that no Gaza refugee had or could ever imagine. Unfortunately for him, Madallah, a blessed woman of God who never told a lie, saw him anxiously shove the two bags inside the improvised metal pipes fastened on top of the house as a safety mechanism to keep the asbestos roof in place. Though the

---

* A sub-machine gun adopted by the Israeli army's elite forces in 1956.

actual size of the al-Badrasawi home had remained unchanged throughout the years, some nominal improvements had been made. The zinc roof was now asbestos, and the mudbrick walls had been replaced with stone. Even the wooden door had been tossed away. In its place, a new sturdy metal door stood as an expression of prosperity. It was painted black, red, white, and green, along with the inscription: "Oh Lord, you who have known my difficult condition, I entrust all of my affairs to you."

Preacher

Gaza was changing, but Ibrahim had neither the intellect nor the desire to understand how his generation was catalyzing this change. Unlike the Nakba generation, who saw Israelis as foreign invaders commanding the kind of firepower that could defeat entire Arab armies, Ibrahim's generation had a more realistic estimation of the enemy. Many Palestinians of this generation saw Israelis as people, not just soulless colonizers who stole land and dropped bombs from distant planes.

The 1967 occupation and the growing dependency of impoverished, occupied Palestinians allowed the oppressed refugee families to see Israelis as a dominating and exploitative economic class. They also saw Israeli military without the uniform—in Ibrahim's case, alternately as revelers sniffing cocaine at Sami Cohen's debauched parties or as customers bargaining for good deals on bananas and oranges. Though hated, this class of people did not inspire the same fear as the European newcomers who colonized Palestine earlier in the century.

Still, it took more than economic dependency to eliminate fear altogether, culminating in Dalal storming Israel on a rubber boat and Ibrahim stealing from his criminal employers.

As Palestinian society became more emboldened, Israel, aware of and concerned about the newly empowered generation, organized to crush it from within by using power-hungry and weak-minded Palestinians.

With the 1976 municipal elections, the Israeli military tried to impose a leadership on the West Bank and Gaza, but failed. The attempt only served to marginalize Israel's Palestinian collaborators and the traditional West Bank clans, who had a stronger allegiance to Amman than Jerusalem. The elections, once a touted Israeli strategy, were a fatal and strategic mistake, as almost all Palestinian towns in the occupied territories elected resistance-oriented supporters of the Palestine Liberation Organization.[78] Not knowing how to respond to their own blunder, Israeli extremists, working with the army, began to assassinate the newly elected leadership, while the mainstream Israeli government exiled or fired the rest.

Even Israel's supposed retaliation to Dalal's daring operation created yet another crisis. Almost immediately after Barak's triumphant photo with Dalal's corpse, the Israeli army invaded Lebanon, bombing at will, destroying everything in its path, forging new alliances, and charting yet more military buffer zones. But Operation Litani didn't end the resistance in Lebanon and instead further exacerbated it, opening another front that would result in the all-out Israeli invasion of the country in 1982.[79] Even though the invasion of Lebanon—whose initial success was the direct outcome of the military support and political backing of the United States and Europe—forced the PLO leadership, and most of its fighters, out of the country, its eventual outcome was the rise of the Palestinian national movement at home, leading to the uprising—intifada—of 1987.

Dalal simply wanted to go home and, if necessary, die there, which she did.

She was most likely too young and inexperienced to appreciate how her single action—a seemingly isolated event without a greater strategy—could lead to changes that could tragically alter the region's entire political map. While Dalal didn't live long enough to ponder such philosophical notions, Ibrahim did, though his single daring action was not done for the sake of liberating Palestine but rather his own family's survival.

In some ways, Shati had become a microcosm of the entirety of Palestine, with the influence of once-disempowered refugees growing to define Palestinian politics and resistance. Such influence grew as a result of lack of economic privileges, which continued to be largely controlled by Israel, and bestowed on those who were sufficiently "flexible," a term used by Israeli intelligence officers to assuage the guilt of potential collaborators. But, in truth, wealth in occupied Palestine seemed to follow a familiar path, with the affluent clans remaining powerful regardless of whether political power was concentrated in Tel Aviv, Cairo, Amman, London, or Istanbul. This would gradually corrupt the Palestinian revolutionary project, at least the one defined by the PLO, leading to its eventual dissolution and seismic shifts in Palestinian society and politics.

But wealth, as a tool of power, never truly mattered to Ibrahim nor the al-Badrasawi family. He rarely used his thousands of liras to make any major improvements to his family's humble dwelling, and certainly didn't alter his own shabby appearance or his behavior. True, he did fix the persistent leaks in the roof, acquired new tiles for the kitchen, dealt, however temporarily, with the rat infestation, and treated Madallah and his father with a few new garments. But Ibrahim mostly converted his newfound wealth into of food and gifts for extended family, neighbors, and friends.

His diamonds became a liability and torment. It took the Israeli police years to locate the original robbers and their accomplices, including Ibrahim. He survived several rounds of police and Shin Bet interrogations and beatings, but the diamonds were eventually found because of Madallah's pathological honesty and inability to tell a lie. She gave him away within a minute of the police raid on her house soon after midnight. "We believe that your son has stolen something important from the state of Israel," an officer began. Before he could continue, and without moving her lips, she pointed her right index finger upward, to the ceiling where the loot had been hidden for years.

In 1982, Ibrahim was sentenced to four years in prison, following, of course, the customary torture at the Saraya military headquarters in Gaza.[80] In prison, he learned about Israel's invasion of Lebanon and the subsequent massacres, including in Sabra and Shatila; however, unlike Palestinian "security" prisoners, he couldn't protest, stage a hunger strike, nor clash with the prison guards; instead, he was held with Israeli criminals, who welcomed the opportunity to abuse yet another Palestinian for no other reason than his identity.

When Ibrahim was released, he was angrier, filled with regrets, and desperate for the kind of guidance he could not find at home. The little money the family managed to save from his work in Israel was spent on a Palestinian lawyer, whose impassioned defense hardly registered with the Israeli judge.

Days after Ibrahim's release, his father, Abdallah al-Badra-sawi, ended his difficult journey in life at forty-eight years of age. While Madallah handled the matter with resolve in public, her companion visited her more frequently in private. In her absence, the family, who had only prospered for a short period of time, was once more orphaned. In this latest chapter of the family's troubled history, characters swapped roles and changed names. Ibrahim became Abdallah, who inherited his father Ibrahim's legacy, who was driven out of Beit Daras twice before, never able to find the way back to paradise.

"Die as martyrs!" Al-Qassam once shouted, but none of that generation of al-Badrasawi men did. Ibrahim was content with the fact that he managed to save his family from the fate suffered by hundreds of Badrasawis during the Nakba. Abdallah lost a piece of his sanity as a result of being tortured, continuing to talk about Nasser's imminent liberation of Palestine years after the Egyptian leader died. And it took years of torture and imprisonment to teach Ibrahim that he wasn't a different kind of freedom fighter but rather a thief, and it was Dalal, a young Palestinian girl with curly hair from Lebanon, who deserved to define her generation by exercising her Right of Return. In some way, she did.

Before regaining the permit that allowed him to resume his life of degradation as a cheap laborer in Israel, Ibrahim spent months in Shati in search of a new meaning of life. He was compelled by his own sense of loss, and also the desire to give his youngest brothers, Wael and Ehab, the kind of insight he had been denied, as a result of the absence of both parents. Since he had little wisdom of his own, he took them to the nearest mosque, where a preacher, himself a refugee, was urging the youth to answer the call for jihad.

Ahmed Yassin was born in Jura, not Beit Daras, but his impact on the al-Badrasawi family changed everything, including Palestine itself.

Chapter Six

Yassin

Ahmed Yassin was a source of pity in Shati, having left Al-Jura*
without his father, who died years before the Nakba, when he
was only three years old. When the family arrived at their new
home in the refugee camp, they, like all those around them,
pitched a tent, experienced long bouts of hunger, begged Egyptian soldiers for food, and dreamed of going back. But home, a
quaint little village close to the coast, had been destroyed by the
Israeli's Givati Brigades.[81]

Human beings respond differently to hardship in life: they
either succumb to despair or cling to hope that, as in the case
of the young refugee, can translate to some form of spirituality. Ahmed spent his whole life advocating spiritual existence.
His father's early death strengthened his faith in a Paradise
unperturbed by loss or grief. The Nakba, however, made him
experience the loss of a different kind of paradise, and a grief no
longer his alone.

Just a few years into his new life of dispossession and des-

---

* The Palestinian village of Al-Jura in the Gaza district was destroyed in the Nakba with the
exception of one single house, and its inhabitants completely ethnically cleansed.

99

perate hope, Ahmed, then sixteen, was fated to break his neck while playing with peers near the ever-harsh sea. The numbness grew with time. It originated in the toes, then feet, then both legs and waist. No doctors, had any ever checked on him, could have reversed that excruciatingly painful process. Yet his faith seemed to grow stronger and faster than his pain. When he became quadriplegic years later, and needed to be carried everywhere, only his tongue and a few facial features remained visibly alive. Strangely, it seemed as if his face was frozen in a permanent state of optimism.

The people of Shati began to see Ahmed's life as a miracle of its own. As they sank deeper into despair, he rose above his own agony to become an educated youth, community leader, teacher, and eventually the man who changed the Palestinian struggle for decades to come. With time, sympathy turned into feelings of inspiration, then admiration, then, at least in the minds of many of his followers, utter adoration. Ahmed Yassin became a living symbol of Palestine—shattered, yet very much alive.

Abdallah, whose UNRWA home was only a few meters away from Ahmed's family home, had much in common with Ahmed. Abdallah passed by Al-Joura on his way to Shati, and remembered asking his father why it was called Al-Joura—which means "the hole" in Arabic—even though he hadn't spotted any large holes in the village as they were running away from Zionist mortar shells. Understandably, he received no answer. The boys lived in adjacent tents, buried their loved ones in adjacent graves, labored together by the sea, and struggled their whole lives with their physical disabilities.[82]

But Abdallah believed in Nasser, and Ahmed didn't, though he had at one point. When the Israeli army left Gaza in March 1957, it was replaced by an international force.[83] Decades of struggle against European colonialism, including Zionism, had taught Palestinians that the Israeli army and international forces often shared the intention of depriving Palestinians of political will. So in March 1957, Gazans gathered in mass rallies to protest the international forces that replaced the Egyptian army following the war. Though he had no wheelchair, and in fact did not acquire one for years, Ahmed attended every Gaza rally, chanting with a voice that grew irreversibly hoarse with time. At one rally, he was held up by helping hands to lead the protesters, mostly angry youth. Like all Gazans, he wanted the internationals out and the Egyptians back in.

Even the mass arrests of members of the Muslim Brother-hood, starting in 1954, had little bearing on Ahmed's view of Egypt or even Nasser himself. [84] Ahmed had yet to adopt the doctrine of the Islamic Egyptian movement, later to become their leader in Gaza. For years Ahmed remained consumed with his own deteriorating health and other life affairs, especially following his graduation from high school in 1958. He then taught Arabic and Islamic education at UNRWA schools, using all his meager income to help his mother, Sa'da, who, for many years bore the task of raising a family of seven on her own. The young man's relationship with his mother grew stronger, to the point that the neighbors only knew him as Ahmed Sa'da, not Ahmed Yassin—an uncommon practice in Arabic culture.

While an UNRWA salary did not provide much, it did give Sa'da, Ahmed, and the family a badly needed income. The woman used the money to improve the life of her children, who had relied on the charity of slightly better-off refugees for years. For Ahmed, job security meant he could spend more time at the mosque, first reflecting on the Holy Quran and reading other books, before eventually becoming a preacher, and a popular one at that. Ahmed first flipped the pages of the Quran with his tongue, before later devising an orally controlled mechanism that allowed him to more easily move between pages and books. For him, reading was an escape from the prison of his body, and the larger prison of the refugee camp. With time, he was revered not just as a man with moral authority, but also as one who possessed a deep knowledge, quickly becoming known as "Sheikh Ahmed" to those closest to him, and "Sheikh Ahmed Yassin" to everyone else.

His circle of followers at the Abbas Mosque in Shati grew larger, with each devotee sitting around him for hours to marvel at the wisdom of a man who used his tongue to obtain and impart knowledge.[85] Ahmed taught them about Islam and the centrality of its teachings in the everyday lives of Muslims, and it followed that when such lessons were given to oppressed refugees, this would culminate in a discussion of jihad. Before long, jihad became a focus of the young sheikh's weekly messages from the pulpit. "Die as martyrs!" he said, invoking Izz al-Din al-Qassam, whose influence shaped his understanding of jihad as a liberation struggle.

The historical, spiritual, and political proximity of the men was often discussed by Gaza's Muslim intellectuals. Ahmed was born on June 28, 1936, seven months after al-Qassam was killed in an orchard near Ya'bad.[86] The Syrian preacher organized a small army of rebels, peasants, and workers who were convinced that only armed struggle could rid Palestine of its European invader. He launched a war that ended almost as soon as it began and died a few hours later in a lonely battle doomed from the start.

Egyptian intelligence suspected that Sheikh Ahmed Yassin was a member of the Muslim Brotherhood. Soon after, the group was accused of trying to kill Nasser in a well-organized operation at the Manshiya Square in Alexandria on October 26, 1954. Mass arrests and much violence followed.[87] Ahmed was among those arrested and held in solitary confinement for nearly a month before he was released, since his interrogators could not obtain, or perhaps coerce, enough evidence to connect the Arabic teacher to the Brotherhood. That experience has "deepened my hatred for injustice," he once said.[88] Injustice, and Ahmed's hatred for it, would accompany him for the rest of his life.

Ironically, the month of imprisonment and torture in an Egyptian-run Gaza prison was one of the main reasons he decided to join the banned Egyptian group. He made this decision after enrolling at Cairo's Al-Azhar University, which was where his views on jihad and liberation took form and consolidated. The historic Egyptian University was a place where an Egyptian-centered pan-Arab identity intersected with history and spirituality to form a unique stream of political thought.

Following the Naksa, Gaza's occupiers were hardly acquainted with their newly conquered society. They oppressed and tormented the masses during the day, and chased *fedayeen*, or rather their shadows, at night. During this period, Ahmed was busy constructing the foundation of a new society, one that required years of molding and educating before being ready for the "the final battle of liberation." Several years after being chosen to lead the Society of Muslim Brothers, he founded Al-Mujamma' Al-Islami, which offered Gazans a variety of services, some catering to the soul, as in religious education, some to the heart, cultural activities and the like, and others to the body, physical preparedness and sports.[89] The choices were not random but were part of the agenda of the new generation of Gaza's Muslim activists, who believed that any permanent change in society would have to start with its most basic elements, and that it should reach all aspects of life.

For this new breed of activists, whose style, ideas, and very ideology directly contrasted with the PLO's nationalist and socialist counterparts, education was key, culminating in the establishment of the Islamic University of Gaza in 1978. Though the Shin Bet watched carefully, it did little to hinder the work of Ahmed and his followers, reflecting general Israeli belief that any schisms in Palestinian society would make it easier to rule the rebellious Strip. This strategy didn't last long, as Sheikh Ahmed's ideas evolved beyond religion, fighting illiteracy, and jumping jacks. In 1984, the teacher, preacher, and nascent political leader was arrested, along with other Muslim activists, by Israeli intelligence. He was charged with forming an armed group, stashing weapons, and conspiring to launch a revolution.[90]

Sheikh Ahmed Yassin didn't spend his entire thirteen-year sentence in Israeli prisons. He was released in 1985 as part of a prisoner exchange.[91] His health condition had worsened, as his quadriplegia was now coupled with permanent chest and ear infections, as well as near-total blindness.[92] By then, the Yassin family had moved to the Sabra neighborhood in Gaza City.

Chickpeas

While the distance between Sabra and Shati was relatively short, this in itself did not explain why Ibrahim al-Badrasawi traveled there once a week to participate in the special Friday prayers. True, others traveled much longer distances to listen to Ahmed preach about the ideal society, resistance to injustice, and the many types of jihad, but Ibrahim's decision to leave

Shati behind, cross the Remal neighborhood, and pray at the Sabra Mosque was not purely spiritual.

At a time when revolt was brewing in Gaza, with the finest of men being tortured or killed, Ibrahim belonged, at least in the eyes of his community, to a different kind of Palestinian. He simply couldn't bear the judgmental looks of his neighbors and most of those who knew him, who did not associate him with national struggle or jihad but rather thievery and a haunting criminal record. His enduring argument that stealing back what originally belonged to you was not theft invariably resulted in raised eyebrows and chuckles.

Thus, every Friday, Ibrahim would get in a beat-up Fiat near his home, and along with Wael and Ehab, his youngest brothers, head to the Sabra Mosque. The two boys enjoyed their weekly outings with their older and more experienced brother, whom they saw as an adventurer rather than a criminal. They relished the stories he told about his exploits, which featured an ever-growing cast of Israeli criminals he managed to beat up singlehandedly, of course.

On every week's holy Friday, the three Badrasawi boys put on their white *jalabiyas* and white *taqiyahs*,* took their prayer beads, and rushed to the mosque. There, they eagerly listened to Ahmed deliver his sermon before joining the group prayer and then finally shaking the hands of other worshippers, as good Muslims are told to do. After these rituals were accomplished, they descended on the old Firas marketplace, a short taxi ride away, for free fresh bread and raw onions, and hummus, falafel, and stewed fava beans. This is how they grew closer, their brotherly bond cemented by Ahmed's sermons,

---

* Skullcap worn by Muslim men.

Ibrahim's embellished stories of past grandeur, and chickpea hummus.

Like many issues in the Middle East, the origin of chickpeas is greatly contested. The exact birthplace of the ancient crop, which originated within the Mediterranean basin thousands of years ago, and the inventor of hummus—a dish of crushed and softened chickpeas mixed with olive oil, garlic, and other ingredients—remain matters of controversy. Chickpeas are also the main ingredients of falafel, balila, and fattet hummus, and are an essential ingredient in *misbaha*, which also includes fava beans.

When the three brothers ordered their meals, they felt like they were feasting on a variety of foods, though they were essentially eating nothing but chickpeas prepared in different ways: smashed, fried, or mixed with other beans. None of this concerned them as they enthusiastically dipped freshly baked flatbread in a large bowl of hummus drenched with locally produced olive oil, another ancient Palestinian ingredient that can be traced back to the region's first human settlements.

On December 9, 1987, the three brothers were not eating hummus in Firas Market but in Jabaliya Refugee Camp. They had no specific reason to be there aside from trying a new restaurant, where Ibrahim taught his younger siblings about life and growing up.

Jabaliya's boundaries, like most Palestinian towns after the Nakba, had expanded to include its own refugee camp, which carried the name of the town. With time, however, the distinction served no demographic purpose, as the camps expanded in all directions, linking refugee encampments to their adjacent cities, and eventually housing the majority of the population.[93]

On this day, a Wednesday, Ibrahim skipped work in Israel,

which was unusual for a day laborer from Gaza. After being regranted permission to enter Israel a year earlier, he had stayed out of trouble by rejoining Nasser and Tal'at in their construction job. The brothers played their part in Israel's economic boom, making enough money to fund a stagnant life that consisted mostly of cheap cigarettes, secondhand clothes, and chickpeas.

A day earlier, an Israeli had deliberately run over Palestinian workers from Jabaliya who were waiting by a bus stop. The Israeli driver came off the main road and rammed into them, killing four. The Israeli evening news persisted in speaking of this as if it was an ordinary car accident, while Israeli leaders, under the impression nothing out of the ordinary had occurred, went on with life and pre-scheduled press conferences, regurgitating the usual meaningless nonsense about existential threats to the state and the endless war against all kinds of terrorists. This was a miscalculation.

Just as the plates of hummus made their way to the table of the three Badrasawi brothers, a cascade of bullets crackled from multiple directions. Hundreds of people began running: youth with rocks and angry faces in one direction, and others, mostly women and the elderly, in the other. "Allahu Akbar!" shouted a young man outside the restaurant, holding a rock in one hand and sandals in the other, while another started smashing the sidewalk to generate more rocks. A chant, hardly audible at first, began to rise in the distance, growing closer, louder, and more harmonious: "With our blood, with our souls, we sacrifice for the martyrs." The three brothers looked at the table, unsure of their next move. What to do? Abandon the hummus, join the protests, or run away, back to Shati?

The dilemma resolved itself on their behalf when the

piercing stench of tear gas made it impossible to stay inside the small and crowded restaurant. As they began running away, Ibrahim realized that Ehab, his scrawny eleven-year-old brother, was running in the other direction. "Rise up for jihad!" the boy yelled in a passionate and forceful voice that surprised the other two. The word *yahud*—Jews—could be heard over the chaotic scene of dust, bullets, and tear gas. "The *yahud* are coming this way!" one boy shouted, as Israeli soldiers seemed to appear everywhere, while another instructed: "The *yahud* jeeps are speeding up that way."

All of this was the outcome of organic fury that followed the funeral of the murdered Palestinian workers. On this day, no press releases were issued from air-conditioned hotel rooms urging Jabaliya Palestinians—and then the entirety of the Palestinian homeland—to revolt. No Arab-conference closing statements or PLO directives had any bearing on the spontaneous revolt. The 1987 uprising, later known as the First Intifada, was the result of oppression, exploitation, violence, indignation, and complete disregard of the rights of an ancient people who trace their very civilization back to the cultivation of chickpeas.

In relaying the Intifada, historians would labor to provide the perfect narrative of how intersecting factors made the uprising inevitable. Such narratives describe how Palestinians felt abandoned by their Arab brethren, the PLO leadership, and the world. They cite Israel's failure to understand the degree of pressure that has been building up in Palestinian society for years, following the 1967 defeat, the Israeli occupation, the expansion of illegal Jewish settlements, the destruction of Palestinian orchards, the demolition of homes, and all the rest. Of course, they are not wrong. But the history of revolution can hardly be summed up in a few lines. If that were the case, then popular revolts could be forecasted with a great degree of accuracy, not only in Palestine but everywhere else.

Jabaliya's revolt—which in a matter of hours became the uprising of Khan Yunis, Shati, Nuseirat, Balata, Nablus, and eventually the whole of Palestine—could conceivably have been inspired by a different logic, largely made up of thousands of Ibrahims, Waels, and Ehabs who grew up in an immovable class position with not even slight improvements on the horizon. They were refugees, sons of refugees, and grandsons of refugees, their future as predictable as that of their fathers and forefathers: disposable laborers who would build Israel, with no rights of their own and no potential to acquire any.

Historians also tell us that when Palestinians rebelled against Israel, they had a justified set of demands: end the military occupation, dismantle the settlements, free the prisoners, allow displaced Palestinians to return to their land, and more. While the youth of the Intifada did not object to any of these demands, it was clear that when the customers of the hummus restaurant at the Jabaliya refugee camp market abandoned their freshly baked bread, raw onions, and chickpeas and ran to join the angry mourners, they were not compelled by a cohesive political program. When yelling "God is great!" they shouted a phrase that has always united Palestinians, underscoring their collective understanding that there is a transcendent force superior to all of us—greater than the soldiers and their guns, the Arab leaders and their empty rhetoric, the PLO's hotel-based revolutionary slogans, and even Israeli drivers who can, at a whim, decide if Palestinians live or die.

Broken Bones

The First Intifada changed the dynamics of the Badrasawi household. Ehab was always missing, Wael was constantly looking for him, and all other brothers, including Ibrahim, were unemployed due to the closure of Eretz. The air in the house reeked, at least for most of the day, of Israeli gunpowder, tear gas, and the smoke of burning tires, a staple of the youth's mostly non-violent revolt. At night, Ibrahim, Tala't, and Nasser smoked until dawn, drinking dark tea and watching the news of an uprising that began on the streets and was now the talk of the world.

As Israeli leaders blamed Iran, Syria, and the PLO for launching the uprising, they arrested 18,000 Palestinians, forcing Israel to expand old prisons and construct new ones, especially in the Naqab desert.[94] Most of the thousands killed or wounded were young people, a third generation of Nakba survivors fighting an old, unfinished war for their land, dignity, and very existence.

Even after Ibrahim ordered him to stop, Ehab continued to participate in the Intifada, mostly by distributing *manasheer*—the flyers that mourned martyrs, announced strikes, and attempted to lift the spirit of the people. He was everywhere, barefoot, breathless, and passionate, and, though a child, acted with a sense of mission that surprised everyone, distressing Madallah, whose love for her youngest son by far exceeded her concern for everything else. Even when his brothers tied him to the olive tree in the middle of the *hakoura* to stop him from joining the rallies outside, he managed to break loose and participate in the Friday protest that followed Ahmed's sermon on a day when many were killed, wounded, and arrested.

Unable to cope, Madallah hid, pleading with God in a voice that was not angry but distraught: "O Allah, my children are all I have in this world, please spare them in the name of the Prophet and the people of the house." But no one was spared, as the youth of Shati, like the youth of Palestine more generally, were determined not to heed the calls of their elders. They paid a heavy price for their defiance. Chanting "with our blood, with our soul, we sacrifice for you, Palestine," they affirmed that Palestine was becoming a real place, not a tent, house of hair, or a life of fear and degradation as cheap laborers in Israel. With a flag, collective chant, and burning tires, Palestinians began to actualize as a nation determined to win its freedom at any cost. Suddenly the road to Beit Daras opened again, at least in the minds of the rebelling youth, who devised a solution to whatever setback they suffered: "O mother of the martyr, ululate, all the children are your sons," they sang, rediscovering the chants of their elders.

Ehab was too young to join the popular committees that sprang up in every refugee camp and town, consisting of local activists, teachers, ex-political prisoners, and unemployed workers, who organized and devised ways to respond to Israel's new and often violent tactics. Soon new committees were created to coordinate the efforts of the small groups throughout Palestine and, in no time, a unified Palestinian leadership had been established throughout the occupied homeland.

The Unified National Leadership of the Uprising operated, at first, largely independently of the PLO and its factions.[95] With time, however, coordination between the UNLU and the PLO created allegiance, and this eventually gave traditional factions direct control over the *Intifada* and its grassroots leaders. The

Israeli army, desperate to reestablish control over the Palestinians, tried every strategy possible. It killed young men, arrested local activists, deported leaders, and assassinated officials abroad.[96] It even resorted to breaking the bones of the children who threw rocks at armed soldiers.[97] Nothing seemed to work.

Ehab was arrested, sometime after midnight, by dozens of soldiers who arrived at the al-Badrasawi family house to capture the boy, now twelve years old. Madallah begged the soldiers to let him go before roaring at them with the thunderous voice of an angry mother. They laughed, pushed her aside, and kicked her repeatedly as she struggled to stand, before handcuffing and blindfolding Ehab. Throughout this affair, he stood with a poise that surprised his own family. As his sisters screamed in agony, their mother collapsed to the ground, a stream of blood trickling from her nose down to her chest and onto the earth below. Wael stood in the corner and cried. Ibrahim and the others tried to use the Hebrew they had learned over the years to persuade the soldiers: "He is too young... he has never hurt anyone... just a child." But the soldiers had clear orders and a long list of names. other Shati boys who threw rocks, chanted the names of martyrs, and demanded freedom.

The family desperately searched for news for days. Eventually, the Red Cross informed them that that Ehab was being held at the Saraya, and that the soldiers had broken both of his arms on the way to prison. Madallah practically disappeared, locking herself in the dark room with the low ceiling, with only an occasional scream telling her children she was still alive. Even when Israeli military curfews were lifted, no one was allowed to leave the house. Ibrahim controlled everything and everyone. They were, once more, at war with life, and it was the eldest brother's chance to redeem himself. While previous struggles involved extreme poverty, this time around, Israel used water, electricity and food as a weapon to control the Palestinian masses, who grew angrier by the day. "Ehab is gone," Ibrahim would scream at his brothers as he tried to block their way, thus preventing them from joining the protests. "We cannot afford to lose anyone else." But loss for the al-Badrasawi family was inevitable.

Wael

Though it lasted only a few weeks, Ehab's imprisonment changed him and profoundly altered Wael as well. The protective older brother could not understand how his younger, shy sibling could be left alone in a small prison cell with broken arms. When Ehab returned, Wael had already joined the youth resistance, distributing *manasheer*, writing revolutionary slogans on the camp walls, and throwing rocks whenever soldiers invaded the neighborhood. The detention of their quadriplegic neighbor Ahmed in 1989, along with hundreds of his supporters, was a watershed moment for Shati, and in fact for the whole Intifada.[98] The arrests were, however, inevitable.

Muslim activists had always presented their ideology as an alternative to the abhorred philosophy of the *ilmanyeen*, the secularists of the PLO. This conflict encouraged the Israeli military administration to pit both sides against each other, as they had done for years. The popular uprising changed everything. For the Islamists, the new society was already in the process of self-animation. For the PLO, the Intifada was an opportunity to reclaim relevance over Palestinian affairs following their forced exile from Lebanon a few years earlier. For Israel, the divide-and-conquer strategy had run its course. For Wael and Ehab, the blood of their peers had to be avenged. "Revolution, revolution, till victory!" they chanted along with hundreds of their peers at every opportunity. "O martyred one, go in peace, we shall carry on with the struggle!"

Hamas was the latest materialization of the Islamic movement in Palestine, whose history dates back to the 1930s, though back then the movement was more Egyptian than Palestinian.[99] Despite the obvious connections, Hamas was different from its Egyptian partners. For years before Hamas's first statement in December of 1987, Gaza's Islamists had been molding a unique version of the Egypt-centric global movement.[100] The Intifada was a decisive moment in which Sheikh Yassin and his followers moved beyond their early slogans and foundational work, focusing mostly on charity and education. Not only did they launch a political movement, but soon its military arm as well. The Izz al-Din al-Qassam Brigades connected Palestine's past and present, reigniting the 1936 rebellion all over again.[101]

It turned out that history never truly concludes, and no amount of violence can suppress the echoes of the past. The call for jihad at Al-Istiqlal Mosque in Haifa many decades ago may have been altered to accommodate the new ideologies and language of new generations, all of which called for a protracted fight for freedom. Izz al-Din al-Qassam was resurrected by Gaza's youth, who adopted his ideology, tactics, and faith that justice will ultimately prevail.

"Die as martyrs" was no longer just a slogan, but an everyday reality throughout the Palestinian homeland. At every possible opportunity, children in Shati shouted at Israeli military "Death is preferred to humiliation!" Their chants, at times, would be the last words they would utter before their legs buckled under the weight of the lead bullets. The blood-soaked bodies would be dragged away from the Israeli firing-squad killers. Those injured would be rushed to a hospital. Those dying would be instructed, by other youths, to repeat "I bear witness that there is no deity but Allah..."

"What does death feel like?" Ehab once asked Wael as they swayed in makeshift wooden swings under the olive tree in the middle of the *hakoura*. His brother replied: "It is like falling gently to sleep, except when you wake up all your pain and suffering would be gone forever and you will be reunited with your loved ones." Mesmerized by this unquestionable piece of wisdom, Ehab kept swinging, breathing in air that still smelled of gunpowder, teargas, and burning tires from a confrontation earlier that morning.

The Swing Set

Khamis Abu Khusa and Wael were killed one week apart. Their lives had revolved around spending time together, from the early days of building sandcastles on the Shati beach to making their own slingshots to chasing after—or, more often, getting chased by—Israeli soldiers. Wael was adamant that the death of Khamis by an Israeli bullet to the throat meant that he, too, would certainly be killed by an Israeli bullet to the throat. His logic was dismissed by his family as an emotional response to the loss of a dear friend. On the day of Khamis's funeral, Wael had made him an *iklil*—a flower wreath of olive branches, lilies, and seashells. In the center of the *iklil* was a photo of both teenagers taken months earlier in a local photography studio. In the photo they stand close, each with his arm on the shoulder of the other, and behind them is a large background image of a waterfall, a blue sky, and a flock of birds, all situated within what seems like a European landscape. They had once made a vow to travel the world together. That photo was the closest they would ever get to fulfilling their childhood dream.

Wael's prediction, which his family later saw as a prophecy, came true on May 20, 1990, with the story of his murder beginning not in Shati but rather in Rishon Lezion, inside Israel. At around 6 a.m., Ami Popper, an off-duty soldier, stopped a group of Palestinian workers on their way to work in Israel. Yousef, Ziad, Zayed, Suleiman, Zakaria, and Abdul Rahim were all young workers who, despite the raging uprising at home, risked everything to provide for their families. They were waiting for their ride when Ami, playing the role of executioner, told them to hand over their IDs and kneel down.[102] Their role in life as cheap laborers compelled them to do so. The Israeli walked around them in a full circle, cocked his automatic rifle, and mowed them down in a matter of seconds. A short moment of final moans and last breaths later, the Gaza youth were gone, their blood merging into a single pool that slowly dissolved in the soil of the Palestinian village of Aion Qara, now part of the Israeli city of Rishon Lezion.[103]

Before news of the massacre spread in Shati, Wael was in the family living room listening to his brothers and neighbors heatedly discuss the Egyptian soccer team's chances in the upcoming World Cup. While interested in the outcome of the conversation, as he cared deeply about soccer and the Egyptian team in particular, he remained silent. Breaking news on the radio changed the unusually jubilant mood, with the Rishon Lezion tragedy confirmed by growing chants rising from the camp center. The older brothers all sprang up, not to join the protests, but to stop Wael and Ehab from joining them. After noisy deliberations, they decided they would all stand together on the street corner, to watch but not participate.

They did. But when two Israeli military jeeps began to head in their direction and sped up, the brothers, neighbors, and everyone else present, panicked. Some fled back home, others froze in place, while Wael ran in the opposite direction. Eventually the commotion subsided, the protesting youths scattered, and the soldiers circled back to their nearby military camp. Ibrahim and the rest ran across the camp yelling Wael's name. When they learned that two youths had been injured in the clashes and that they had been taken to the Shifa Hospital, they all piled into a small Fiat and rushed there as well. The chants outside the surgery ward were enough to tell them that at least one of the two boys had died. The word *shahid*—martyr— seemed to be on everyone's lips—the strangers mourning a fellow Palestinian they had never met, along with the medical staff, the local reporters, and others. Leading his brothers, Ibrahim forced his way inside. "I am looking for my brother, Wael al-Badrasawi," he said. A young doctor was the first to answer his pleas. "Be strong," the doctor said, pressing gently on Ibrahim's right shoulder. "He is in Paradise now."

Just before the brief conversation finished, Ehab trailed behind. When they arrived at the ward, he stood at the doorway, separating the crowd outside from the doctors and his brothers inside. Knowing the fate of his beloved brother hung on a few words, he wanted to be close enough to know if he was fine, and also far away enough for "he is in Paradise now" to be muffled or mistaken for something else entirely. Hearing the doctor's words, Ehab clung to the hope that he might be referring to a different boy, brother, or paradise. His hopes evaporated as the body of Wael, fully wrapped in white sheets with only his kind and gentle face protruding, emerged from a partially darkened room filled with the stricken faces of medical staff. "Praise be to God," declared Ibrahim, his once melodious voice ruined by the puffs of a million cheap cigarettes. His attempts to hide his tears failed, as heavy breaths turned into soft, then intense but mostly mute sobs. The bodies of his brothers began to shake in a similar motion, as if Ibrahim's decision to break down was all the permission they needed to do likewise.

Ehab stood still. Drawing closer, he looked at Wael and was surprised by the gentle smile that adorned his face. The first thought that crossed his mind was their conversation while swinging under the olive tree: "It is like falling gently to sleep, except when you wake up all your pain and suffering would be gone forever and you will be reunited with your loved ones." Gazing at his brother's face once again, he saw that Wael looked quite comfortable, at ease even, as if telling him not to be afraid. When the Badrasawi boys learned the bullet had lodged in Wael's throat, Ehab knew the prophecy was true: there is a Paradise, and his brother was already there.

Chapter Seven

Without Wael

He had experienced the same torture techniques before, though at the hands of the Israelis, not fellow Palestinians. His interrogators denied him sleep for days, while officers took turns beating him for hours on end. Between bouts of punishment, often conducted methodically and scheduled in orderly shifts, he was left shackled to a chair. The chair was designed to be flawed, perpetually slanted forward, making it impossible for his contorted body to find any degree of stability, let alone relief. Once his face and other parts of his body stopped bleeding, the torturers would return and carry out the same process all over again.

Ehab al-Badrasawi was not the only Palestinian being tortured at the hands of other Palestinians in the Saraya prison in February 1996. Hundreds of Hamas members, affiliates, and supporters were brought into the Saraya in several waves of mass arrests. Ehab was among the first wave of detainees, which included Abdul-Aziz al-Rantisi, Mahmoud al-Zahar, and Younis al-Astal among others.[104]

At only twenty years of age, Ehab was incarcerated and tortured with the leaders of Hamas, a movement that by then

had proved to be the main obstacle to whatever private agreements had been reached between Israel, Washington, and those
who claimed to speak on behalf of Palestinians. Curiously, top
leaders of what became known as the Palestinian Authority (PA)
consisted mostly of former revolutionaries of the PLO, particularly its dominant Fatah faction. Though the Hamas-Fatah
dispute had been festering for years prior to the establishment
of the PA, it was now morphing into something else entirely,
superseding political ideologies and becoming a struggle for the
very soul of the Palestinian nation.

The question of how the freedom fighters of yesteryear
became the torturers of the present was a recurring subject
of conversations between the leaders of Hamas in the Saraya
prison. The common wisdom at the time resolved that the illusion of power, and the wealth that is often obtained through
political power, were the main reasons behind moral corrup-
tion—a notion not entirely unfamiliar to Palestinian society.
Though Ehab routinely nodded his head in agreement, he was
too young to appreciate the irony. Indeed, he was only a child
when he joined Hamas, a decision that he made impulsively and
almost instantly after the murder of Wael. In Hamas he found
a family that understood his rage and his grief, for each Hamas
member had a Wael, if not several Waels, in their lives that they
had lost to a sniper's bullet. The only language that appealed to
Ehab and other youngsters like him after such formative events
was found in the profound spirituality of Hamas and the comforting words of preachers, particularly those of Sheikh Yassin.

Though the First Intifada was winding down, Ehab's enthusiasm for the struggle remained potent. In his new lexicon, the
struggle was jihad. His dialectics were as innocent and pure
as his age: if he ceased to be active in the local resistance, the

legacy of his brother would end, his martyrdom would have been in vain, and neither worldly nor heavenly paradises would be attainable. Where else could he be reunited with his brother if his Paradise was lost forever? Since the boy could not entertain the thought of abandoning the struggle, he carried on, sometimes alone. His activities involved throwing rocks, distributing flyers, and urging others to join him, while listening, ever so attentively, to the sermons of Sheikh Yassin at the Abbas Mosque in Shati. Here he learned that the struggle for justice is an obligation, not a choice, a mantra Ehab spent the rest of his life embracing and repeating.

Even when many Palestinians were fixated on their television screens, watching Haidar Abdul Shafi, the head of the Palestinian delegation to the Madrid talks, issue an impassioned plea for justice for the long-suffering Palestinians, Ehab was alone on the Shati streets, looking for soldiers to chase away with his rocks.[105] But he found none. Instead, he began spraying graffiti over the gray walls of the camp denouncing the fools who put their trust in the United States government, Western laws, and institutions. "The Quran is our constitution," he wrote. When, two years later, "Madrid" was abandoned in favor of an agreement reached secretly in some orchard near Oslo, thousands of miles away from Gaza, Ehab again denounced the traitors using the walls of his refugee camp.[106]

Saraya

The Oslo Accords of September 1993 were only the start of this new era, one riddled with internal conflicts that eventually culminated in outright civil war. As polished men in black suits celebrated the inception of a "peace process," Hamas and its allies in other Islamic and socialist movements instead decried the squandering of the Palestinian people's legitimate rights. But such objections were moot to those Palestinians who acceded simply because they personally benefited from the generosity of US allies, including Japan and Saudi Arabia.[107] For this new breed of Palestinian leaders, the decision to substitute Western-style uniforms for military fatigues seemed to be motivated purely by financial calculations.

The cynicism felt by Hamas and other Islamic and socialist political forces in Palestine following the Madrid talks turned into outright rejection after Oslo, serious anxieties after the Gaza-Jericho Agreement, anger at Jordan for normalizing with Israel, and total war following the signing of yet another accord in September 1995.[108] Between 1993 and 1995, signs of an impending conflict became evident. The parties involved in this conflict were no longer just Palestinian and Israeli, as the Palestinian front became more fragmented than ever. The PLA of the past became the model of another army, the Palestinian Security Forces. In the view of the newly-formed PSF, Israel was no longer the enemy, or at least not the only one. The Palestinian political leadership had experienced its own purges and transformations. Those within the PLO who rejected Oslo and its consequences were marginalized in the new political setup. The others began returning to Gaza and the rest of the occupied territories in stages, a less than triumphant return that culminated in the arrival of Yasser Arafat himself in the Strip in July 1994.[109]

Most of Gaza welcomed Arafat, who remained committed to the same old revolutionary slogans, attire, and language. His supporters spoke of a different kind of revolution, a phased one that would culminate in the full liberation of Palestine and the return of the refugees. For most Palestinians, however, the line between love and allegiance to Arafat began to blur with realistic fears that the new era would not deliver all on its promises. When times grew harder, an unrehearsed speech and a few slogans like *Revolution, Revolution, Until Victory* would buy the PA time to churn along until the next crisis arose.

Not long after the PA began official operations in Gaza, Jericho, and eventually other areas of the West Bank, Palestinian class divisions began growing at a rate unparalleled in their modern history.[110] No speeches, no matter how passionate or compelling, could hide the obvious truth: Palestinians were divided along many lines, divisions that had grown tremendously over a short period of time. Large residential towers were erected close to the Shati refugee camp as it sank even deeper into disrepair and poverty. Black limousines, often in large convoys, were increasingly spotted on the dusty and crowded roads of Gaza, pushing their way past old Fiats, donkey carts, and perplexed onlookers. As the new PA infrastructure and economy, consisting mostly of residential homes, towers, hotels, beach resorts, and police stations, rose and became established across the Strip and parts of the West Bank, a large number of Israeli settlements also expanded across occupied Palestine.[111]

The euphoria that initially accompanied the return of the rugged-looking Palestinian officers with PLO insignias and Palestinian flags was soon replaced by confusion and even anger. Those who promised phased liberation seemed to have found a way to coexist with Israel, all within the boundaries of occupied Palestine. Though Palestinian resistance, still nascent and disorganized, avoided directly confronting the old revolution's *nouveau riche*, a new type of military operation targeting Israeli interests quickly became the norm. Palestinians called them "martyrdom operations," Western media spoke of "suicide bombings," while Israel raged against the "terrorist attacks," urging its new PA partners to act. Regardless of the name, these attacks spoke clearly of the despair growing among Palestine's poor classes, who felt orphaned, encircled, and without much to lose.

At first, Arafat seemed to be caught in what looked like an impossible dilemma, which he had tried to resolve by arresting hundreds of Hamas leaders and members in a move that received full US support and guarded Israeli approval. In his thinking, the once revolutionary, now statesman had no alternative. The PA's existence depended on a simple calculation: without donor money, the political apparatus would crumble, and the new class of wealthy Palestinians would cease to exist. But cracking down on Palestinians would bring an end to the idea that the PA was an outcome of a revolutionary process, and that the liberation of Palestine was a matter of principled politics that could be achieved through yet more polite negotiations.

It did not take long for the PA to settle this quandary. Hundreds of Palestinian activists in Gaza were thrown into the Saraya, the Strip's notorious gulag. Others were rounded up on the West Bank and sent to prison. All Gazans arrested and tortured in the early 1996 were familiar with the Saraya, which they dreaded because of what they or their loved ones had experienced there at the hands of the Shin Bet.

The Saraya's history is one of conquerors and resistors. When the Palestinian rebellion was in full bloom in the 1930s, the British began building new prisons in Gaza and the rest of Palestine. The Saraya prison, completed in 1936, was used to detain and torture many rebellious Palestinians. When the

British left Palestine, the Egyptians took over the prison, made some repairs, and resumed the war against Gaza's political dissidents. When they left, the Israelis took over, repainted the walls, and placed Hebrew signs on top of the Arabic ones that had once replaced the English. There, the Israelis perfected various torture techniques, including the use of deafening music and electric shocks to the genitals.[112] When the PA took over the Saraya, Israel had redeployed its occupation army only a short distance away, although always within the borders of Gaza.

Ehab was not concerned about the details of Oslo nor the Saraya's history. In his mind, the entire Oslo gambit was an act of national suicide by a small group of power-hungry men who manipulated Palestinian emotions and symbols to temporarily win popular support. For him, the most important question was justice, regardless of who was committing the injustice: "O you who have believed, be persistently standing firm in justice, witnesses for Allah, even if it be against yourselves or parents and relatives. Whether one is rich or poor, Allah is more worthy of both," was one of many verses that he had memorized, then imparted, first to his fellow refugees in Shati, then to his fellow prison inmates.[113]

It was that boldness, despite his young age, that singled him out to the snooping PA *mukhabarat** in Gaza, later earning him repeated visits to the prison basement's solitary confinement cell. In one dramatic episode, his Palestinian interrogator began shouting insults at him in Hebrew. This was one of the few occasions where Ehab felt truly baffled, as neither his limited experience in life nor knowledge of the holy book was enough to guide him through

---

* *Mukhabarat* refers to intelligence agencies or secret police forces in various Arab countries.

this bizarre spectacle: "Were you imprisoned and tortured by the Israelis yourself?" Ehab asked the Palestinian interrogator, genuinely hoping to understand why the Gaza-born man was torturing him using the enemy's language. "I am the one who asks the question, *ya ibn Izzuna**," the Palestinian said, in Arabic, again using a Hebrew slur. Instead of yelling back in defense of Madallah and Abdallah, who were no adulterers, Ehab took a deep breath: "God said in the Quran," he began, oblivious to a fresh stream of blood trickling from his mouth and seeping down his chin to his neck. The interrogator interrupted: "You, your God and your Quran are under my dirty shoes," in language redolent of the Shin Bet officers who spilled their fair share of Palestinian blood in the prison, in fact in that very same dimly-lit room.

How Ehab managed to leap forward from his position while fully tied to his chair, throwing himself like a rapidly descending boulder at the well-dressed interrogator remained a mystery, even to Ehab. Using his head alone after falling perfectly on top of the officer, Ehab repeatedly struck the interrogator's face. "*Ya ibn Izzuna*," the officer insisted, gagging on his own blood and Ehab's. The guards rushed into the room, separating the two. They were bewildered by the unusual sight. To help the bleeding officer control his rage and restore some of his dignity, the guards, without prior orders, attacked Ehab with all their might. By the end of the beating, it looked as if the young man's face was no longer his own. Contortions and bruises grew from his brow to his feet. His eyes sunk deep below his fully broken cheekbones and jaw. Not once did he plead for his life or implore his tormentors to stop.

---

* *Ya Ibn Izzuna* is a derivative phrase from Arabic that has been Hebraized. It refers to a person born out of wedlock and can be considered the equivalent of "bastard."

Per the orders of the officer, who was busy checking his own facial injuries throughout the whole episode, Ehab was taken to the prison's lowest circles, a dungeon deep below earth reserved for the most dangerous and unrepentant. He stayed there for months, but his recollections of that period were those of someone neither dead nor living. For reasons unbeknownst to him, he managed to hold on to his humanity, though circumstances were pushing him to the brink of madness.

The Voices

Ehab's *jinn* were not the friendly type, like his mother's companion who often appeared during difficult times. His were of the category of the *shaytan*, the demonic variety whose enduring mission is to seduce humankind to stray from the natural order of things as commanded by God. Even before regaining consciousness in his new underground cell, he could hear them, talking, laughing, urging him to give up, to break down, to surrender.

Ehab knew that he was underground because his first meal, a dry loaf of bread, was lowered to him from above. Then "Eat *ya kalb*," a voice was heard, followed by an echo. Being referred to as a "dog," the heavy footsteps, the loud slamming of metal doors, and the engulfing darkness reminded him that he was a Saraya prisoner, no longer kept alongside the rest of the Hamas prisoners.

"Eat *ya kalb*," another voice whispered in his ear, followed by many others, then fiendish laughter by his new hostile companions. Instinctively, he answered with Quranic verses, the two closing chapters of the holy book known to protect the faithful from evil.[114] For hours, then days, he incessantly repeated: "Say,

'I seek refuge in the Lord of daybreak. From the evil of that which He created. And from the evil of darkness when it settles. And from the evil of the blowers in knots. And from the evil of an envier when he envies.'"

Followed by: "Say, 'I seek refuge in the Lord of mankind, The Sovereign of mankind. The God of mankind. From the evil of the retreating whisperer—who whispers into the breasts of mankind—From among *the* jinn and mankind.'"

As a child, Ehab heard his mother and many other refugees repeat these verses whenever they sensed danger. During the Intifada, prayers became a shield that many refugees raised to protect their families against the soldiers who, often in the darkest hour of the night, appeared, like demonic figures, moving from one house to the other, terrifying children and breaking mothers' hearts. Unfortunately for the al-Badrasawi family, praying was not enough to prevent Ehab's arrests, Wael's murder, and the life of constant fear and insecurity that they have always faced under the Israeli occupation.

But Ehab was devoted to his faith. He believed that Islam was not granted to humankind to promise earthly possessions, secure against harm, or guarantee life itself. A good life, Ehab once argued against Ibrahim's constant regrets for the jewels lost all those years ago, is not a life of material wealth, but a just life that cannot be obtained through human laws and institutions, but through the Quran. "Islam is the solution," he would declare whenever an argument seemed to have reached an impasse.

In his dungeon, such arguments were moot. He had nothing to tempt him, reassure him, or keep him company, aside from the Quran. Memorizing it occupied long hours of his sentence. Even when the guards strapped him to the ceiling and gagged his mouth with a dirty cloth, he carried on reciting, emitting a muffled but melodious sound.

All of this kept him strong enough not to sink into the kind of madness usually compelled by the presence of the *shaytan*. He invited kinder company. His favorite was his mother's gentle voice, which would suddenly appear in his mind as if it was a child's dream. She talked to him about Beit Daras. "Being in Beit Daras feels as if I died and went to heaven," she would say. Ehab would smile and imagine himself a child in the village, chasing swallowtail butterflies and climbing fig trees. She would talk to him about how kind, generous, and brave the Badrasawis were: "If your grandfather was still alive, he would have been so proud that you followed in his footsteps," she told him once, but only once, when she realized that he had joined the Al-Qassam Brigades. She feared for him and had every reason to be afraid, all the youth who joined the armed wing of Hamas killed in battle or executed in the street. "Why would my son be the exception?" she often asked herself and Ehab. When the Palestinian authorities arrived in the darkest hour of the night to arrest him, Madallah was confused. To her the Palestinian police were "*khawaja*"—Westerners—a word reserved for foreigners, never for Palestinians. When they were gone, she let out a shriek of pain that was heard throughout the neighborhood. Even at her old age, Madallah's agony was still piercing and powerful.

Other friendly voices also visited him in his lonely prison cell: "Jihad is our pride, fighting is our pride, martyrdom is our pride, surrender is the path of humiliation and servitude," Sheikh Yassin had urged his followers.[115] "Die as martyrs," announced al-Qassam in the very month of Yassin's birth in Al-Joura, an ancient Palestinian village that has been wiped off the map but not from memory. The voices often interloped all at once. "But how do I resist when my torturer is my brother?" he yelled at the empty, dark space under the Saraya. The answer arrived quickly.

As soon as the Second Intifada started in September 2000, Israel resorted to aerial bombardment, with the aim of showing Palestinians that any attempt to launch a long and grinding rebellion would be costly and easily crushed. Israel was wrong. The Intifada lasted for years, resulting in the deaths of thousands, the majority of whom were, of course, Palestinians.

The Israeli bombing of the Saraya in December 2008 was meant to achieve more than one goal.[116] It was a message to the Palestinian leadership, whom Israel had wrongly perceived as the instigator of the uprising. It was also an attempt to eliminate, in a single military stroke, the Hamas leaders holed up inside that citadel of human misery.

Ehab couldn't hear any of the commotion outside, not the explosions, cries of "Allah Akbar!" from inside the prison walls, or the chants of thousands of people trying to break into the prison. He felt deep thuds coming from the walls of his cell as dust from the ceiling fell on his pale, exhausted face. Months inside his lonely dungeon taught him not to pay heed to what seemed at first unimportant details. Then, a door slammed open, and another, followed by shouts of "God is great!," hurried steps, and anxious but reassuring faces. The strangers helped him stand on his feet, wiped the dust off his face, and called him a brother.

No words can describe what Ehab al-Badrasawi felt in that moment, as his faith in his Palestinian identity was restored despite four years of torture by his fellow nationals. The world outside gave a feeling of serenity and vigor. The air of the Mediterranean filled his lungs, replacing the dust that had nested in his chest for years, as the sun slowly breathed life into his ashen skin. Even the swooshing sounds of the fighter jets above didn't detract from the beauty of Gaza and the people of this ancient land. Thousands ran in all directions. More explosions followed. Distraught voices gave directions: "Take cover!" "Free the prisoners!" "Haul the wounded!" "Stay your ground!"

Ehab stood in the midst of all of this. He straightened his back despite the crackling noises sounding from every bone of his body. He was alive and ready to fight. "Glory to the martyrs," he shouted along with the crowd. "Glory to the martyrs."

The Bodyguard

Israel tried to kill Abdul Aziz al-Rantisi four times. It only needed to succeed once, and eventually it did. On that Saturday, April 17, 2004, Ehab took the day off guarding Rantisi, the Hamas leader, a job he had done for years. Even if he had been riding in the doomed car at the exact moment it was evaporated by two Israeli precision missiles, he could have done very little.

How he—the freed Hamas prisoner of the Saraya—became the bodyguard of Rantisi, the most wanted Palestinian at the time, was no mystery. Ehab was physically strong, with the kind of prowess that brought him much attention and adulation from his peers. In the summer of 1995, he rashly decided to become a boxer, though he had no prior experience in the field of boxing or any other contact sports. His training consisted of punching a sandbag which he tied to the tree in the middle of the family's *hakura*. The sand was collected from the beach, and the bag itself was devised from the hide of a cow, stitched by his ever-accommodating sister Warda. The odd contraption leaked as slowly and consistently as an hourglass, requiring constant refilling. Using his bare knuckles, he pummeled his bag daily following the dawn prayer, and again after the evening prayer.

When he declared his sudden entrance into the world of boxing, the middleweight champion of Gaza had no reason to accept the unscheduled duel. He went along with it anyway on the advice of his coach, who had been promised a good number of shekels and certain victory. The confused champion buckled under Ehab's relentless jabs before the first round had officially ended. The celebration in Ehab's neighborhood, which had never claimed a sports title of any kind, carried on for hours before abruptly ending when Ehab declared that he had no intention to fight anymore.

"I am as strong as a lion," Ehab would often declare to his older, teasing brothers, while flexing his biceps and forearms. "You are as strong as a jackass," Ibrahim would respond, provoking laughter, including from Ehab himself. As the boy grew older, he devised an exercise regimen that was consistent with the instructions of the Prophet when he said, "Teach your children swimming, archery, and horse riding."[117] Ehab was an excellent swimmer and a superb diver, going as deep as the bottom of the half-sunken ship Satia, which had been stranded at the Shati beach for decades.[118] On that same beach, he learned horse riding, first for joy, later as part of his training with Al-Qassam.

Ehab obtained his first gun when he officially joined the Brigades' intelligence unit. Eventually he was trained to use a host of weapons, some homemade, others smuggled, whether by the sea, through the border tunnels that connect Gaza to Egypt, or even from Israel itself. But this is not exactly why al-Rantisi chose Ehab from all the fighters to be his most trusted companion. The true answer lay in the Saraya. When Ehab was kept in solitary confinement, Rantisi was also singled out for repeated interrogation, and therefore torture. When Ehab was thrown in the dungeon, it was Rantisi who pleaded his case, offering to take his place underground.

Though the Israeli government regarded Rantisi as a notorious militant leader who ordered many attacks on Israeli targets, he was also a trained pediatrician who worked in the Nasser Hospital in Khan Yunis for many years. His many supporters noted how he never charged a poor person for medical treatment before spending a decade in Israeli prisons, mostly for refusing to pay taxes to the Israeli occupation. A refugee himself, originally from the village of Yibna, he experienced poverty at a very young age.[119] Born only months before the Nakba, he had witnessed every episode of Palestinian loss, tragedy, destitution, and resistance.

Like many refugees, Rantisi managed to carve out a measure of success for himself. He often spoke about how he shared the same pair of shoes with his brother, how his father's ill-timed death sunk the family even deeper into poverty, and yet how he managed to complete his medical degree at the University of Alexandria. Egypt played an important role in Rantisi's life, as it did in the lives of Al-Qassam, Sheikh Yassin, and many other Islamic leaders. Like other religious Palestinian students in Alexandria, he frequented the Salam Bastanly and Commander Ibrahim mosques, gravitating to the impassioned sermons of Mahmoud Eid and Ahmed al-Mahalawi, the intensity of their calls for jihad against Western colonialism matched by their mutual hate for Anwar Sadat, Egypt's third president.

It didn't take much to convince Rantisi that he should hate Israel, which epitomized all the pain, humiliation, and injustice that he, his family, and Palestinian people had experienced over the years. But the Muslim Brotherhood preachers helped him consolidate his political thoughts within a framework different from nationalists, socialists, and all other breeds of politics and ideologies so influential across the Arab world at the time. Unlike other young ideologues, Rantisi, who embraced political Islam at a young age, remained committed to it until two Israeli precision missiles smashed through the cracked windows of his car on a dusty Gaza road, killing him at the age of fifty-six.

Israel's assassination of Rantisi was arguably one of the most predictable events in Palestine during that period. Israel had tried to kill him three times before, each time killing his companions or injuring members of his family, including one attempt in South Lebanon. In December 1992, Rantisi and 415 other Palestinians, mostly members of Hamas and Islamic Jihad, were exiled to the "Meadow of Flowers," a mountainous area in southern Lebanon, not far from what Israel had demarcated as its own border. Some believe this mass deportation was the key event that transformed Hamas into a mass movement, not only in Palestine but also throughout the Middle East more generally. The Israeli army had driven them there in a large convoy of buses and simply left them in the middle of nowhere. Stranded, the Intifada activists quickly adapted. They pitched a university, a library, a mosque, a parliament, learned arts and crafts, and cooked their own food. They even had representatives. The equivalent of a minister of foreign affairs fostered relations with the nearby villages. Rantisi was the spokesman.

This was when and where the first assassination attempt took place. Two men entered the media tent to conduct an interview with Rantisi, who had just finished his daily press conference outside to an ever-growing crowd of Lebanese, Arab, and foreign journalists. One, who introduced himself as a

Japanese reporter, and another who claimed to be his translator were actually would-be assassins.[120] The large duffle bag they left behind following the sham exploded soon after the two departed the camp. While no one was hurt, Rantisi now clearly knew that his demise could arrive at any moment.

Rantisi's role in the First Intifada, and the public spectacle of his daily press briefings from the wilderness of the Lebanese border, irked Israel. But his role in the Second Intifada, especially following his dramatic escape from the Saraya, made his assassination a top priority for Ariel Sharon and the Israeli government.

Unlike the First Intifada, the second uprising had a warlike aspect. Palestinians resorted to bombing attacks at a faster rate than before, and the Israeli military treated all Palestinians as if they were combatants in an existential war. The death toll was extreme. Nearly 5,000 Palestinians were killed.[121] The new Intifada moved in several parallel fronts. The first front was that of Israel, whose obsession over its own security blinded it from seeing the reasons why such security was absent in the first place. Thus, it invaded cities, gunned down children, assassinated activists, destroyed homes, and built yet more walls—the most prominent being its "Separation Wall," which served to annex more Palestinian land.[122] In doing so, Israel fueled the very response that had caused its "insecurity" in the first place.

The second front was that of the United States, which remained unconditionally committed to Israel without reflecting on how its support deprived Palestinians. While blaming Palestinians for incitement and, far less frequently, urging Israel to use restraint, the US continued to support a process that ultimately led to normalizing illegal settlements, gradual annexation, and ethnic cleansing.

The third front was that of the Palestinian Authority, which had lost its ability to find the balance between its commitment to the US project and its lip service to a revolution that never was.

The last front belonged to Ehab al-Badrasawi, whose political discourse had never intersected with any of the aforementioned. His commitment was to his mother Madallah, now aging and depleted by the hardships of an unkind life, to Wael's legacy, to his fellow fighters, each carrying their own heavy share of commitments and tragic memories, and to whichever paradise he was to achieve first.

"Life is cheap, trifling. What we seek is eternal life," said Sheikh Yassin. Unlike Rantisi, Sheikh Yassin escaped death only once before. Though Israel had declared its intention to kill him months earlier, the quadriplegic man continued to frequent the same mosque, at the same time, five times a day. In June 2003, he survived a quarter-ton bomb dropped over an apartment in the Al-Daraj neighborhood with minor injuries.[123] On March 22 of the following year, Israel killed him as he was returning from Fajr prayer.

This is how Rantisi became Hamas's new leader, a position he would hold for less than a month. His assassination, or, in the language of his enemies, "liquidation," served no practical purpose, aside from the fact that Hamas's new Gaza leaders, from that day on, rarely appeared in public. "The most I hope for is that my Lord will let me enter Paradise." Here, he was no longer speaking of Yabna. That earthly paradise, at least for Rantisi, though a short distance away, seemed unreachable.

When the Second Intifada ended, some of the lines intersected in a bizarre and unexpected manner. Israel restored its military supremacy over much of the West Bank and Gaza, but redefined its occupation of the Strip as military "disengagement."[124] The Palestinian Authority, especially after the death or poisoning of Yasser Arafat, resolved its quandary by leaning toward the Israeli camp and abandoning most of its rhetoric about resistance and revolution.[125] As the United States distanced itself from the conflict, Hamas and Ehab, now the commander of the Shati Brigade of Al-Qassam, went underground.

Ehab's war was yet to begin.

Chapter Eight

Ehab's War

On March 8, 2003, a young Palestinian girl walked down a busy street in Gaza City. Her destination was, and remains, unknown. Perhaps she was on her way to or back from school, a grocery store, a friend's house, her own home, or playing hopscotch in the street. We will never know if she saw any of the five missiles fired from three different Israeli Apache helicopter gunships as they came towards her. All we know is that the impact exploded her body, later collected in shreds from the sidewalk, the main road, various street corners, and a nearby *hakoura*.

The girl was just additional "collateral damage," a familiar term deployed by Israeli military spokesmen and analysts to describe the fate of Palestinian people killed by the thousands during the Second Intifada. The main target of the missiles was a man from Beit Daras called Ibrahim al-Makadmeh.

Israel briefly rationalized the murder of al-Makadmeh, along with three of his companions and the unfortunate little girl, as the direct response to a bombing that had killed seventeen people in Haifa a few days earlier. Whether al-Makadmeh was involved in engineering that specific bombing, it mattered little in Israel's war on the Palestinian people and their resistance during the Intifada. In actuality, al-Makadmeh, at least by then, was focused largely on his role as a member of Hamas's political bureau. Like the deaths of many other Hamas leaders, his assassination served little purpose in ending the Palestinian uprising. The Intifada continued, along with the unprecedented rate of Israeli killing of Palestinian civilians, and Palestinian counterattacks, which proved more painful for Israel than ever before.[126]

Like Ehab, Al-Makadmeh was born into a prominent clan from Beit Daras. There are two explanations as to why the Badrasawis were overrepresented in Hamas's political and military leaderships. The historical explanation attributes this to the Beit Daras massacre at the height of the Nakba, and more specifically to the radicalization, irrespective of previous political ideology, of this once serene, now destroyed Palestinian village. The popular explanation insists that the secret to Beit Daras and her people lies in the curiously large skulls of the Badrasawis. Though some Gazans truly believe that people from the village carry larger heads than others, some use the reference to illustrate stubbornness or pride. This means that the Badrasawis's fight against Israel does not only aim to recover the Palestinian homeland, but is in part due to their particular relationship and love for Beit Daras itself. This argument, of course, could apply to every one of the nearly 500 villages destroyed during the Nakba. The survivors and the descendants of each town, village, and locality have their own logic for continuing to resist.

Beit Daras in particular was at the center of many conversations between Ehab and Ibrahim al-Makadmeh during their difficult detention at a Palestinian Authority prison, which began in early 1996. Even the best and most amusing arguments of other prisoners could not convince them that Hamas's demographics were drawn from a diverse representation of all refugee groups, in fact all Palestinians, or that they were not special. The uniqueness of Beit Daras aside, al-Makadmeh's life pattern was similar to that of other Hamas leaders. He was born in the Jabaliya refugee camp, studied at UNRWA schools where he excelled, and earned a seat at an Egyptian dental school where he developed an ideological affinity with the Egyptian Muslim Brotherhood. Back in Gaza, he worked at the Shifa Hospital, befriended Sheikh Yassin, spent time in Israeli and Palestinian Authority prisons, survived torture, and wrote books before Israel killed him with five missiles fired from three different Apache helicopter gunships. Long before his assassination, however, he helped establish the first military wing of what would become Palestine's strongest armed resistance movement.

Glory

The idea to start Al-MAJD was not al-Makadmeh's or even Sheikh Yassin's. It was the brainchild of Yahya Sinwar, a refugee from Majdal Asqalan.[127] Years before the First Intifada, leading to the rise of Hamas and its military wing, Sinwar believed that the first course of action to ensure the success of any resistance movement was the capture, and, if necessary, the elimination of collaborators. Without collaborators, the Shin Bet would not have been able to subdue Gaza as it had managed to with relative success since the start of the military occupation after the Naksa. When Sheik Yassin agreed to the proposal, Sinwar, al-Makadmeh, and a few others established MAJD, an acronym that also meant "glory."[128] Over the years, the movement became an intelligence unit gathering information on Israel's operations in Gaza before evolving into something else entirely. Israel eventually discovered the Islamic movement's attempt to build a serious military presence in Gaza. Al-Makadmeh was arrested in 1984 and sentenced to eight years in prison. Sheikh Yassin was sentenced to thirteen years. Sinwar was also captured, though his first imprisonment in 1985 lasted only eight months. After his second trial, in 1988, Sinwar was sentenced to four life sentences of which he served twenty-two years until his release among 1,026 others in a 2011 prisoner exchange for Israeli soldier Gilad Shalit.[129] Sinwar emerged from prison with a plan that would fundamentally change the relationship between Palestinians and their Israeli occupiers.

The crackdown on the Islamic movement which later became Hamas and MAJD followed years of Israeli intelligence failure. Israel's Gaza military administration had wrongly concluded that the Islamists were merely interested in religious affairs, specifically building mosques, holding educational seminars, and arranging mass weddings. When the Israeli intelligence raided Sheikh Ahmed Yassin's house in 1984, they found not only copies of the Holy Quran and other religious texts, but also a weapons cache, which, by the standards of the time, shocked the Shin Bet and the Israeli government. The cache included twenty pistols, eleven M16 assault rifles, three AK-47 Kalashnikovs, one Carlo Gustav submachine gun, one IMI Galil rifle, one inoperative hand grenade, one anti-tank rocket launcher (also inoperative), and five Uzi submachine guns. The Israeli military presumed that this discovery had thwarted what could have been a disaster for its military occupation of Gaza. But neither the arrest of the Muslim activists nor the relentless assassination of these leaders in later years could slow the movement. Those killed were quickly replaced by others, who, with greater experience, demurred from fighting aboveground and instead built an army beneath.

"Our homeland will not be liberated and our people will not be freed . . . without sacrifices. Freedom has a price, and the price is blood," al-Makadmeh said just days before his "deserved liquidation" on March 8, 2003.[130] The "blood" al-Makadmeh was referring to was, of course, his own. He, or whatever remained of him, was hurriedly buried in Gaza amidst chants calling for freedom and revenge, which reassured his family that "the people [would] carry on with the struggle." Many Hamas leaders who attended the funeral were also killed in the months and years to come as Israeli missiles "liquidated" their cars, homes, civilians, and small boys and girls on their way to unknown destinations.

Young Ehab al-Badrasawi was also there, delivering a short sermon to whoever cared to listen, emphasizing how much he and Ibrahim al-Makadmeh had in common, sharing a relationship that started long before they were born in two separate but nearby refugee camps in Gaza. For him, it all started in Beit Daras, a fact that gave his cause even greater meaning.

A few years after al-Makadmeh's assassination, a homemade Palestinian rocket carrying his name was born. It was called M75, where the letter M stood for Makadmeh, and the number 75 indicated the range of the rocket in kilometers. Israel was shaken by the unfamiliar spectacle of an M75 flying over Rishon Lezion, Tel Aviv, and even the Jerusalem area. Though Israeli military intelligence studied every aspect of the new rocket, it never connected Rishon Lezion to the massacre that killed Palestinian laborers on Black Sunday on May 20, 1990, subsequently resulting in eighteen-year-old Wael al-Badrasawi being shot in the throat while standing between the alleyway and the main road. Nor did they concern themselves with understanding the link between Wael's murder and Ehab's haunting memories, including a conversation the two brothers once had about God, martyrdom, and Paradise while swaying on a homemade swing set beneath the olive tree in the middle of the *hakoura*. If the Israelis had paid close attention, they would have realized that the rockets had passed over an empty site on which a village called Beit Daras had stood for millennia before its inhabitants were expelled amid a massacre that shapes the collective identity of the survivors and their descendants to this very day.

Sardine Cans

Even as Madallah's ailments mounted in the latter part of her life, she remained hopeful that all things would be restored to some kind of a natural order, an order that can only be established through the will of God, not the dictates of man. Despite everything she had been through in her life, she never begged or implored anyone for her own sake. The exception was always her children. On many occasions, she beseeched soldiers—both Israelis and Palestinians—to leave her family alone, or to release her incarcerated sons.

When Ehab was in the Saraya, Madallah spent countless days camped outside the notorious prison, though she was not allowed to see the youngest of her boys for months on end. Whenever she was allowed to see him, she would put on a brave face, maintaining false courage until she returned home, only to hide in her special room and cry, pray, and beseech God as she had her whole life.

In the Saraya she met al-Rantisi, al-Makadmeh, and Salah Shehade, the man who, with Emad Akel and Mohammed al-Mabhouh had formed the Al-Qassam Brigades nearly a decade earlier.[131] For her, such meetings were of no consequence. Her relationship with her son's prison mates was only that of a mother, equally torn to see others taken away from their families the way Ehab had been taken from her. She prayed constantly to God for all their freedom.

When the prisoners escaped in the early months of the Intifada, the Palestinian Authority, at least for a while, sought their return. PA officers repeatedly raided the Badrasawi family home, searching every corner of the house, breaking doors and furniture, and swearing at God, Hamas, and every family member who questioned their violence. Almost every time, Madallah, weaker than ever, sustained some kind of injury that required days, or even weeks, to recover.

While on the run, Ehab met Asia al-Masouabi, whose family sought no dowry for their daughter, as was and remains the custom among religious communities. The marriage was finalized quickly, though the traditional celebrations were kept to a minimum so as not to alert the PA to Ehab's whereabouts. In the first few years of Ehab and Asia's married life, they met only a few times, always in secret, enough for Asia to become pregnant with their daughter Mariam, whose eyes Madallah declared were the exact same eyes as those of her mother, Mahasin.

The al-Badrasawi house, on the same plot of land allocated to them by UNRWA decades earlier, went through many stages of development. Following the death of their father, the older brothers divided the house into two sections, one for Nasser, who insisted on marrying first, and the remainder for everyone else. When Tal'at married, it was impossible to further divide the remaining space. So Tal'at and his wife moved out, though they remained within the borders of the Shati refugee camp. When Ibrahim finally decided to get married, he did what many refugees in Shati have done before, expanding the house upward to construct what Palestinian refugees in Gaza know as the "sardine can system": vertical cubicles of concrete stacked on top of each other in a seemingly haphazard fashion in order to accommodate the growth of a population with no other means of expansion. The bottom part was left to Madallah and her unmarried children; the second floor to Ibrahim, his wife, and kids; and the third to Ehab, Asia and, over the years, their six children.

The strange structure of the improved UNRWA house, which often solicited laughter from passersby, served its purpose until Israel attempted to assassinate Ehab for the first time in 2002. An Israeli drone struck the top floor and carved the house into two vertical structures, one of which immediately fell while the other remained in place. Miraculously no one died, though all thirty-six members of the household—the brothers, their wives, families, Madallah, and the married and unmarried sisters—had all clustered in the small living room on the second floor. They thought they were safer together. They were wrong. Everyone agreed that the presence of Madallah, a blessed woman, was the reason the missile spared the whole family.

Ehab was miles away when Israel attacked his home. He was being chased by a drone on the other side of the refugee camp. His options were limited: stand in place and die, or return home and cause the death of everyone else. Not knowing that the family home had been blown up anyway, he devised a third option: running in circles in the hope that the drone would eventually run out of fuel or ammunition. This story was always retold with the same degree of excitement and laughter as if it were another ordinary event in the life of the al-Badrasawi family. Despite the laughter, Ehab felt a degree of pride conveying the story, as it demonstrated yet again that his will was stronger than that of an Israeli killing machine. "The cowards tried to kill my family since they couldn't kill me," he would say, and his mood would shift from comical defiance to sheer anger.

Hidden Reality

The armed component of the Intifada presented the perfect pretext for the Israeli army to eliminate Hamas's political and military leadership. Ehab, a well-known Al-Qassam fighter and recruiter, was therefore someone Israel had to assassinate. For its part, Al-Qassam also saw the uprising as an opportunity to develop its combat capabilities, restructuring its crude military into a guerrilla army.

The Second Intifada brought more military operations, more recruits, and more chances to wage jihad, always emphasized in political discourse but rarely evidenced on the battlefield. This struggle was no longer confined to Gaza and instead extended to various parts of the West Bank, which was evolving away from the passivity of Oslo and toward active armed combat.

Israel's military strategists could clearly see that in order for its colonial forces to attempt to control the Palestinian families and communities living in the West Bank and Gaza, many had to be "liquidated" or detained. They also resorted to massacres in attempt to inflict the kind of shock needed to suppress a nation that was collectively determined to remain sovereign.[132] Finally,

the Palestinian Authority also needed to reinvent itself in order
to serve its intended mission—at least as seen by Israel and the
United States—prioritizing the security needs of Israel.[133]
Arafat was blamed by both the Israelis and the Americans
for rejecting Israel's supposed peace overtures, and for igniting
the Intifada.[134] Israel punished him by sending tanks to blast his
office in Ramallah. In April 2004, Israeli Prime Minister Ariel
Sharon said he was "released from the pledge" of not physically
harming Arafat, hinting he might be targeted for assassination.[135] Arafat was only allowed to escape his confinement
once, in October 2004, to a French hospital, where he was pronounced dead a month later.[136] Palestinians, it seemed, were
finally defeated. Israel's allies within the Palestinian Authority
were once more in charge. Those Palestinians who were not
killed or imprisoned, like Ehab, went on the run, often literally
living underground.

Hidden from TV news headlines, however, another reality
was forming. Palestinian society was undergoing a grassroots
evolution that was neither dictated by Israel, financed by the
United States, nor implemented by the Palestinian Authority.
In contrast to the claims of Israeli leaders in general elections,
Hamas had in fact emerged from the Intifada much stronger.
The movement had replaced its assassinated or detained
leaders, recruited hundreds of fighters, and began forging alliances outside of Palestine, taking advantage of the political
shifts underway in Lebanon and the rest of the Middle East.[137]

For the United States and Israel to continue to manage Palestinian reality, some kind of legitimacy to Palestine's new
rulers was needed. It started with the January 2005 election of
Mahmoud Abbas as the new "moderate" president of the Palestinian Authority. Unpopular, corrupt, and associated with the

intrigues of Oslo, Abbas quickly solidified his power over all aspects of Palestinian institutions, including the PLO.[138] Along with Israel, he used arrests, torture, and soft power to subdue the West Bank. Gaza, however, remained untamable, a group of refugees who called themselves the *fedayeen* carrying on the war for liberation soon after the Nakba.

Believing that Gaza had little strategic value in terms of Israeli territorial expansion, Sharon, still the prime minister of Israel, decided to leave the Strip. His disengagement plan, starting in August 2005, was not popular among the settlers, but received political support from the rest of Israeli society.[139] In truth, the Israeli army never truly left Gaza. It simply deployed from densely populated areas to impose a tight land, air, and sea blockade on the Strip.[140] A new type of warfare followed. Israel used malnutrition, the denial of medicine, and restrictions on freedom of movement as new weapons in its ongoing war. In early 2006, Dov Weisglass, then a senior advisor to Prime Minister Ehud Olmert, stated that Israeli policy aimed "to put the Palestinians on a diet, but not to make them die of hunger." In 2012, it was disclosed that in early 2008, Israeli officials had prepared a document calculating the minimum caloric intake needed for Palestinians to avoid malnutrition. This was done to restrict the amount of food allowed into Gaza, ensuring sufficient rations to prevent starvation, but not more.[141] Palestinians responded with homemade rockets, compelling, at least in Israel's own logic, the Israeli army to "mow the lawn" of Gaza—a figure of speech referring to the wholesale slaughter of Palestinians. Ex-CIA analyst Elizabeth Murray has noted that this expression has been used in Israel since Operation Cast Lead assault on Gaza in 2008–2009 that killed over 1,400 Palestinians, which one hardline Israel supporter at a think tank seminar brushed off by saying: "It's unfortunate, but every once in a while, you have to mow the lawn."[142]

Soon in Paradise

Madallah Abdulnabi—the "extension of God" and "servant of the Prophet"—died in 2006. She needed surgery to eliminate the early traces of cancer that were nesting in her colon. It was the early months of the siege, and no hospitals in Gaza could carry out the operation. Israel's refusal to grant her a permit to leave Gaza for a better-equipped West Bank hospital meant certain death. According to family members, her last prayer was: "Oh, Allah, I only ask that you spare my *karameh* in my old age." He did. Madallah died in her sleep surrounded by every member of her family. Even Ehab, who snuck into the house in the middle of the night, was there. He hugged her briefly, held her right hand, kissed it, laid it gently by her side, closed her eyes and told her: "God willing, I will see you soon in Paradise." No one knew if her companion had departed her body, or if he died with her on that very mattress, in that same room with the low gray walls.

Without Madallah urging him to be careful, stay safe, and focus on his long-delayed master's degree in Islamic studies, Ehab had no reason to reject the post of commander of the Shati battalion. The redeployment of the Israeli army, though it did little to help Palestinians achieve their political goals, gave Ehab and Al-Qassam Brigades the space needed to form their guerilla army: five brigades, each consisting of five to seven battalions, including an elite battalion, each divided into small units.[143]

As the battalions grew in both number and quality of fighters, their weapons became more sophisticated. Gone were the days of the twenty pistols of Sheik Yassin and an inoperative rocket launcher. As the Israeli military was now fortified in buffer zones within or just outside the vicinities of Gaza—an area that became known as the "Gaza Envelope"—the range and quantity of Al-Qassam's missiles increased, in preparation for future, imminent wars.[144] As a message to Israel that the assassination of its leaders was not the end of the fight, Al-Qassam named its missiles after its iconic leadership, killed by Israel over the years. As M75 stood for al-Makadmeh, J80 stood for Ahmed al-Ja'bari, R160 was dedicated to al-Rantisi, and A250 to Yahya Ayash.[145] With time, Palestinians produced weapons of greater power and range, each one named in honor of a fighter who had given their life to the Palestinian struggle.

But in times of quiet, Ehab focused on recruiting and training the newcomers and keeping a watchful eye over his refugee camp. In his new role as the area commander, he was granted the power to issue certificates for moral and religious commitment to young Gazans who wished to join Hamas's newly established military academy. Those who graduated from the academy with high marks were often selected to join the *nukhba*—the elite units entrusted to carry out complex operations.

Asia

It is largely believed that Arabic calligraphy was developed over the course of fourteen centuries and that current Arabic scripts and early Canaanite and Aramaic alphabets have similar origins. Whether or not Ismail al-Masouabi was aware of this, his artistic skills displayed the evolution of many generations and various civilizations that inhabited not only the Levant, but also Iraq and the Arabian Peninsula as well. Though Ismail experimented with most Arabic fonts, he spent most of his free time designing the Diwani script, which adorned the walls of Abdullah bin Omar Mosque in the Shati refugee camp for many years.[146]

On June 6, 2021, shortly before he drove a car laden with explosives to an Israeli military camp in northern Gaza, Ismail was at that very mosque to perform his dawn prayers. He led the faithful as they conducted their obligatory *rakats*, and went home to kiss his mother's hand, insisting that she forgive him. She did, not knowing why her ever-respectful son was seeking forgiveness in the first place. After showering and putting on the new clothes he had purchased for special occasions, he left the house, never to be seen again.

Within days, the quiet, deeply spiritual artist of Shati became a legend, not only in his refugee camp but also throughout the Gaza Strip, after killing and injuring numerous Israeli soldiers by detonating a car full of explosives.

Dugit was a small, new settlement located at the northern point of the Gaza Strip, somewhere between Al-Majdal, the town from which Ismail's parents were driven out during the *Makba*, and Shati. After the Israeli military finally released the little that remained of him, two mass rallies were held to honor Gaza's latest martyr: one immediately after his death, following a symbolic burial at the historic Omari Mosque, and the actual burial of his remains at the Abdullah bin Omar Mosque in Shati.[147] As thousands of people flooded the mosque for the *janaza* funeral prayer, many were alerted that the beautiful Arabic calligraphy throughout the mosque was Ismail's hand-iwork.

Thus, when Ehab took a delegation of elders from his neighborhood to ask for Asia al-Masouabi's hand in marriage, the entire process went smoothly. He was a brother of a martyr from the First Intifada, and she was the sister of a martyr from the Second. It was understood, in fact expected, that no money would exchange hands. "We are buying a man,"* al-Masouabi elders told the al-Badrasawis. They were sure that Ehab, then a leader in Al-Qassam, the same group to which Ismail belonged, was that very man.

Asia, however, was worried. Ismail was not her family's first martyr, and marrying the commander of the Shati Brigades made her fear that he wouldn't be the last. They married anyway, agreeing that one of their shared goals was to invest in a large family. Within a decade, she and Ehab had six children, the first four arriving in consecutive years. That made already difficult financial matters worse. Ehab's salary with Al-Qassam may have improved slightly over the years, but certainly not enough to look after such a large and growing family. "Sustenance comes from Allah," he reassured her often, and, whether she found these words comforting or not, she nodded in agreement.

Asia was a Majdalaweih, a woman from Majdal Asqalan. She was not born in Al-Madjal, but like most Palestinian refugees, continued to identify with her parents' or grandparents' villages in Historical Palestine even decades after the Nakba. The term also has another meaning. Al-Majdal was a town significantly larger in size than Beit Daras. While Beit Daras and

---

* In Palestinian culture, the term "buying" in this context doesn't refer to a financial transaction. Instead, it signifies a deep emotional investment in a person, applicable to both men and women, and is especially common during marriage arrangements, though used in other scenarios as well.

numerous other villages in southern Palestine were the food basket of that whole region, Al-Majdal was a center of industry, mainly textiles. Even when the Majdalawis, like the Badrasawis, were displaced, dwelling in the same refugee encampments after the Nakba, they maintained a unique dress style, a more elegant accent, and, at least for the first post-Nakba generation, an elevated sense of social status. Asia never subscribed to that mindset, partly because she was a third-generation refugee who could no longer relate to the socioeconomic modes of the past; and partly because she was a humble, innately anxious woman whose anxieties were compounded by her relationship with Ehab.

Asia rarely complained, even when money ran low and eventually dried out completely following Israel's 2007 blockade on Gaza. To supplement the family income, she gave private Arabic classes to elementary school children and sold embroidered scarves and other garments from her home. She was even forced to sell some of the art left by her brother Ismail. She regretted that decision for years, although at the time, she had no other option.

Though Asia was not the stereotypical Majdalaweih, Al-Majdal meant to her precisely as much as Beit Daras meant to her husband: a lost paradise. Ehab asked her once in a teasing manner, "If Palestine is liberated, shall we go back to Beit Daras or Al-Majdal?" He had hoped to exchange barbs about the difference between city dwellers and *fellahin*. "My paradise is wherever you and my children are," she responded quietly and without any hesitation, as if she had already given the subject much thought.

The Other Majdalawi

Yahya Sinwar was another Majdalawi, an assertive and fiercely intelligent man from Khan Yunis, in southern Gaza, who spent over two decades in an Israeli prison. Unlike Ehab, Sinwar only experienced two years of the first uprising, none of the second, and only learned about the transformative events that affected Gaza and Palestine from inside an Israeli prison cell. When he was finally released in 2011, he quickly ascended through the hierarchy of Hamas, first elected as a member of its political bureau and, six years later, as the leader of the whole movement in Gaza.[148]

Sinwar was often linked to much of Hamas's political savvy and military prowess, though Hamas's military strength was on an upward trajectory prior to his release. Regional politics were rapidly changing, and Hamas, once a marginal movement whose leaders were on the run, was becoming the uncontested power in Gaza. A series of successive events made this possible. Israel's redeployment in Gaza had helped Hamas demonstrate its unmatched influence over the Strip by defeating the dominant PLO and PA party, Fatah, in Palestine's first democratic elections in January 2006.[149] The outcome of the elections, which angered Israel, the United States, and the post-Oslo Palestinian leadership, resulted in brief but deadly strife among Palestinians, which helped cement Hamas's position as the new ruler.[150]

Sinwar was not involved in any of those events, which spiraled into open violence between Palestinians in the terrible summer of 2007. In fact, after returning to Gaza, he used negotiation skills that he had perfected during his long imprisonment to bring the various factions together. Ehab, whose efforts to stop or at least minimize the bloodshed of 2007 had failed, rallied behind Sinwar in anticipation of a unified Palestinian front.

But Ehab was developing his own conflict with Hamas, or at least with some of its leadership in Gaza. For years before Sinwar's release, Ehab and others in the military command of Al-Qassam had grown wary of the political path taken by some within the upper echelons of the movement. In a meeting involving some of Hamas's top political and military leadership, Ehab crossed every line when he reprimanded "those who travel through Gaza in black limousines," a reference to Hamas's politicians imitating the lifestyle of their Palestinian rivals in the West Bank. As voices rose in anger and objections were made to the offensive remarks voiced by a mere field commander, Sinwar silenced everyone when he agreed that Ehab was within his rights to make such a statement. Soon after that incident, Ehab acquired the title "Abu Obeida al-Badrasawi." Though it was unclear who had given him that name, Ehab was proud of the new *nom de guerre*, which replaced his actual first name among his peers.[151]

The legitimacy gained by the second tier of commanders within Hamas was not just the outcome of the release of Sinwar and the redefining of Hamas's political priorities, which had, until then focused mostly on breaking the Israeli siege. The younger leadership felt empowered because Israel's attempts to break the Hamas movement through war had failed.

The first such failure came in 2008.

Chapter Nine

Tunnels of War

On April 29, 1273, an Andalusian man by the name of Mohammed bin Ahmed al-Qurtubi died at the age of fifty-nine in an Egyptian city located nearly 150 miles south of Cairo. It is not clear why a man born in the city of Qurtuba, now Cordoba, would leave his home, a thriving hub of culture, religion, and scholarship, venture across Gibraltar and then the entirety of North Africa to Egypt, before taking another detour south to Minya, to live and die by the Nile.

History, however, left us a few clues. Al-Andalus was largely under the control of the al-Muwahhidun.[152] In fact, al-Qurtubi was a citizen of that Islamic state-turned-empire. It all started when some Berber Muslim tribes in a small village in Morocco's Atlas Mountains used their strict interpretation of Islam to form an army and state in the Maghreb region, before extending it to the Iberian Peninsula.

While ruling over Al-Andalus, the tribal kingdom changed its capital on more than one occasion to accommodate administrative and military needs. Their first capital was in Seville, before it was moved to Qurtuba and eventually back to Seville. Al-Qurtubi was born and raised in Qurtuba when the kingdom reached its zenith in terms of military power, political, strength and cultural influence. The slow and painful demise of the kingdom, purportedly created to restore the centrality and oneness of God in the affairs of Muslims, may have been a reason why one of its greatest religious scholars, al-Qurtubi, died in Minya, Egypt, not in his birthplace, the legendary city of Qurtuba.

Though Ehab al-Badrasawi adhered to the Shafi'i school of Islamic jurisprudence, he was fascinated by al-Qurtubi, an advocate of the Maliki school. All four major schools of Sunni Islam emphasized the centrality of the Quran and the traditions of Prophet Mohammed, known as *hadith*, or sayings, regarding them as the pillars of all Islamic beliefs. Differences between these schools, apparently minor to uninformed observers, helped shape Islamic history throughout the centuries.

However, there is a major irony in Ehab's choice to study and promote al-Qurtubi's logic. Only a few miles away from the Badrasawi's home in the Shati refugee camp, a man by the name of Mohammed Idris al-Shafi'i was born nearly thirteen centuries ago. His legacy, ideas, and brand of Islam gave birth to one of the greatest and most enduring schools of thought, which influenced many Muslim societies throughout the years and even to this day. Unlike al-Qurtubi, al-Shafi'i was born into utter poverty in the city of Gaza.[153] He was only two years old when his mother resettled in the city of Mecca, seeking survival and a potential future for her son. There, the boy memorized the Quran at the age of seven and, before turning twenty, acquired the kind of knowledge that permitted him to issue *fatwas*, religious decrees that are usually the sole prerogative of the oldest and wisest religious scholars.

Many of Hamas's supporters in Gaza, like most Palestinians, are followers of the Shafi'i school, rather than the Maliki school. History teaches us that Muslim communities who lived in relative isolation—for example, within vast deserts or amid mountain ranges—adopted a stricter interpretation of Islam, while coastal communities sought a more moderate practice. For Palestinians, the Shafi'i represented a middle view of the world. In addition to its emphasis on the centrality of the Quran and the traditions of Prophet Mohammed, Shafi'i followers apply *qiyas*, a religious form of deductive reasoning. This concept allows Muslims to respond to worldly matters whose exact rulings may have not been revealed precisely in the Quran or elsewhere.

Ehab was an astute follower of Imam Shafi'i until he joined the Islamic University of Gaza, where he pursued his interest in jurisprudence. Sometime in 1995, he began reading *The Interpretation of Al-Qurtubi*, one of the most influential volumes that attempts to explain the entirety of the Quran. The task of reading and understanding al-Qurtubi's seminal book was too great of a task for a single class. Ehab then launched his weekly *halaqa*, a religious circle that included medical doctors, teachers, and other university students. Ehab's *halaqas* would typically consist of twelve people, whose conversations would ricochet from Islamic rulings to Islamic history to the reasons behind the decay and weakness of Muslim societies.

For Ehab, as for many Islamic activists, the history of Islam was always linked to the fate of Palestine, and the sorry state of the *ummah,* the global community of Islamic people. He believed the colonization of Palestine by Zionists and the West's hegemony over Arab and Muslim nations could not be viewed separately from the splintering of Muslim states hundreds of years ago, including the Iberian Peninsula. To Ehab's *halaqas*, past and current Muslim disunity was most obvious in the case of Palestine, which had been left to fend for itself against the designs of Israel, the United States, and the whole Western world.

Thus, Ehab did not only study Islamic scholars of the past to obtain knowledge on religious matters, but also to understand what had gone so terribly wrong for Muslims everywhere—starting with the loss of Al-Andalus all the way to the loss of Palestine. Ehab argued that gaining a true understanding of al-Qurtubi could be the starting point of correcting a historical injustice that began when Muslims turned against each other all those years ago.

This is how Ehab's political discourse and everyday language shifted over time to become situated within an Islamic intellec-tual framework. Modern ideologies were no longer relevant to him except as illustrations of the fatal mistake by Muslims who entrusted their destinies to foreign entities, whether capitalists, socialists, nationalists, or anything else. This kind of thinking was not his alone, but that of a whole generation left to rule over Gaza after the Israeli redeployment in 2005 and the pivotal fight between Hamas and Fatah in 2007. Even the language that Hamas ascribed to its subsequent wars with Israel carried deep spiritual and historical meaning. When Israel attacked Gaza with unprecedented ferocity on December 27, 2008, the Israeli military called its war "Operation Cast Lead." Hamas referred to it as the "Battle of Al-Furqan," named after the twenty-fifth chapter of the Quran. The word *furqan*, "the criterion," was a reference to the holy book itself, meaning the decisive factor that separates good and evil.

But the three-week war was hardly decisive in any sense. Rather, it was the start of a different kind of war between

Israelis and Palestinians. Israel killed more than a thousand Palestinians and destroyed almost 50,000 homes, leaving tens of thousands homeless.[154] Hamas, already struggling to manage the impoverished and besieged Gaza Strip, now had to contend with the devastation wrought by the war.

Israel's surprise war was meant to make it impossible for Hamas to exist as both a civilian authority and a resistance movement. When a truce was declared on January 18, over 100,000 Gazans were left homeless, and many of the wounded continued to die due to a lack of proper medical care. Poverty deepened as Israel targeted factories, farms, and civilian infrastructure. The Israeli war was also meant to restore the status quo that had existed in the period between the Israeli redeployment from Gaza in 2005 and the Fatah-Hamas clash of 2007.

Yet none of Israel's plans were actualized. Despite unprecedented devastation, Gaza remained standing and unified.

From the onset, it seemed that the Battle of Al-Furqan would change nothing on the ground. The Israelis maintained that their latest onslaught was merely "self-defense," and Washington and other Western governments wholeheartedly agreed. Arab and Muslim countries condemned Israel but did little to help the Palestinians. The Palestinian Authority and the Israeli army continued with their security coordination in the West Bank. The United Nations investigated the alleged war crimes, but took no action to hold the war criminals accountable; Western media, as always, continued to toe the Israeli line.[155] But certain things did, in fact, change, such as the Israeli realization that Hamas was a growing military force to be contended with. Equally crucial, it was now recognized that if the Resistance was to survive, a different style of warfare would have to be adopted. That was the moment that Ehab al-Badrasawi put down his favorite book by al-Qurtubi and picked up a shovel.

Tunnels

When the Macedonian army under the command of Alexander the Great finally conquered Gaza in 332 BCE, Batis, the leader of the Gazan forces, was killed in a way that was considered brutal even back then.[156] The fighters at the Gaza fort had pushed back Alexander's army three times in his three-month siege of their city, almost completely thwarting the Macedonian's attempt to occupy the entirety of the Mediterranean coast. A local fighter almost succeeded in assassinating Alexander, who was twice injured in his Gaza campaign—once on the battlefield and also by the daring would-be assassin.

When the war was over, historians tell us that all of Gaza's men were put to the sword and all its women were sold into slavery.[157] Batis, still alive, was dragged by a chariot around the walls of fallen Gaza. The ropes that fastened his bleeding and bruised body to the horses were forced through holes in his heels drilled by the triumphant soldiers. This cruelty was carried out so that rebellious Gazans would understand, for generations to come, that resistance was futile.

Batis was punished for failing to kneel to the man who had conquered his city and destroyed its homes, temples, and people. The stubborn Badrasawi kneeled before no man and fought with the ferocity of an ancient warrior against the Macedonians and their merciless sieges and torture techniques. If Ehab represented the natural evolution of the warrior spirit, unleashed long before Batis's time, then there must have been many Batises and Ehabs throughout Palestinian history.

It is equally true that Gaza's resistance throughout history has been linked to Palestinians themselves, not to the specific heroic figures we encounter now and then. We know this because of the consistency of the collective resilience of the Palestinians often invoked in the word *sumud*, which does not seem to be linked to any specific period, mode of thinking, or religious belief. Otherwise, how can one explain the Gazans' legendary resistance against the Romans, the Crusaders, Napoleon's military campaign, the British and, finally Israeli settler-colonialism?[158]

The perplexing thing in all of this is that in terms of its topographic formation, Gaza was never truly ready for these kinds of wars and sieges. A flat, small coastal area, it was always vulnerable to invaders who attacked from the sea, charged from the desert, and converged from every direction. Yet Gaza and the rest of Palestine always found a way to resist. To fight Alexander, Gazans built artificial hills from mounds of dirt. In later wars, they dug massive trenches. When modern warfare made these tactics ineffectual, they dug tunnels. Geography and landscape can be a blessing or a curse to those fending off foreign invasions, but an ingredient far more precious is required for resistance to matter: the human spirit. The same factor which compelled Batis and his people to fight Alexander with the determination to vanquish the ruthless Macedonians compelled Ehab to dig tunnels all around his Shati refugee camp in order to keep the enemy at bay.

The period between the end of the 2008–9 war and the start of the 2012 war were dedicated to creating the foundation of Gaza's resistance tunnels, which proved to be one of the most successful guerrilla war tactics, not only in Palestine, but anywhere in the world, ancient or modern.[159] The Gaza tunnels began not as a resistance tactic, but as survival strategy, to cope with the Israeli siege imposed on Gaza after Hamas won the 2006 election.

The earliest tunnels were dug in the southern Gaza city of Rafah. When the Rafah residents first began digging, Hamas as a political movement with a military wing did not yet exist. Following the 1979 Egypt-Israeli treaty, the two countries resolved that the border between Gaza and Egypt needed to be redrawn, a process not completed until 1982. Consequently, Rafah was divided into an "Egyptian Rafah" under Egyptian control and a "Palestinian Rafah" under Israeli military occupation.[160] The dividing line disfigured whole neighborhoods, separating families, even splitting houses into two.

So Palestinians began digging tunnels.

The tunnels were initially dug so that fragmented families could occasionally unite, especially during times of great joy or sorrow. Most of the tunnels started in family basements, living rooms, or *hakouras*, emerging after a few meters, and eventually a few hundred meters, in corresponding family homes on the other side, whether Egyptian or Gazan. This method, which helped Rafah maintain a degree of social unity for at least a few more years, became Gaza's economic salvation after the Israeli siege was tightened in 2007.

Even before the Israeli redeployment of 2005 and the full imposition of the blockade in 2007, the Rafah Crossing between Gaza and Egypt was always a source of hardship for Palestinians. Some Gazans who were allowed access by Egypt were denied entry by Israel. The latter excluded any Palestinians or their relatives who had a concerning "security record"—anyone suspected of challenging the Israeli occupation, even if only by word. At times, Israel would shut down the border crossing as a form of collective punishment. Sometimes the Egyptians would be the ones who shut down the border, often at Israel's behest. The tunnels became critical as they helped Palestinians avoid a massive apparatus of control involving governments, militaries, and an American largesse dedicated to ensuring Palestinians were besieged.[161]

When the Israeli siege created shortages in basic products, the tunnels helped alleviate the suffering, bringing food, medicine, cement, gas, seeds, livestock, and eventually clothes, even zoo animals, and weapons. Though often the tunnels were referred to as the "Hamas tunnels," in actuality, most of them were privately owned by families, clans, and local businesses. A 2015 UNCTAD report noted that during the five-year period following 2007, there were more than 1,532 tunnels under the border, all which were closed by mid-2013. It was claimed the tunnel trade exceeded official trade.[162] As their role became fundamental to sustaining the Gaza economy, the ever-expanding tunnels became a lifeline for all of Gaza. They were even subject to taxes, and managed by an unwritten set of rules and regulations.

Israel's 2008–9 war on Gaza made the tunnels even more critical to the people's survival. Since Israel didn't allow Palestinians to rebuild the thousands of homes, housing units, and other civilian and government infrastructure it destroyed, the tunnels filled some of the gap, enabling Palestinians to rebuild what had been destroyed in the war in the span of a few years.* Yet just when Gazans were celebrating the rebuilding of their

---

* The tunnels were originally constructed from concrete salvaged from buildings destroyed during Israel's wars on Palestinians. Some of these tunnels, particularly those near the Rafah border between Egypt and Gaza, were used to funnel essential goods like cement into the Strip. This cement was also used to fortify the tunnels themselves.

cities, Israel destroyed the Strip again starting with the war of 2012 and the far more devastating war of 2014.

During this period, Egypt changed more than once, undergoing the kind of seismic political shifts that greatly impacted Palestinians, especially those living in Gaza. Hosni Mubarak, who was ousted in 2011, for example, restricted Palestinian movement through the Rafah Crossing and carried out many aggressive measures to halt the operations of many tunnels.[163] Mohammed Morsi, the first post-revolution president, opened the Crossing more often and largely turned a blind eye to many of the tunnels that were still in operation. Abdul Fatah al-Sisi, who overthrew Morsi in 2013, cracked down once again on Palestinian movement with great resolve. His army operated the Rafah Crossing according to the most arbitrary rules, and largely destroyed the tunnels—ostensibly all of them. Yet Palestinians kept digging. The more restrictions that were imposed on them aboveground, the more freedom they found below. Though the tunnels as an economic lifeline were no longer relevant after the Sisi campaign, the tunnels of the Resistance kept growing, no longer confined to the Rafah area. Initially under Mubarak, and then to a much greater extent under Sisi, Egypt sought to destroy Gaza's tunnels. Their methods included constructing an underground barrier, creating and expanding a buffer zone, and pumping toxic gasses, sewage, and sea water. Families suspected of digging tunnels were punished with heavy fines and home demolitions.

Palestinians were digging everywhere, around their refugee camps, near areas adjacent to the Israeli fences and walls east of Gaza, even close to the beach, starting near Shati in the north and ending in Rafah. At the time, the logic of digging seemed erratic and confusing, or possibly meant to mislead the Israeli drones in their around-the-clock reconnaissance missions over the Strip. Only time would prove that the digging beneath Gaza was done in anticipation of a future war even the Israelis couldn't foresee, let alone win.

Instead, the Israelis continued with their "mowing-the-lawn" tactics, which, starting in November 2012, included destroying tunnels. What Israel called operation "Pillar of Defense" was countered the Palestinian "Operation *Sijjil*," another Quranic reference of good ultimately triumphing over evil.[164] Unlike other wars, the short but deadly conflict started with a resounding Israeli success—the assassination of Ahmed Al-Ja'bari.[165] The killing of the man responsible for turning Al-Qassam into a fighting force that could withstand a prolonged Israeli war was considered by Israel to be a fatal blow to the movement.

It was a difficult blow, but not a fatal one. Thanks to al-Ja'bari and other leaders of Al-Qassam, the brigades were structured so as not to depend on an individual leader or a set of leaders to carry on with the fight. Though the man was responsible for shaping the new vision of the Hamas military wing, his death was not the end of armed resistance in Gaza. The war continued. As Israel began to strike thousands of targets in Gaza, Palestinians pounded Israeli cities. Though the Palestinian's homemade rockets were not as deadly or effective as Israel's, more than 1,456 rockets were fired from Gaza into Israel, some traveling as far as the city of Tel Aviv, and even beyond.[166]

For Israel, 2012 was just another year of war ended with Egyptian mediation and yet another flimsy ceasefire agreement. For Palestinians, however, the war meant something greater. Al-Qassam's leaders recognized that no matter what type of weapons Palestinians used aboveground, winning a war against Israel would require that the Resistance would have to be mostly staged underground. For that to happen, the tunnels could no longer be used solely for smuggling weapons or storing supplies. It was time to move from the position of defense to that of attack.

The case for the "attack tunnels" had been demonstrated years before the 2012 war. In 2006, a group of Palestinian fighters emerged from underground at the border between Rafah and Israel, taking their enemy by surprise. It seemed as if the masked Palestinian fighters sprung from the bottom of earth as they pointed their automatic rifles, hitting their targets with accuracy amid shouts of "God is Great!" Two Israeli soldiers were killed and five were injured in that unusual episode, whose consequences would alter the tactics of the Israelis and the Palestinians, possibly forever. But more important for the Palestinians than the killing and wounding of soldiers was the capture of a scrawny, bespectacled Israeli Corporal by the name of Gilad Shalit.

The capture of Shalit, who was forced to live in Gaza—mostly underground—for years, was an earthshattering event for both Israel and the Palestinian resistance. The speed and audacity of the operation, the Resistance's ability to conceal the captured soldier for five years without any traces or clues of his whereabouts, and the heavy price exacted for his release, were all indicators of an end to the conventional relationship between Israel and Gaza. Shalit's release in 2011, in exchange for 1,027 Palestinians proved for the first time that Palestinians in Gaza can do more than merely challenge the Israeli occupation and siege. By obtaining leverage, Palestinians managed to force Israel to negotiate, if indirectly. For the Resistance, the outcome of the story meant greater legitimacy. For Israel, humiliation.

The 2012 war on Gaza was Israel's attempt to reset a relationship that had existed since the Nakba. It was Israel's way of stating, through overwhelming firepower, that it was still in control. But the message was not received, leading to the war of 2014—codenamed "Operation Protective Edge" by Israel and the "Eaten Straw" by Palestinians. Israel's primary goal of the war was to destroy the tunnels, thus denying Palestinians their last lifeline. All that Palestinians needed to do, through military ingenuity and *sumud*, was deny Israel any achievement in that war.

Ehab al-Badrasawi and many of his generation fully appreciated the meaning of that historical juncture, one that he felt could determine the future of the Resistance and Gaza. So he and thousands like him kept digging. They dug tunnels of all sizes and for all purposes, mostly unaware of the logic behind the number or locations of the tunnels—how, why, or where they intersected or parted ways. But they understood that they were digging tunnels in preparation for another war.

When that war finally arrived, the fighters moved underground, staying there for fifty-one days. They only emerged for brief moments to hit a target, or, from the perspective of the Israeli army, to be killed. Often a single second made the difference between life and death. Many survived. In fact, the 2014 war, though it destroyed much of Gaza, was the first time in modern history where the Gaza fort was not conquered. Batis was still very much alive, regardless of the return of the Macedonians, ready to take his chances defending Gaza against a brutal enemy.

Al-'Asf al-Makoul

On July 21, 2014, Palestinian fighters from the Al-Qassam Brigades emerged from a narrow tunnel that started in Gaza and ended in an Israeli military area near Kibbutz Nir Am, not far from the Sderot settlement.[167] One of the fighters took aim and fired an anti-tank missile. Others shot in multiple directions to create a protective shield before returning to their tunnel as quickly as they had emerged. The Israeli army admitted to the killing of four soldiers, including a commander from the elite Nahal battalion. It was not the first time that Hamas's attack tunnels were used in the 2014 war.[168] Just four days before the storming of the Israeli military base, another Al-Qassam unit emerged in a similar fashion in the Sufa area, near Rafah, a relatively long distance from Sderot. Here too, the Israeli army was also taken by surprise, and five soldiers were killed.[169] After many years of trying, Hamas, and other Palestinian groups in Gaza altered the most basic equation of their war against Israel.

The war of July 2014 was different from other wars, clashes, or popular uprisings, though it borrowed specific elements from previous encounters.[170] Hamas built on the attack of 2006, which led to the capture of Shalit; retained the highly defensive nature of the 2008–9 and 2012 wars; and relied on the popular support of the Gaza masses to negotiate a more dignified ceasefire.

For Israel, the war was a failed experiment, one that provided an important lesson. The inconclusive outcome of Israel's 2012 "Protective Edge" had troubled the Israeli political and military establishments. Losing military deterrence, which had long governed the relationship between Israel and all Arabs, was agonizing and unacceptable. The pretext to return to war in Gaza didn't emerge from Gaza itself, as Hamas and other resistance movements largely adhered to the ceasefire mediated by Egypt. The pretext was found in the West Bank.

On June 12, three Israeli settlers—ages sixteen to nineteen years old—were kidnapped and killed in the settlement of Gush Etzion. Their case, due to their ages, became a rallying cry for another, even bigger war among Israeli officials. The propaganda campaign lasted for weeks, finally causing one of the deadliest wars against Gaza. The war began with a lethal aerial assault. Between July 8 and 16, an estimated 1,700 targets in Gaza were hit.[171] The number may have been higher. The Israeli army, per its habit, said that the strikes had only targeted "terrorist infrastructure," but hundreds of civilians were killed. Hospital morgues were inundated with the dead and the bereaved. But even then, though destructive and tragic, the war was a typical one. A series of events, this time initiated by the Palestinians, would soon change the course of the war.

Palestinian tunnels now reached Israel itself, a realization that shocked the Israeli military to its core. First there was the July 17 tunnel attack, then another attack on July 21. Between these two events, something extraordinary took place: an actual battle in a Gaza neighborhood called Al-Shuja'iyya. Despite the overwhelming superiority of the Israeli military in terms of numbers, equipment, air power, and overall technology, they still lost the battle to a group of Palestinian fighters who manufactured their own arms and assembled their own explosive devices underground.

To appreciate what happened in this small, historic, and overcrowded neighborhood, it is necessary to reflect on the battle's wider military context.[172] Israel attacked Gaza with three military divisions, each consisting of several brigades. The brigades were supported by one of the world's most powerful combination of military intelligence, air force, and navy. All of them conspired to defeat a few bands of local fighters, whose numbers were estimated at merely eight hundred.[173]

The First Golani Brigade, which operated under the command of the 36th Division, is considered one of the Israeli army's most elite fighting forces. Formed in February 1948, it operated in the Nakba, and two of its five battalions can trace their origin back to that time. When the Brigade first advanced into Shuja'iyya on July 19, 2014, it must have been certain of the success of its mission, to locate and destroy the tunnels of the Resistance. Still, the decision to advance into the largely destroyed neighborhood was made with great care and careful planning. The rest of the 36th Division was involved in a maneuver in the north and east of Gaza to distract from the intricate operation which was about to take place. Yet the moment the Golani forces crossed the fence into Gaza, specifically into Shuja'iyya, they came under fire. The deception maneuver failed, and ultimately the whole operation. A single Palestinian strike at an American-supplied Israeli M113 armored personal carrier with an RPG anti-armor shell killed seven Israeli soldiers, in addition to the brigade commander.[174] Other commanders from the same battalion were wounded. Trapped, the Israeli army on the ground called for air support.

The Arabic word *shuja'iyya* is derived from the word *shuja'a*, which means bravery. But bravery was found all over Gaza, whose basic elements of resistance are not mere guns or bullets, but the collective tenacity acquired through many generations. This tenacity has never been weakened by high explosive shells, artillery, war planes, and the ceaseless march of military battalions. Even the one hundred 2,000-pound bombs dropped over Gaza during the war could not alter the outcome of the battle of Shuja'iyya or anywhere else in Gaza.[175] When the battle ended on July 12, the Israeli army admitted that thirteen of its soldiers were dead and many wounded, along with scores of dead Palestinians, mostly women and children.[176] But to some extent, Shuja'iyya emerged enlivened by the battle, as the Palestinian spirit soared once again over the military might of its colonial oppressor.

Israel was desperate to escape a war it had started. This time it was Hamas that rejected the ceasefire initiative pressed by the Sisi government in Egypt and Israeli allies in Washington. Palestinians wanted a fundamental change in the status of Gaza: an end to the siege, an expansion of the fishing zone, the release of those rearrested since the Shalit exchange, and an international force to monitor the border area.[177] Unable to retreat, Israel decided to invade Gaza with no clear objectives, since every area it designated as a legitimate target had already been destroyed.

Thousands of civilians were killed from the air, shelled by advancing Israeli tanks, or mowed down as they attempted to escape. Yet the Israeli army could not advance into most populated areas, and whenever it tried, it could not hold its positions for more than a few hours or days. Rockets continued to fall on Israel, as the launchers were no longer hidden in olive groves and open fields, but underground. Frustrated by the unusual limits imposed on its military, Israel struck civilian areas without mercy. By August 26, Palestinian losses surpassed that of any of the previous wars.

Among the thousands of wounded, many were maimed for life. Whole neighborhoods were erased. High rise buildings were reduced to dust. Israel's new targets included hospitals, schools, mosques, and as always, homes along with their owners. Yet when the war was over, practically all of Gaza celebrated victory over Israel. Crowds carried the children of the martyred and roamed the streets chanting for the Resistance. Old men attempted to do the traditional *dabka* dance while waving their canes in jubilation. Women ululated. Children grasped balloons resembling the color of the Palestinian flag. Traditional dessert shops hurriedly made baklava, distributing it freely to the ecstatic crowds who sang for the Resistance like they had never cheered for an Arab army before. A new lexicon was born, exceeding the factional language of the past to a more encompassing discourse, in which Yasser Arafat was celebrated alongside Ahmed Yassin and Mohammed Deif.

Thousands chanted in unison, "Stack the sword by the sword, we are the children of Mohammed Deif." Israel's attempts to kill the leader of Al-Qassam had failed. Deif's wife, seven-month-old son, and three-year-old daughter had been killed when Israel bombed a house in the area, but Deif was alive.[178] News emerged that the leader of the Resistance, who lived most of his life in tunnels, might have been badly wounded, that he had lost an eye and sustained serious wounds in one leg.[179] But Deif continued to issue statements, directives, and inspirational speeches from below the ground, where he was already preparing an even more decisive battle.

This was Deif's war. It was Gaza's war. But also, in many ways, it was Ehab's war. At thirty-nine years of age, Ehab's body was still strong enough to engage in direct combat. He moved underground with the ease of a child, emerging rapidly from the furthest point of the camp to the other, giving directions, orders, and reminding his fighters of the virtue of dying as martyrs. "Always go for the *burj* ... go for the *burj*," he would advise his fighters, pointing them to the towers of the Israeli Merkava tanks, one of its most vulnerable spots. He went for the *burj* himself, and more than once, scored direct hits before shouting "God is Great!" and diving back into a tunnel as if he was being swallowed by quicksand.

Whether Ehab took part in the planning or execution of the successful naval commando operations that penetrated southern Israel during the war cannot be known. The Frogmen of Hamas have always been shrouded with secrecy. Yet Ehab spoke of these operations proudly and often after the war. As one of the early divers of the Al-Qassam naval force, he had argued that if the land fights on the side of its rightful owners, so should the sea. In fact, the Gaza Sea, which once snatched the bodies of Nakba refugees buried not far away from the beach, was finally at peace with its refugee neighbors. Indeed, Palestinians have befriended the sea; in fact, they have fought for every inch of it, because the more access they had, the greater their chances of survival became.

Did the sea weep for Palestinians on July 16, 2014, when four children—Ismail, Zakaria, Ahmed, and Mohamed—were killed by an Israeli warship as they played at the beach?[180] Some of those who witnessed the incident said that the cousins, ages nine to eleven were playing soccer. Others said they were playing hide and seek. They were all children of fishermen. Huts belonging to their Bakr clan have dotted the beach for many years. The boys died in the very place where their ancestors learned how to survive. But not even the murder of the Bakr boys would break Gaza, which mourned its dead while celebrating its martyrs. Every neighborhood, refugee camp, village, or town in Gaza had a funeral procession in August 2014.

Writing the Last Chapter

After the war, Hamas looked as if it was ready to translate its achievements on the battlefield into politics, namely acquiring the kind of legitimacy it was denied following its election victory in 2006. Moreover, an earnest push for the normalization of the status quo had begun, where ensuring calm at the Gaza front by Hamas would be rewarded by Israel with the easing of the siege. International envoys arrived in Gaza to meet with Ismail Haniyeh, the Hamas leader. Robert Serry, the UN special envoy for the Middle East peace process, met with Haniyeh and urged him to consider a "reconstruction *hudna*," a ceasefire of at least three to five years. Paul Garnier, the Swiss representative to the Palestinian Authority, who was coordinating with Serry, also discussed the proposal with Hamas officials.[181] Hamas began promoting its own vision of a long-term *hudna*, a state of truce that would not involve the recognition of Israel as a legitimate nation-state.[182]

Hamas was willing to consider "no-war, no-peace" under the condition that Al-Qassam would not be disbanded or disarmed. Without the brigades, Hamas, and all of Gaza would lose their main leverage and would once again become vulnerable to Israel's habitual "mowing of the lawn."

Israel began to sense a shift in the attitude of the Palestinian movement. Israel's Western allies began to try to appraise the change underway in the seemingly new, more pragmatic Hamas. Tony Blair, the former British prime minister and now envoy relegated to carrying out tasks assigned by Washington and Tel Aviv, was on the move. He met with Khaled Mishal, then head of the political bureau, more than once, urging him to release the bodies of two Israeli soldiers believed to have been held in Gaza from a previous war. At first the talks seemed serious and encouraging, but they lasted for years and ultimately yielded nothing but promises of yet more talks.[183]

As the talks and the siege continued, Ehab al-Badrasawi, once the fastest and strongest of fighters in the whole northern command, was growing old. In his mid-forties, his body was no longer able to meet the physical demands of a Hamas soldier. Though his body remained strong, his agility petered out. He grew heavy and tired. Without fighting in the field, what was his worth as a Gazan, a Palestinian, a Muslim, a fighter, and a human being? His whole life, since the early years of the First Intifada, had revolved around his dangerous activities countering Israel's colonial encroachment—throwing rocks as a child, painting revolutionary graffiti as a teenager, and, as a fully grown man, carrying a gun, digging tunnels, firing RPGs, and chasing soldiers or getting chased by them and their drones.

"Hamas wants me to become an administrator of a prison," he told Ibrahim once with evident sarcasm. "They want me to be the warden of the very prison in which I was held and tortured," he said, raising his voice in annoyance. "But it is not Ehab Abdallah al-Badrasawi who would imprison his own people, no matter the circumstance or the crime." Ehab always used his full name whenever he made such important declarations. Ibrahim urged him to reconsider his decision, to think of Asia and the children. To think of his own future. "No one remains a fighter forever, and life is not a constant revolution," the older brother reasoned. Ehab scoffed and stormed out of the house, the same family home of many years ago. Though the scars of war had changed parts of it, it essentially remained the same house of Madallah and Abdullah al-Badrasawi. They were long gone, but the memories of pain and joy they left behind were still infused within the walls of a place that had been offered by the UN as a "temporary shelter" for families displaced by the Nabka. The election of Yahya Sinwar as Hamas's new leader in Gaza in February 2017 renewed hope that the movement would soon return to the field. But Sinwar continued to pursue the path of reconciliation with Fatah. The two movements signed an agreement to end the division in October of that same year— just another piece of paper, signed but not honored. Despite the promises, the siege remained in place. Israel monitored Gazans from all directions, and occasionally shelled them as a reminder that Israel was always there, listening, watching, counting calories, granting life, assigning death.[184]

March 2018 was a breaking point. The Great March of Return was the outcome of a combined effort by all Palestinian political factions, including Hamas and various civil society organizations. Tens of thousands of civilians advanced to the eastern borders of Gaza, close to the Israeli fence which had caged them in a kind of open-air prison for many years.[185] They shouted at the soldiers to let them free. They held placards carrying the names of their ancestral villages while chanting for the Right of Return. Behind the fence there was a paradise, one they have heard about, fought and died for, but never visited or even seen. The Gazan masses protested without guns. Despite sporadic bouts of rock throwing by some of the youth, Gaza wanted the world to understand what they had been going through for generations. Israel summoned hundreds of its best snipers, who dotted the Gaza horizon, and when the masses refused to leave, they pulled the trigger. One bullet at a time, over months, Israel took hundreds of Palestine's young people.[186]

The transformation of an armed struggle to a popular, largely nonviolent one garnered little attention in the international media. Only when frustrated Gaza youths began flying incendiary balloons into Israel, at times burning agricultural land, did the story of the protests begin acquiring mostly negative attention.[187] Another round of indirect truce negotiations was held, abruptly ended, started again, then completely stopped. The rounds of useless talks were repeated, along with the cycle of violence, most notable being the brief but deadly wars of May 2019, May 2021, and August 2022.[188]

At times, Hamas didn't get involved, leaving the Islamic Jihad to carry the brunt of the confrontations with Israel on its own. Such conduct raised questions and doubts about Hamas's objectives. Was the "unity of the squares" an illusion aimed at conveying the mere impression of unity among Palestinian groups? Hamas insisted that the mini wars fought alone by the Islamic Jihad were coordinated through the Joint Operation Room—a united front of armed factions in the Gaza Strip—and that Hamas's absence from the battle was tactical, as the group was busy rebuilding its defenses that had been destroyed in previous wars. Hamas also claimed that they never stopped digging tunnels and that the recruiting of new fighters to replace those who were killed or retired was still underway.

But Hamas did fight in an eleven-day war it launched after Israeli forces stormed the Al-Aqsa Mosque on April 15, 2022, injuring at least forty-two Palestinians.[189] This was the first time in years that Palestinians felt truly united. Gaza rose in solidarity with the pleas and chants of Palestinians in Jerusalem, the West Bank, and even historic Palestine.* But even in

---

* Historic Palestine, or Filasṭīn al-Tārīkhīya, traditionally encompasses the territory between the Jordan River to the east and the Mediterranean Sea to the west, extending from the Lebanese border in the north to the Sinai desert in the south. In this specific context, however, it refers collectively to the occupied Palestinian Territories of 1967—East Jerusalem, the West Bank, and Gaza—as well as what lies within the borders of the modern state of Israel.

the event of a ground war, Ehab would not have been able to fight or, to be more precise, he would not have been allowed to. He was told that his place was no longer in the trenches, that he should leave combat to those more physically capable than he. Though the new Al-Qassam leadership saw Ehab's age and battle scars as reasons he should put down his gun, he saw them as testament to his prowess as an untiring and invincible warrior.

On October 6, 2023, he sat alone in his room, the very room to which Madallah had escaped from life outside, seeking solace and an unearthly companion. The room, like the whole house, was enclosed in darkness, save for a few candles that labored to maintain a semblance of light in the poorly furnished place. This was not the typical daily outage resulting from the lack of fuel due to the Israeli siege, or the repeated bombardment of Gaza's main electric grid. Al-Badrasawi's home had no electricity simply because Ehab no longer had the money to pay the many overdue electric bills. Though Asia had implored him to use his contacts with the movement so that the Shati municipality would forgive his burgeoning debt, he vehemently refused. "I didn't join Hamas to win favor with bill collectors," he once told her. She never asked again.

But why had Ehab joined Hamas in the first place? Speaking in the heated voice and manner he reserved for politics, he once told his brothers he believed that a single decisive battle would be the difference between dying in a refugee camp or returning home to Beit Daras. That was years ago, when he was young and agile. Though he wanted to believe that such a battle was still possible, he felt that Gaza, browbeaten and alone; the West Bank, betrayed and segmented; the Arabs, weak and at times treacherous; and the whole world were all moving on.[190]

Yet, at precisely 6:30 a.m., on Saturday, October 7, 2023, a new battle began. Hamas called it the "Al-Aqsa Flood," and Ehab al-Badrasawi was ready to write his own final chapter.

Chapter Ten

The Flood

A new generation of al-Badrasawi boys grew up, all under Israeli siege. Not one of them had ever set foot outside Gaza. Even the sea, the only respite from what became known as the "world's largest open-air prison" was at times off limits.[191] Over the years of colonial oppression, many Shati fishermen were shot or drowned for daring to venture beyond whatever arbitrary line Israeli warships drew on any given day.

Wael's martyrdom in the First Intifada had sealed the fate of the fourth generation of the al-Badrasawi family, just as the Nakba had sealed the fate and legacy of the first generation. But unlike previous generations, including those who sought cheap employment in Israel—namely Ibrahim, Tala'at and Nasir—the new Badrasawi youth had different priorities. Their chance of having a life of dignity and freedom was blockaded by Israel. For many of them, the less dignified life of running away from the Gaza prison was unacceptable. The only option was to stay home and fight.

Without telling anyone, shortly before dawn on October 7, 2023, Baha' al-Din al-Badrasawi rode his motorcycle to a destination only known to him and a few others, somewhere inside the Gaza Envelope. This was the first time that he had entered *liblad*—the homeland—as Israel is known to Palestinian refugees. No one knows exactly what he did on that day, or how he felt when he breathed the air of Historical Palestine for the first time. Indeed, no one could have possibly known. The previous night, Nasir's oldest son, Baha', had been quiet and reflective, seeking forgiveness from everyone, kissing his mother's right hand, demanding reassurance from his father that he had been a good son. He prayed more than was required before huddling with his children, a five-year-old boy and a three-year-old girl, to watch the Arabic-dubbed version of *SpongeBob*, staying with the children until they fell asleep. Baha' was never seen or heard from again.

Baha' al-Din, whose name translates to something akin to the "glory of religion," had joined Al-Qassam's Nukhba elite forces soon after graduating from the Al-Ribat University College.[192] He did so against his father's wishes. Nasir, who spent his whole life "chasing after the loaf of bread," a famous family reference to his desperate quest to survive, was hoping that his children would stay out of danger. But even those who did not join the Resistance were in danger, as medicine ran scarce, food supplies would often deplete, and Israeli war planes didn't distinguish between a fighter and a child.

Over the years, Baha' grew fond of his uncle Ehab, whose struggle for Gaza and Palestinian freedom was no longer affected by any familial pressures. After Madallah's death, Ehab had no reason to worry about family demands to put down his gun. Ibrahim's gentle reprimands to Ehab in the early years shifted to pressure on his own children not to follow the same path. Two of Ibrahim's children ran away from Gaza. No one knew how they snuck into Egypt before joining the arduous path taken by countless refugees desperate to reach Europe. The harrowing stories they told about the road to their supposed salvation in the West forced their parents into the odd position of imploring them to return to besieged Gaza.

Ehab's own children stayed. They pursued whatever education was available to them in Gaza, obeyed their parents as dictated by religion, and shuffled through Instagram photos of celebrities and their safe, happy lives whenever their parents were not looking. Except for Abdulrahman, Ehab's third of the six. He had no social media accounts and cared little for the trivial matters that consumed other teenagers. His good performance at school was only paralleled by his passionate recitation of the Quran. When he memorized the holy book in full, his proud father threw him a party: several trays of baklavas, many pots of tea with *maramia*, an intricately designed flower wreath, and a seemingly endless stream of guests, mostly family, neighbors, and Ehab's Hamas circle.

Abdularahman had already joined Al-Qassam. He had wanted to fight in the Sword of Jerusalem battle in 2021, but there was not much ground fighting back then, and he was too young. He had wanted to join his comrades in the Al-Quds Brigades—the military wing of the Palestinian Islamic Jihad Movement—when Israel singled them out in May 2023, thus avoiding an all-out confrontation with Hamas. Back then, he was told to hold off. When he protested, he was reminded that there were far more capable men making these decisions, and that a Qassam fighter should know this. So, when the news came out that Baha' and hundreds of Qassam fighters had cut the fence encircling Gaza's eastern borders, and that they had crossed into Israel, Abdulrahman al-Badrasawi knew that his first real battle had just begun. And when, in the late morning

of October 7, he walked into the house with a machine gun
and a green bandana wrapped around his forehead to tell his
parents that it was time for him to join the other fighters, he
found his father also brandishing a gun, and still in the process
of tightening his own green bandana. Ehab and Abdulrahman
hugged without saying a word. As the young man's lower lip
began to quiver, his father reminded him that real men don't
cry before wiping his own tears. "We live in freedom," Ehab said
in the tone of someone expecting a response, looking into his
son's eyes. "Or we die as martyrs," the boy answered.

Past, Present, Fate

The al-Badrasawi women didn't immediately leave the house,
along with their children and whatever they could carry. They
held on long enough to beseech their husbands, brothers, or male
cousins to join the mass of people fleeing Shati. At one point, Ehab
too wanted Abdulrahman to leave with the rest of the family. But
he didn't have the courage to tell his son not to fight. Asking him to
abandon the battlefield when resistance mattered most would be a
betrayal of everything Ehab had stood for and taught his children.
Nonetheless, he tried. He told his son that protecting one's family
is also a duty, and that if they both died, the family would be left
vulnerable to the endless hardships of life in Gaza. Abdulrahman
disagreed, retorting with the Quran verses that demonstrated
beyond doubt that jihad against injustice is obligatory. He told his
father that the whole of Gaza is a single family, and that it was his
duty to protect that larger family as well. Ehab had no choice. He
nodded in hesitant agreement. Asia looked on, mumbling in an
almost inaudible voice: "Please, Abdulrahman. Please, son." She
never saw her son or husband again.

The assault on the Gaza Envelope was unprecedented. Few could have imagined that Palestinians would dare carry out such a complex operation. The profundity of the attack was not in the number of Israelis killed on that day, though many had been killed. What the resistance assault had done was alter the equation governing the relationship between the whole of Occupied Palestine and Israel since the very beginning.

Isolated, impoverished, and largely unarmed, Palestinians were expected to always be on the defensive. Going on the offensive required superior weapons, first-class intelligence, and hundreds of thousands of well-trained combatants.[193] Even this would not have been enough, as Gazans also needed an effective air force, or, at least powerful anti-air defenses. They had none. Yet, on that morning, hundreds of fighters simply drove into Israel in their pickup trucks, old Fiats, and motorcycles. They cut the fences from which the Israeli snipers had killed many Gaza youth in previous years, and attacked those snipers while they were in their offices, or even in their sleeping quarters. But not all Palestinians crossed the fence, or drove through the Eretz checkpoint. Some parachuted directly into Israeli military bases, fortified settlements, and intelligence units. According to Israeli sources, around 2,900 Palestinian fighters infiltrated Israel. After attacking the Eretz Crossing, they reached Sderot, Re'im, Be'eri, Nahal Oz, Zikim, Nir Oz, and Kissufim, and attacked other bases. In addition to this, Hamas fired around 5,000 missiles and shells at Israel.[194]

Hundreds of Israelis were killed on that day. They included top military brass, officers, soldiers, settlers, and civilians. No one, aside from those who were there, truly knew what transpired exactly in the early hours of that unusual morning, since most Palestinians who entered into Israel from Gaza, including

Baha' al-Badrasawi, never returned. Their version of the truth died with them, and the initial Israeli account was confused, contradictory, and rife with disinformation.[195] But certain facts could not be contested, even by the Israelis themselves. One such fact is that the theory of military deterrence, the backbone of Israeli policies against Palestinians and Arabs over the years, had collapsed, shattered forever.

Even the concept of a siege as a method of permanent containment of the enemy suddenly seemed a myth promulgated by Israel and even accepted by Palestinians. Since the imposition of the siege, seventeen years before the Flood, Gazans had implored the world to intervene, to force Israel to end the siege, and to enforce the humanitarian laws that never seemed to matter in the case of Israeli's occupation and illegal settlements. No one listened. No one cared. The Al-Aqsa Flood was their way of taking matters into their own hands, by whatever means or cost. When Hamas combatants crossed the fence into Israel, many layers of Israeli myths and defenses simply collapsed without any resistance, as if they were figments of the collective Israeli and Palestinian imaginations.

But Hamas too became a victim of its unforeseen success. It hadn't anticipated that the operation's effectiveness could lead to such unpredictable consequences. Indeed, when ordinary Palestinians learned the imaginary line had been breached, large numbers rushed into Israel to join the attack. Hamas neither expected its "flood" to drown the Israeli army within hours, nor that ordinary Gazans would join the operation. Al-Qassam's goal was to capture as many Israeli military personnel as possible to use as bargaining chips in negotiations for political concessions such as freeing imprisoned Palestinians, easing the siege, and ending the raids on Al-Aqsa Mosque. However, the ordinary Palestinians who rushed across the border also took hostages, without distinguishing between soldiers, civilians, and even children.*196

Many Israelis were taken captive on that day, and by a strange turn of events were forced, for the first time in their history, to enter into the Palestinian matrix, not as invaders, but as hostages, some in their military fatigues, others barefoot, half-naked, bewildered. No amount of training could possibly have prepared them for such encounters. None of this could have happened if it were not for the fact that Palestinians had disabled the military communication system in southern Israel and rendered Israeli defenses useless by launching hundreds of rockets all at once. Israel's much-touted "Iron Dome" was overwhelmed beyond its capacity. No amount of US-funded or supplied military technology could have saved Israel from defeat and humiliation.197

It all felt surreal, a parallel reality unfamiliar to both sides. When Al-Qassam's leader, Mohammed Deif, spoke on the morning of October 7, officially announcing the launch of Operation Al-Aqsa Flood, he offered some clarity regarding what had happened, although many questions remained unanswered. This hardly mattered to Ehab al-Badrasawi, who felt

---

* As of late 2025, the events of October 7 have not yet been investigated by an independent international body. Nevertheless, evidence suggests that various acts of violence went beyond the acceptable limits, even of guerrilla warfare. This is not surprising—neither considering the historical pattern of Israeli colonialism in Palestine and the resistance of the indigenous Palestinian people, nor within the broader global context that has marked similar situations throughout history.

Pan-Africanist political philosopher Frantz Fanon offers perhaps the clearest explanation. In his influential work *The Wretched of the Earth*, he argued that violence is a "cleansing force" for the colonized, helping them to break free from the psychological inferiority imposed by colonial rule through revolutionary action. "The violence which has ruled over the ordering of the colonial world ... that same violence will be claimed and taken over by the native at the moment when, deciding to embody history in his own person, he surges into the forbidden quarters."

that Deif was speaking to him directly, personally summoning him to the final battle of Palestine's liberation. "The enemy will understand that the time of their rampaging without accountability has ended," Deif declared.[198] For years Ehab had raged at the docility of the movement, for practically abandoning the Palestinian struggle and focusing instead on pity, factional fights, and mere survival in Gaza. A few months earlier, his anger turned to sobs when he saw Palestinian women at Al-Aqsa Mosque savagely beaten by Israeli soldiers. "If I lay my hands on them, if I just lay my hands on them," he shouted as he clasped both fists, while watching the same scenes of violence against Palestinian worshipers on the news and over and over again on social media. Finally, his opportunity had arrived. Ehab sensed that it was the most decisive battle in the history of Palestine. It was the battle that would define his legacy, as a Gazan, a refugee, and the son of Abdallah and Madallah of the long gone but never forgotten Beit Daras. For him, this was the moment when justice needed to be exacted in a historic finality. His determination, mixed with the uncertainty of the operation, brought numerous erratic but profound images to his mind:

The swing set. Paradise. Beit Daras. Madallah.

The Saraya. Sheikh Yassin. Rantisi. Firas Market.

Angry Israeli officers shouting in broken Arabic. Angry Palestinian torturers shouting in broken Hebrew.

Gaza. The sea. The past. Al-Aqsa. Wael.

The past became an urgent matter that needed to be resolved. Zionist gangs once again at the gates of Beit Daras, Shati, Gaza. The voice of Izz Al-Din Al-Qassam yelling to his men: "Die as martyrs" echoing throughout Ehab's refugee camp.

The Nakba. The Naksa. The Arab betrayal. Western duplicity.

Endless streams of displaced Palestinian families, many dying on the road to Gaza, perishing from disease and succumbing to hunger.

The graveyard summoned by the tide of an angry sea.

Generations of martyrs. Abdallah's torture, and his death. He fizzled into forgottenness as if he never existed. Madallah's final, unintelligible words. Was that her voice, or someone else's? The Intifadas. The sieges. The wars. Al-Aqsa.

Wael. Wael. Wael.

As soon as the Israeli planes, tanks, and drones began pummeling Gaza from all directions, Ehab went to the *hakoura* to train for a ground war he believed was imminent. Asia, watched, amused and puzzled, as he jumped in place, crawled on the floor with an intense look on his face, and leaped from one side to the other.

Pregnant with their seventh child, Asia knew that Ehab had made a decision, a final one. She thought about being left alone in Gaza, raising a large family and a newborn. Explosions went off all around them, drawing nearer by the minute. The deafening thuds were often followed by screams or defiant chants. The al-Badrasawi household was encased by noise emanating from all directions, including the shouts of Asia herself, ordering her children to carry whatever they could as she too stuffed clothes into a large duffle bag. She didn't know where she was supposed to go, but was certain that she had to leave immediately.

Before her hurried departure, Ehab, now donning his military fatigues and brandishing a Kalashnikov, stopped her for a brief moment. He wanted to tell her that he loved her, that she had given his life meaning, that in her eyes he saw more than a faithful wife, but heaven itself. But he didn't. Time froze in a single moment, the loud thuds grew closer, and they looked into each other's eyes and said nothing.

He hugged his children in frantic haste and told them to join other family members on the other side of the camp. He thought that the high concentration of UNRWA schools and clinics in that area might provide a measure of safety to fleeing women and children. He was wrong. The bombs didn't fall on Gaza with any kind of logical order. Nor did the shells whizzing over Shati from the sea have a particular destination. Everyone and everything was a target.

Ceaseless Israeli bombardment quickly turned much of Gaza into rubble. According to UN data, after the first 100 days, "more than one Gazan person in every 100" had been killed, a rate which exceeded that of any other armed conflict in the twenty-first century.[199]

The "total blockade" promised by Israel's Minister of Defense Yoav Gallant was being delivered. In a video statement, Gallant said: "We are putting a complete siege on Gaza... no electricity, no food, no water, no gas—it's all closed."[200] Gallant said that his country was fighting "human animals," and that his country would "act accordingly."[201] Washington didn't find Israel's language or behavior problematic. Instead, it sent aircraft carriers to the eastern Mediterranean to ensure that no one dared obstruct Israel's collective punishment of Gaza.[202]

American weapons continued to flow to Israel at an unprecedented rate. By June 28, 2023, the US had armed Israel with at least 14,000 MK-84 2,000-pound bombs, 6,500 500-pound bombs, 3,000 Hellfire precision-guided air-to-ground missiles, 1,000 bunker-buster bombs, and 2,600 air-dropped small-diameter bombs, along with other munitions.[203] The most devastating of such weapons to Gaza's civilian population are the 2,000-pound bombs.[204] When they were dropped into overcrowded neighborhoods, few would survive the impact. Even animals and trees perished.

Israel repeatedly bombed residential areas, towers, hospitals, schools, mosques, and churches, any place where refugees sought shelter. In the first three months of the war, Israel destroyed at least 1,000 mosques, killing at least 100 Muslim preachers.[205] No place and no one was secure in Gaza. Even the "safe zones" declared by the Israeli army during the early part of the war became targets.[206] Exhausted, hungry, and trapped, Palestinians could do nothing but run without a clear destination in mind. This was another, even bloodier, Nakba.

The Al-Ahli Baptist Hospital massacre on October 17, 2023 was gruesome but was not a singular event. The Gaza Health Ministry reported that 471 people were killed and 342 injured, with US intelligence agencies estimating between 100 and 300 casualties.[207] The hospital massacre was only one of many others to come. Thousands of displaced Palestinian families would be killed in the very places where they thought they had found safety. Palestinians beseeched the world to help them, but when America's president arrived in Israel, he only promised that "the US will continue to support Israel."[208] Palestinians, whose corpses quickly filled the streets of Gaza, didn't factor into America's decision to continue to arm Israel. Other Western leaders fell in line behind the United States. They too flocked to Tel Aviv, parroting the same lines as if reading from the same script, though sometimes in different languages.[209] For Western leaders and media, the history of the conflict began on October 7, 2023. Nothing before that date and nothing after that date mattered or existed.

The world continued to watch as Palestinians in Gaza

were left alone, defending against powers that exceeded their capacity to comprehend. Western intelligence officials gathered in Israel, not far from the Gaza border, to plot the Strip's downfall.[210] Political leaders met to discuss the future of the region without paying the slightest heed to what the Palestinians of Gaza—or Palestinians anywhere—had to say about their own future, their political aspirations, or their generational quest for freedom.

On October 27, Israel was ready for what it called the "second phase" of what would become a genocidal war: the ground invasion. They invaded from several directions: northeast, towards Beit Lahia and Beit Hanoun; west to Shati; and east to occupy the small town of Juhr al-Dik. Coupled with an intense bombing campaign, the relentless violence was meant to bring Gaza into total submission. The Israeli army entered Gaza without moral constraints or codes of conduct. Within the first weeks of war, the bombs Israel dropped on Gaza were equivalent to two nuclear bombs.[211]

Palestinians, however, stood their ground.

New Nakba

The Israeli army sealed off Gaza City from the east, north, and south. To fully surround the city, Shati also needed to be subdued. The Resistance brigade responsible for the refugee camp had always served as the frontline of defense of the western walls of Gaza, but this war was different from all others.

When Israeli forces stormed the northern parts of the Strip, they attacked homes, hospitals, mosques, and schools, leading to a mass exodus of refugees from the north to the south.[212] The Resistance brigades, each unit assigned to protect a different neighborhood, tried to hold the Israelis back. Some succeeded, others didn't. By November 2, the city of Gaza was besieged, though resistance continued in Shejaiya, Zaytoun, Sheikh Radwan, and elsewhere. In the east of Gaza, the Resistance desperately hung on. Scores of fighters attempted to block the path of thousands of Israelis sheltering inside their tanks as they tried to reach Shifa Hospital. Large crowds of newly displaced families had taken shelter inside the hospital. A massacre was inescapable. Israel had bombed, shelled, or besieged all the other major hospitals in Gaza—Nasser Hospital in Khan Yunis, and the Kamal Adwan Hospital and Indonesian Hospital in northern Gaza.[213] The Israeli army claimed that Hamas had fashioned secret headquarters inside or underneath some of these hospitals, especially Shifa.[214] No such offices were ever found.[215] Israel's claims were used as rationale for the ethnic cleansing of all Palestinian communities from northern Gaza.

As soon as government, civil defense, and media offices were destroyed in the early days of the war, medical centers in Gaza took on a role beyond providing treatment for the sick and injured. Doctors and other medical staff began to serve as spokespeople of the Palestinians. Their discourse was not factional or ideological, but humanistic and universal. For Israel, having articulate, passionate, and professional voices represent the Palestinian cause to the world was intolerable. They needed to be silenced. Israel was particularly angered when the daily casualty count produced in Shifa became a credible reference picked up by many global media organizations. Thus, on November 11, 2023, Israel attacked the Shifa hospital. Many displaced families, patients, and medical staff were killed or wounded. Some buildings in the Strip's largest medical center caught fire when Israeli shells bombarded the orthopedic department. Israeli snipers zeroed in on the hospital from all directions, opening fire at anyone who approached or tried to flee. Eventually thousands were ordered to leave, and many did. Doctors and nurses were seen pushing gurneys into the destroyed and dusty streets of Gaza, unclear where to go next. A mass of refugees joined them, distraught, terrified, and uncertain.

But this was only the start. The hospital, like other hospitals, was attacked again and again. As long as these relatively large spaces remained available to the stream of displaced Gazans, the plan to push all of Gaza to the south would be delayed. For Israel, time was critical, as the emerging genocide it was committing was becoming clearer to the rest of the world. Israeli officials began to devise quick and brutal solutions. Some spoke of their desire to expel all of Gaza to the Sinai desert, rekindling an old plan that had never been realized.[216] On November 5, Israel's heritage minister, Amichai Eliyahu even said that dropping a nuclear bomb on the Gaza Strip was one of the options open to his government.[217]

The West ignored desperate pleas from Palestinians to be spared a horrific fate while trapped in hospitals, schools, and neighborhoods. Like previous generations of Palestinian victims of colonial violence, their calls on the world to intervene went unanswered. Most of the internationals working for humanitarian organizations in Gaza prior to the war escaped for their lives whenever the Rafah Crossing was intermittently opened.[218] Palestinians who had enough money to bribe the Egyptian military fled as well. The rest were trapped in what a United Nations report came to describe as genocide of "colonial erasure."[219] An estimated 2.3 million Palestinian survivors of displacement and war now faced the US-armed Israeli war machine alone.

The siege of Shifa continued, alongside the bombing of other hospitals. It became clear that the Israeli declaration that "Palestinians [are] human animals and Israel will act accordingly" was not released as part of a psychological operation against the Resistance, but as part of an increasingly open policy of colonial erasure that the Israel would execute with weapons provided by the United States. Patients were killed as they lay on their hospital beds.[220] Displaced families were murdered en masse, often while huddling together inside temporary shelters. People who had been detained or imprisoned were executed without mercy.[221] Israel has slaughtered hundreds of families who opted to stay in, or couldn't flee, their own homes. A whole nation was being systematically eradicated or expelled. When Shifa was finally fully occupied five months later, hundreds of people, including women and children, were found buried together in mass graves.[222] The Israeli army even handcuffed children before executing them alongside their families.[223] The UN reported that hundreds of bodies were "buried deep in the ground and covered with waste" at Nasser Hospital in Khan Younis, central Gaza, and at Al-Shifa Hospital in Gaza City in the north. More than 280 bodies were recovered at Nasser Hospital, of which at least forty were identified. "Among the deceased were allegedly older people, women, and wounded, while others were found tied with their hands... tied and stripped of their clothes," said Ravina Shamdasani, spokesperson for the UN High Commissioner for Human Rights.[224]

The protracted episode of horror could be read on the faces of all Gazans. Their blank stares, sunken cheeks, and gaunt bodies told a story of human atrocity unseen in a century.

One year after the war began, the UN issued a report that

said, "The violence that Israel has unleashed against the Palestinians post-7 October is not happening in a vacuum, but is part of a long-term intentional, systematic, State-organized forced displacement and replacement of the Palestinians."[225] Despite every attempt by mainstream Western media to ignore daily evidence of that conclusion, Palestinians voices escaped. With time, the narrative evolved. What began as an "Israeli retaliation against the Hamas attack" shifted into the "Israel-Hamas war" and "possible war crimes" then finally and clearly became "genocide" and mass "extermination."[226] Though no tragedy that had afflicted Palestinians in their modern conflict with Zionism could be compared to the atrocities which followed October 7, the tenacity of the Palestinians was the stuff of legend. The steadfastness of ordinary people in the Strip made Israel's mission of crushing the Resistance impossible to achieve.

The al-Badrasawi family, which had remained together for decades after their original exile, was finally forced to separate. Ibrahim's family was split between the homes of his married daughters, who eventually fled to UN-run schools and hospitals. But real tragedy didn't strike until the night of October 25, 2023, when a 2,000-pound bomb was dropped on a neighborhood in the south of Shati. Among scores of other victims, it killed Ibrahim's youngest daughter, Ala', her husband Mohammed, and Zain, the younger of her two boys. It only spared 'Amro, who was critically injured. He miraculously survived, though the bones of his right leg and arm were shattered into many pieces. Shrapnel dotted every part of his tiny, frail body. For months he was not told that his whole family had died.

Ibrahim and his wife, Hanan 'Ashour, had been planning to spend that night at Ala's home. Hanan did, but Ibrahim changed his mind at the last moment, as he felt that he had to check on his other grandchildren at a UNRWA-school-turned-shelter. His grief over his daughter and her son was only matched by his guilt of having survived the ordeal. His wife was critically injured.

Ala' was the most beautiful of Ibrahim's children. Many good men had sought her hand in marriage, yet she refused them all. Until Mohammed came. He was rugged, handsome, and educated, but it was his kindness that attracted her the most. Their wedding had brought the whole of Shati together. For one night, until the early hours of the morning, people sang, danced, and ate without worry. The collective joy felt on that day was seen as a good omen for the happy life that awaited her. She returned to school and vowed that her children would receive the best education, despite the siege and the recurring wars. When her lifeless body was finally pulled out, she was still holding onto her little son. Zain seemed at peace in the arms of his mother, as if he had fallen gently to sleep.

Ehab and Abdulrahman were first to arrive at the destroyed neighborhood. Ibrahim was not present when the bodies were excavated from beneath the slabs of concrete. He was rushing in an old Fiat, which he had borrowed from a neighbor to transport the broken and bleeding bodies of his wife and grandson. But the hospitals were under siege, burning, or both. He did not recall being angry. Like many other Gazans, he felt numb, unable or perhaps unwilling to understand what had befallen his family. "Oh, Allah we have no one but you to turn to," he repeated mechanically, over and over again.

After gathering the remains of Ala' and Zain, Ehab yelled to his son to return to the battlefield. "The camp cannot fall," he screamed at Abdulrahman. The polite and sensitive boy, who had just finished his first university semester, was no longer an aspiring computer programmer, but now officially a warrior. His first battle was defending the last bastion of the Palestinian struggle. The father had learned to accept that the son was destined to continue a fight that started generations ago, even before Izz al-Din al-Qassam urged his men to fight until the end. The boy rushed back, as if he was to singlehandedly hold back the thousands of invaders closing in on Gaza from every direction.

Ehab and others buried the bodies in a mass grave. There was no time for religious sermons about the eternal salvation of martyrs as the bombs continued to fall on Shati and all of Gaza as if fiery rain. "Do not say that those killed in God's path are dead; they are alive, though you do not realize," he muttered before rushing back.[227] He didn't go back to the front line, but home. The murder of Ala' and Zain had changed his plan. This time he was not acting upon anyone else's orders, but his own.

One Last Time

"No soul knows what it will earn for tomorrow, and no soul knows in what land it will die. Surely Allah is All-Knowing, All-Aware." This Quranic verse from Surah Luqman is known to those living in Gaza because in Gaza, death often happens suddenly, without introductions or warnings.[228] Ehab had used the verse repeatedly to illustrate that the path he had chosen for himself did not mean that his end was in any way foretold. He maintained the same attitude when a whole generation of fighters in Shati—childhood friends, neighbors, and comrades—were killed in previous wars. He would often help bury them, offering, even if uninvited, a few words of wisdom during their *janaza* funeral prayer before alluding to the same verse: "and no soul knows in what land it will die." But does this eternal truth apply to those who choose the time, place, and method of their own death?

The killing of new members of his family added a new dimension to Ehab's struggle against Israel. The crushed bodies he had salvaged from the rubble and buried with his own hands revitalized the past, all of it. The original Nakba, as conveyed by Madallah's many painful stories and demonstrated in the everyday life of the refugee camp, began to take on a real form. The Nakba was no longer in the past. It was now. It became immediate. Urgent. Raw. Deadly. While many around the world were beginning to speak of the "New Nakba," Ehab felt it in the bodies he had buried, the burning smoke of flesh he breathed, and the unfathomable destruction he had witnessed.[229] But for Ehab, this new or continued Nakba was not an historical or intellectual notion for study and consideration. It was his life. His past, his present, and, at least in his own mind, his sealed fate as well.

There was nothing that Ehab could have said or done to alter the Nakba of 1948 or its outcome. This time, however, he felt that he had options. Unlike his son, Abdulrahman, he could not scale high walls, leap over mountains of rubble, or wedge himself through the smallest of tunnels. But Ehab was still a warrior, because, as he often argued, courage can never be degraded by age. Indeed, in every station of his life in Gaza, Ehab had always maintained a degree of bravery that impressed everyone around him. Nothing could possibly stop him now.

When he arrived home, he found his neighborhood mostly empty. Even the fighters were scarce, as many of them had rushed to the battlefront to counter the siege imposed on the Shifa or other areas in Gaza City. We will never know exactly what Ehab did between the period of October 25—the murder of Ala's family—and November 9, 2023, the date of his last battle. Between these two dates, much of northern Gaza was destroyed in the invasion. Many neighborhoods were bombed, some completely flattened, leading to the digging of yet more mass graves. Not everyone was so lucky: nameless, often unrecognizable bodies continued to dot the desolate streets of Gaza.

Amidst all of this, Ehab remained at home. The evidence he left behind showed that he must have prayed, cooked small meals, mostly eggs, assembled an explosive belt, listened to the radio, and demolished the wall between his house and the neighbors'. In fact, over the course of his solitary stay, a series of walls were also demolished, starting at the al-Badrasawi home, going through other houses, and ending at Rashid Street, which separated the camp from the sea. He also must have read from the holy book, because in the center of the living room there was a copy of the Quran which had been removed from its place on the shelf. On the main wall, the one guests immediately see when they enter, was a large, framed poster of Sheikh Ahmed Yassin and another of Wael. Other framed images of Madallah, Abdallah, the map of historic Palestine, Quranic verses illustrated in Arabic calligraphy, and more were scattered in no particular order on the other walls. Somehow they remained in place despite the constant bombardment of the area, which violently shook any walls that remained standing.

Just when it seemed that Shati was fully conquered, and the remaining Resistance units had been killed or disappeared into the tunnels below, Ehab emerged, initially alone, in the streets of Shati. These were the same streets where he had once, as a teenage boy, painted revolutionary graffiti and distributed flyers for the Resistance. Looking across the street, he saw the spot where an Israeli bullet killed Wael. This time, however, Ehab was not in the mood to chase or to be chased by anyone. He wore a large green coat, hauling on his shoulder a Yassin-105, a Palestinian-improvised anti-tank missile named after the quadriplegic sheikh himself.[230] He ascended to the top of the rubble of a destroyed house with ease and leapt from one pile of concrete to the other. Those who saw him on that day claimed that he moved with the ease of a teenage boy, not the heavy steps of a middle-aged man. "Allahu Akbar," his voice echoed in the empty neighborhood, summoning the remaining fighters. "Allahu Akbar," some shouted back as new fighters began to emerge from the rubble. Another battle was about to commence.

The noise of Israeli tanks drew nearer, drowning the gentle susurration of the sea. The fighters retreated into more secure positions, but Ehab stood still. He carefully aimed his Yassin-105 and fired, striking the tower of one of the Merkava tanks. The impact of the explosion, and the large fire it ignited, transformed what was meant to be the smooth takeover of Shati into a chaotic scene. Some tanks tried to maneuver; others completely stopped. A military personnel carrier was trapped between the monstrous killing machines, which froze in position, unable to surpass the blown-up tank or to retreat into the camp's narrow roads.

Palestinian fighters emerged from their positions. No one knew what political faction they belonged to; no one cared. They all opened fire at the beleaguered Israeli force. Ehab didn't join in. He calmly reloaded his weapon and fired again, striking another tank. Some soldiers who had survived the initial blow jumped out of the Merkava, and scattered into the alleyways of the camp. Instead of running in search of a safe position, Ehab tossed his weapon aside. He took off his green coat and ran towards the personnel carrier.

"God is great," he yelled one last time.

Epilogue

Ehab was never buried.

Weeks passed before the Israeli army left the area where he carried out his martyrdom attack. When they did, Ehab's sons searched for hours with the hope of finding his remains.

None were found.

"He is in Paradise now," the boys resolved, before returning to their UN shelters to convey the news to Asia.

Abdulrahman learned of his father's death while in Jabaliya, fighting to prevent a major invasion by the Israeli army, which struggled to conquer the ever-tenacious town.

His comrades say that he was proud of his father.

Abdulrahman also ascended to Paradise on November 20, 2023, eleven days after Ehab's death.

The circumstances of his killing were conveyed to his mother, Asia, many days after her son was struck by an Israeli drone.

As soon as the first temporary truce was declared on November 24, 2023, she braved the Israeli military siege, which remained in effect in many parts of northern Gaza, to search for Abdulrahman.

Despite the massive destruction and numerous other corpses, she found him.

His lifeless body was resting against the wall of a mosque. His arms were holding onto a rifle—presumably a Kalashnikov. His feet extended in front of him and his eyes were closed. Twenty days after his death, she swore that her son was smiling.

Those who survived the attack said that their group was hit by an Israeli military quadcopter soon after they received their evacuation order.

They survived, but he died. A large piece of metal shrapnel was lodged in his back.

Asia was desperate to bury her son. She couldn't find anyone to help, so she covered part of his body with her scarf and promised him that they would soon meet in heaven.

His body was never seen after that day, likely buried in a mass grave or eaten by stray dogs.

Nasir was also killed on February 6, 2024, in the same way he spent his life, "chasing after the loaf of bread."

Following his son's death on October 7, Nasir became responsible for Baha's children. When famine hit Gaza due to the Israeli siege, Nasir was desperate to preserve the lives of his grandchildren. He spent many hours standing in long lines with the hope of receiving bread and water.

During one of these quests, an Israeli plane bombed a crowd of Palestinians waiting for aid.[231] His initial injuries were not fatal, but the immediate impact of the bomb severed his right hand.

With no access to a functioning hospital, Nasir bled to death. His left hand was still holding a plastic bag that contained a piece of bread and a small bottle of water.

Ibrahim's wife, Hanan, was one of the lucky few allowed to

leave Gaza for medical care. She was treated at an Egyptian hospital in the city of Arish, in the Sinai Desert. She survived but lost the ability to walk.

Ibrahim gathered the surviving family members and took shelter in the Shifa Hospital. They were spared the initial massacre. They fled south, where they took shelter in the European Hospital in Khan Yunis, before fleeing again.

Tal'at and two of his sons were detained and tortured by the Israeli army. They escaped from a makeshift military camp in northern Gaza. Their whereabouts remained unknown until October 21, 2024, when Israeli soldiers executed all of Tal'at's children, alongside a large number of men and boys, in the Jabaliya refugee camp.

Asia and her family fled to Rafah, where she remained until Israel invaded the southern part of Gaza city. Then they fled to the Mawasi area, between Rafah and Khan Yunis. Israel had declared Mawasi a "safe zone," but bombed it repeatedly, forcing the family to flee to the center of the Strip.[232]

On February 6, 2024, Asia gave birth to her seventh child, Ala', named after her aunt who was killed in the early days of the war.

Ala' was born with a congenital heart defect and Down Syndrome, but with no operating hospitals, doctors couldn't perform surgery or even offer her any medication.

With her newborn and five surviving children, Asia spent months on a seemingly endless journey, looking for safety.

As of the time of this writing in May 2025, Israel's war on Palestinians has killed at least 52,000 people and wounded 118,000 since October 7, 2023.[233] Thousands more missing under the rubble are presumed dead. Almost all of Gaza has been destroyed.

No heavenly paradise has yet been found.
Only Paradise above.

Historical Timeline

10000 BCE—The Palestinian city of Jericho is founded as a camping ground for Natufian hunter-gatherers.

3300–3000 BCE—Arab Canaanite tribes settle in the southern part of the Tel As-Sakan area, in the Gaza region, before later spreading across Palestine.

12th century BCE—"Peleset" (cognate for Palestine) people fight against Egyptian Pharoah Ramses III, according to temple inscriptions. Recent archaeological evidence from 3,000 years ago indicates that the Palestinian "sea people" were actually the settled indigenous population.

8th–7th century BCE—Assyrian inscriptions refer to "Palashtu" and "Pilitu," cognates for Palestine.

6th–4th century BCE—Cities of Philistia develop their own monetary system.

5th century BCE—Greek historian and philosopher Herodotus refers to Palaistine or Phalastin.

4th century BCE—In *Meteorology*, Greek philosopher Aristotle refers to "a lake in Palestine," apparently the Dead Sea.

332 BCE—After a long siege and several battles, Alexander the Great conquers Gaza.

96 BCE—After being part of the Ptolemaic and Seleucid Kingdoms, Gaza is besieged and later destroyed by the Hasmonean king Alexander Jannaeus.

63 BCE—Gaza is rebuilt after being conquered and incorporated into the Roman Empire under the command of Pompey Magnus.

100–170 CE—Alexandrian mathematician, astronomer, and cartographer Ptolemy refers to Palestine.

284–305—Palestine is divided into three Byzantine provinces.

July-August 634—Arab Muslim forces, under the command of Amr ibn al-As, defeat the Byzantine (Roman) army but cannot take control of Gaza, which is conquered only after a three-year siege. In the summer of 637, al-As finally manages to take control of Gaza, vanquishing the Byzantine garrison but granting the city's inhabitants safety.

683–1099—Palestine becomes Arab "Jund Filastin."

1100—The Crusaders conquer Gaza and convert mosques into churches, ruling over the city until they are defeated by Muslim commander Salah al-Din al-Ayyubi in 1187.

1100–1165—Filastin appears on the world map of Muslim geographer and cartographer Muhammad al-Idrisi.

1260—Ayyubid rule abruptly comes to an end when the Mongols Tatars invade and destroy Gaza. Subsequently the Mamluks, under the lead of general az-Zahir Baybars, drive the Mongols out of the city and defeat a Mongol army of around 20,000 soldiers in the Ain Jalut battle, in southeastern Galilee in the Jezreel Valley.

1517—Palestine falls under the control of the Ottoman Empire, which lasted until 1918.

16th century—*Filastin* (Palestine) as a political entity with a proto-national sense begins to develop, as showed by *fatwas* composed by Mufti Khayr al-Din al-Ramli (1585-1670), which mention on several occasions the concept of *Filastin, biladuna* or "Our Country, Palestine."

1765—Zaher al-Umar al-Zaydani, a local leader in the Ottoman Sultanate provinces, establishes an autonomous kingdom in northern Palestine, which would later extend throughout the Galilee, Tiberias, Acre, and Haifa. He controls the entire Palestinian territory between 1770 and 1775.

August 1775—The Ottoman navy attacks al-Umar's stronghold in the northern Palestinian city of Acre, killing him.

February 1799—Napoleon Bonaparte launches a campaign to occupy Palestine, starting with Gaza. Fierce Palestinian resistance contributes to the foiling of the French colonial plans.

19th century—Palestine experiences a literary and cultural *nadha* or renaissance. Cities grow and agriculture flourishes.

1878—Petah Tikva, the first Jewish colony in Palestine, is constructed in the central region of Palestine. It becomes a permanent settlement in 1883.

November 1917—Britain pledges to construct a Jewish state in Palestine. The Balfour Declaration promises the Zionist movement "the establishment in Palestine of a national home for the Jewish people."

December 11, 1917—During the First World War (1914-18), Ottomans are defeated and the British army enters Jerusalem.

October 1918—Following the Battle of Megiddo, Ottoman forces are defeated by the British under the command of General Edmund Allenby, leading to the British occupation of Palestine that same year.

June–July 1919—The King-Crane Commission, an American delegation, visits areas in Palestine, Syria, Lebanon, and Anatolia to dispose of the regions formerly administered by the Ottoman Empire.

July 1922—At a private meeting of the Council of the League of Nations in London, Britain is given formal international recognition for its Mandate over Palestine.

1920s–30s—Sheikh Izz al-Din al-Qassam, a Syrian Muslim preacher, leads local struggles against French and British Mandatory rule in the Levant, later becoming a fierce opponent of Zionist colonialism in Palestine.

1918–1939—Zionist colonies grow under British military protection. Zionists are appointed to senior positions in the British administration.

1936–39—The Great Revolt, a popular uprising against British and Zionist colonialism, breaks out in Palestine. Between 5,000-6,000 Palestinian fighters are killed in suppression of the uprising, including Sheikh Izz al Din al Qassam. More than 100 are executed. Collective punishment is regularly used against the civilian population.

May 23, 1939—The White Paper is issued by the British government in response to the Great Revolt. The paper calls for the establishment of a "Jewish national home (to be founded) in Palestine" within an "independent Palestine state," rejecting the partition of Palestine, and formally limiting mass Jewish immigration.

November 1947—The UN General Assembly adopts Resolution 181, which calls for the division of Palestinian territories into separate Jewish and Arab states, with Jerusalem as a *corpus separatum*, an internationally governed area.

1947–48—Zionist militias and gangs carry out the Nakba, or Catastrophe, ethnically cleansing approximately 800,000 Palestinian natives from their land. Over 500 towns and villages are destroyed or depopulated. The Palestinian refugee crisis begins.

October 1945—The Muslim Brotherhood opens a Palestinian branch in Jerusalem under the leadership of Sa'd Ramadan. The Gaza branch is established on November 25, 1946.

December 1948—The UNGA passes Resolution 194, calling for the Right of Return for Palestinian refugees, stating that "refugees wishing to return to their homes and live at peace with their neighbors should be permitted to do so at the earliest practicable date."

1950s—From Palestinian refugees expelled from their villages during the Nakba, the *fedayeen* freedom fighter movement emerges.

October 1956—Britain, France, and Israel launch the Tripartite Aggression against Egypt. In November, Israel installs a military government to oversee Gaza before it withdraws on March 7, 1957.

October 1959—The Palestinian National Liberation Movement (Fatah) is established. Fatah's main founders are Salah Khalaf, Khalil al-Wazir, and Yasser Arafat.

January–June 1964—The Arab League establishes the Palestine National Council (PNC), the Palestine Liberation Army (PLA), and the Palestine Liberation Organization (PLO).

June 1967—The Naksa, or "Setback" takes place, where Israel occupies the remainder of historic Palestine—the West Bank, the Gaza Strip, and East Jerusalem—along with the Syrian Golan Heights and the Egyptian Sinai Peninsula.

November 22, 1967—The UN passes Resolution 242, calling on Israel to withdraw from newly occupied territories.

October 3, 1973—Egypt and Syria attempt to reclaim Arab territories illegally occupied by Israel. The war leads to a UN-brokered ceasefire on October 25.

September 1, 1978—The Camp David Accords lay the ground-work for a mediated agreement between Israel and Egypt.

March 26, 1979—Egypt and Israel sign a peace treaty, leading to Israeli withdrawal from Sinai. Palestinian and Arab territories remain under Israeli occupation.

December 9, 1987—The First Intifada, a popular uprising against the Israeli occupation, erupts in the West Bank and the Gaza Strip.

December 14, 1987—The Islamic Resistance Movement (Hamas) is founded by a quadriplegic local imam and activist Sheikh Ahmed Yassin following the outbreak of the First Intifada. Though Hamas had its roots in Gaza-based organizations for many years, its first statement as a political and militant movement was issued on December 14, 1987. The word "Hamas" itself is not used until January 1988.

July 31, 1988—Jordan renounces all legal claims to the West Bank.

December 1988—PLO talks are held in Tunisia following statements by PLO chairman Yasser Arafat renouncing violence (armed struggle), among other US demands.

Mid 1991—While, during the First Intifada, the military arm of Hamas, initially MAJD, developed into a different organizational structure known as the Palestinian Mujahideen, sometime in mid '91, it became known as the Izz al-Din Al-Qassam Brigades, and then later as the Al-Qassam Brigades.

October 30, 1991—The Madrid Peace Conference initiates direct negotiations that involve Israel, Egypt, Syria, Lebanon, and a joint Jordanian-Palestinian delegation.

September 13, 1993—The Oslo Accords are signed, allowing the establishment of the Palestinian Authority (PA).

May 4, 1994—The Gaza-Jericho Agreement kickstarts the implementation of the Oslo Accords, leading to limited Israeli military withdrawal from Gaza and Jericho and the transfer of governing responsibilities to the PA.

October 26, 1994—Israel and Jordan sign a peace treaty often referred to as the Wadi Araba Treaty.

September 28, 1995—Oslo II is signed, technically granting the PA greater autonomy over more of the West Bank and setting up governance structures in preparation for a final peace agreement, which was never reached.

July 2000—Talks between Israeli and Palestinian leaders are hosted by US President Bill Clinton in Camp David. No agreement was reached.

September 28, 2000—The Second Intifada erupts following Ariel Sharon's provocative visit to the Haram al-Sharif Muslim sanctuary, leading to widespread violence which lasts until 2005.

June 23, 2002—Israel commences the construction of a Separation Wall, mostly built over West Bank territories. Palestinians dub it the Apartheid Wall.

March 22, 2004—Sheikh Ahmed Yassin, the founder of Hamas, is killed by a missile fired from an Israeli helicopter gunship while returning from Fajr prayer.

July 19, 2004—The International Court of Justice (ICJ) delivers an advisory legal opinion on the Israeli West Bank wall, deciding that it contravenes international law and should be removed.

November 11, 2004—PLO and PA President Yasser Arafat dies in a Paris hospital. Various investigations suggest that the Palestinian leader was assassinated, most likely by polonium poisoning.

August 15, 2005—Israel redeploys out of the Gaza Strip, though it maintains control over borders, airspace, and the coastline.

January 25, 2006—Hamas wins Palestinian elections, leading eventually to its control of and isolation in Gaza.

2006—Israeli authorities impose a land, sea, and air blockade on the Gaza Strip.

June 25, 2006—Hamas fighters capture Israeli soldier Gilad Shalit, who would be held captive until his release on October 18, 2011 following years of indirect negotiations.

January 26, 2008—George Habash, the founder of the socialist Popular Front for the Liberation of Palestine, dies in Jordan. Habash and the PFLP strongly opposed the Oslo Accords.

December 27, 2008—Israel launches a deadly war on the Gaza Strip, killing nearly 1,400 Palestinians and wounding over 5,000.

December 14, 2012—Israel launches an eight-day war on the Gaza Strip, killing over 170 Palestinians and wounding nearly 1,400.

July 8, 2014—Israel launches its deadliest war on Gaza yet, which they call Operation Protective Edge, killing over 2,200 Palestinians and wounding over 17,000.

December 6, 2017—The US formally recognizes Jerusalem as Israel's capital. The recognition extends to reach the occupied Palestinian city of East Jerusalem.

March 2018—The Great March of Return starts in Gaza. Tens of thousands of Palestinians, mostly youth, rally at the fence separating besieged Gaza from Israel, demanding an end to the siege and the Right of Return.

March 25, 2019—The US recognizes Israeli sovereignty over the occupied Syrian Golan Heights, illegally annexed by Israel in 1981.

January 28, 2020—The Trump administration unveils the so-called Deal of the Century, a regional peace plan developed without Palestinian involvement.

September 15, 2020—Bahrain and the UAE normalize relations with Israel. Other Arab countries join in.

May 2021—Israel launches an eleven-day military campaign on Gaza, killing over 250 Palestinians. Palestinians retaliate with the Unity Intifada, exemplifying cooperation between all Palestinians throughout the occupied territories.

May 2022—Israel launches a major operation in the West Bank, making 2022 the deadliest year since 2005, according to United Nations estimates.

August 5, 2022—Israel conducts nearly 150 airstrikes in Gaza allegedly targeting Islamic Jihad sites. The strikes kill forty-nine Palestinians, including seventeen children.

October 7, 2023—Hamas, along with other resistance groups in Gaza, carry out the Al-Aqsa Flood Operation in southern Israel. Subsequently Israel launches its deadliest war on the Strip.

War and Genocide Timeline

October 7, 2023

6:30 a.m. Gaza time—Air raid sirens are activated in southern and central Israel. Mohammed Deif, the commander of the Al-Qassam Brigades, announces in a prerecorded message the start of the Al-Aqsa Flood Operation.

7:40 a.m.—The Israeli army confirms that Hamas fighters have infiltrated southern Israel.

10:47 a.m.—The Israeli Air Force launches air attacks on Gaza.

11:35 a.m.—Israeli Prime Minister Benjamin Netanyahu declares: "Citizens of Israel, we are at war."

October 8, 2023—The Lebanese movement Hezbollah starts military operations against the Israeli army in occupied south Lebanon and northern Israel.

October 9, 2023—Israeli Defense Minister Yoav Gallant announces a total blockade of the Gaza Strip, cutting off water, electricity, food, and fuel. Gallant declares that Israel is "fighting human animals."

October 11, 2023—Netanyahu declares that the war's main goal is to "crush and destroy Hamas."

October 12, 2023—US Secretary of State Antony Blinken visits Israel to express solidarity. Following Blinken's visit, Israel is visited by many Western leaders, including President of the EU Commission Ursula von Der Leyen on October 13, US President Joe Biden on October 18, and British Prime Minister Rishi Sunak on October 19, among others.

October 13, 2023—Israel issues its first evacuation order for the Palestinian residents of northern Gaza.

October 14, 2023—The first rally in solidarity with the captives is held in Tel Aviv, with protesters calling on Netanyahu to resign. Protests will continue throughout the war.

October 16, 2023—The USS Eisenhower aircraft carrier reaches the eastern Mediterranean with the aim of providing support for Israel.

The Al-Qassam Brigades releases its first video of Israeli captives in Gaza.

Abu Obeida, the Al-Qassam Brigades military spokesman, declares that over 200 Israeli captives are being held by Hamas while other resistance groups also hold dozens of detainees.

October 17, 2023—Israeli forces strike an UNRWA school for the first time in the war.

Israel commits the largest massacre yet by bombing the Al-Ahli Baptist Hospital, killing at least 500 Palestinians and wounding many more. Following international outcry, Israel denies responsibility.

October 18, 2023—The US vetoes a UN Security Council (UNSC) resolution calling for "humanitarian pauses" to deliver lifesaving aid to millions in Gaza.

October 20, 2023—US Secretary-General António Guterres visits the Rafah Crossing, calling on Israel to open an aid lifeline for Gaza.

October 27, 2023—Israel announces an expansion of its ground forces at the Gaza border. This coincides with a total communication blackout in Gaza. Later in the evening, Israel begins the ground invasion of the Gaza Strip.

November 2, 2023—Israeli forces besiege Gaza City.

The Geneva-based Euro-Med Human Rights Monitor reveals that in the first weeks of the war, Israel has dropped more than 25,000 tons of explosives on the Gaza Strip, the equivalent of two nuclear bombs.

November 3, 2023—Israeli forces launch an eleven-day siege at Gaza's largest medical center, Al-Shifa Hospital in Gaza City.

November 14, 2023—Israeli troops storm the Al-Shifa hospital, which houses hundreds of staff and patients along with several thousand people who sought shelter in the hospital's courtyards. According to the Safeguarding Health in Conflict Coalition, during the first week of war, there were ninety-four attacks on healthcare facilities in Gaza. According to the World Health Organization, as of June 2024, Israel had attacked 464 healthcare facilities, killing 727 healthcare workers, injuring 933 healthcare workers, and destroying 113 ambulances.

November 22, 2023—The Palestinian death toll passes 10,000.

November 24, 2023—A ceasefire comes into effect. Around 240 Palestinian detainees are released in exchange for around 105 captives, including eighty-three Israelis.

November 2023—Students occupying administrative buildings at Brown University in Providence, Rhode Island in solidarity with Gaza are arrested at the request of college administrator. Protestors join in at various universities throughout the US before student protests become a global phenomenon.

December 1, 2023—The seven-day ceasefire ends at 7:00 a.m. Gaza time. The Israeli army resumes combat operations.

December 7, 2023—Israeli forces kill renowned Gaza intellectual Refaat Alareer.

December 8, 2023—The US vetoes a second UNSC resolution calling for "an immediate humanitarian ceasefire."

December 9, 2023—The military spokesman for Yemen's Ansarallah group, Brigadier General Yahya Saree, warns shipping companies against cooperating with Israel, saying that all Israel-bound ships in the Red Sea will become a target.

December 15, 2023—The Israeli army launches its first major attack on the southern Gaza Strip's town of Rafah and the Philadelphi Route, separating Gaza from Egypt.

December 22, 2023—The Palestinian death toll passes 20,000.

December 29, 2023—South Africa files a case against Israel at the International Court of Justice (ICJ) accusing Israel of genocidal acts in Gaza. (Many countries in the Global South take action to express their solidarity with the Palestinian people, including Namibia, Nicaragua, Colombia, and Bolivia, among others.)

January 3, 2024—Israel assassinates top Hamas official Saleh al-Arouri in Beirut.

January 11–13, 2024—The genocide case is discussed at the ICJ.

January 12, 2024—The US and the UK, supported by Australia, Bahrain, Canada, Denmark, the Netherlands, and New Zealand, launch a series of airstrikes against the Ansarallah in Yemen.

January 23, 2024—Israeli forces encircle the city of Khan Yunis and launch a major assault.

January 26, 2024—The ICJ judges find that "at least some of the rights claimed by South Africa and for which it is seeking protection are plausible," including "the right of the Palestinians in

Gaza to be protected from acts of genocide and related prohibited acts."

January 28, 2024—The killing of six-year-old Hind Rajab by Israeli forces as she pleads with paramedics to rescue her from inside a car surrounded by tanks shocks the world.

February 5, 2024—A convoy of trucks waiting to bring humanitarian aid to Gaza is hit by Israeli fire. (According to the UN Office for Coordination of Humanitarian Affairs, as of September 13, 2024, Israel has struck at least sixteen humanitarian convoys.)

February 6, 2024—A statement issued by UN experts, including Irene Khan, Special Rapporteur on the protection and promotion of freedom of opinion and expression and Francesca Albanese, Special Rapporteur on the situation of human rights in the Palestinian Territory, condemns the killing of journalists in Gaza. (As of August 26, 2024, 171 Palestinian journalists have been killed, according to the Gaza government media office.)

February 20, 2024—Despite international pressure, Netanyahu vows to invade Rafah "no matter what."

The United States vetoes for the third time a UNSC draft resolution on Israel's war on Gaza, thus blocking a demand for an immediate ceasefire. (Zhang Jun, China's envoy to the UN, expresses "strong disappointment and dissatisfaction" with the US. Russia's Ambassador to the UN Vassily Nebenzia says that the US veto marks "another black page in the history of the Security Council.")

February 22, 2024—Addressing the ICJ, the Chinese representative Ma Xinmin says that the Palestinians' use of armed struggle to gain independence from foreign and colonial rule is "legitimate" and "well-founded" in international law. The statement is made during hearings on the legal consequences of Israel's occupation of the West Bank and East Jerusalem at the ICJ.

February 25, 2024—Aaron Bushnell, a twenty-five-year-old officer of the US Air Force, sets himself on fire in protest against the genocide in Gaza.

February 29, 2024—The Palestinian death toll passes 30,000.

March 1, 2024—Nicaragua institutes proceedings against Germany at the ICJ under the Genocide Convention due to Berlin's support for Israel in its war on Gaza.

March 18, 2024—Israel invades the Al-Shifa hospital for the second time. (On April 2, after fourteen days of siege, journalists and humanitarian workers find at least 300 bodies inside the hospital. On April 15, two mass graves in the vicinity of the hospital are also found.)

March 25, 2024—A draft UNSC resolution demanding an immediate ceasefire is approved by fourteen members of the Council. The US abstains.

April 1, 2024—Israel bombs the Iranian embassy in Damascus, killing two top Iranian generals.

April 10, 2024—An Israeli airstrike on the Shati refugee camp kills three sons and four grandchildren of Hamas's top political leader Ismail Haniyeh.

April 13, 2024—Iran's Islamic Revolutionary Guards Corps (IRGC) launches retaliatory attacks against Israel and the Israeli-occupied Golan Heights with loitering munitions, cruise missiles, and ballistic missiles, in an operation codenamed Operation True Promise.

April 20, 2024—The US House of Representatives passes an aid package that would provide Israel with $26 billion in emergency aid, with $17 billion allocated to military assistance.

May 2, 2024—Colombian President Gustavo Petro announces the cutting of diplomatic ties with Israel over its genocidal war on Gaza.

May 6, 2024—Hamas accepts an Egyptian-Qatari ceasefire proposal, calling for a gradual end to the war.

May 7, 2024—Israeli ground forces seize control of the Gaza side of the Rafah Crossing, and initiate the Rafah offensive.

May 16, 2024—Tlaleng Mofokeng, UN Special Rapporteur on the Right to Health, says in a statement that she is "horrified" by the death of a Gazan surgeon while in Israeli detention and calls for an independent international investigation. (As of September 2024, over 885 medical personnel have been killed and 310 detained since the beginning of the war, according to the Gaza government media office.)

May 20, 2024—The International Criminal Court Prosecutor Karim Khan files applications for arrest warrants before the Pre-Trial Chamber for Israeli Prime Minister Benjamin Netanyahu and Israeli Defense Minister Yoav Gallant. The arrest warrant application is also filed for Hamas's political leader Ismail Haniyeh, Al-Qassam Brigades commander Mohammed al-Deif, and Hamas leader in Gaza, Yahya Sinwar.

May 31, 2024—US President Joe Biden announces an Israeli ceasefire proposal.

June 7, 2024—UN Secretary-General Antonio Guterres notifies Israel he is adding it to the "blacklist" of nations that kill and injure children in conflict zones.

June 8, 2024—Israel announces the rescue of four Israeli captives from the Nuseirat refugee camp in central Gaza. During the military operation, 276 Palestinians are killed and nearly 700 are injured.

June 9, 2024—Israeli minister and opposition leader Benny Gantz announces his resignation from the Israeli war cabinet.

June 10, 2024—The UNSC adopts a resolution calling for a three-phase comprehensive ceasefire agreement in Gaza.

June 11, 2024—Hamas accepts the UNSC ceasefire resolution.

June 17, 2024—Netanyahu dissolves the Israeli war cabinet.

June 23, 2024—Netanyahu rejects the possibility of a permanent ceasefire.

June 25, 2024—Israeli forces bomb Haniyeh's family home in the Shati camp, killing ten people including his sister.

July 25, 2024—Netanyahu addresses a joint session of the US Congress. 135 Congress members boycott the speech, while Palestinian-American Congresswoman Rashida Tlaib holds up a banner reading "War Criminal" and "Guilty of Genocide."

July 30, 2024—Israel carries out a strike in the suburbs of Beirut, assassinating Hezbollah's top military commander Fouad Shukr.

July 31, 2024—Hamas's political leader Ismail Haniyeh is assassinated in Tehran.

August 3, 2024—Following an investigation, Iran's IRGC announces that a short-range projectile is behind Haniyeh's killing. Tehran blames the assassination on Israel and vows retaliation.

August 15, 2024—The Palestinian death toll passes 40,000.

August 22, 2024—Retired Israeli General Yitzhak Brik issues a stark warning in an article published in the Israeli newspaper *Haaretz*, stating that Israel could face collapse within a year if the war continues.

August 25, 2024—Hezbollah launches over 300 rockets, drones, and missiles at military targets in Israel, stating that the attack is a first phase of retaliation for the killing of its top commander Fouad Shukr.

August 28, 2024—The Israeli occupation army launches a military operation in the West Bank, stating it is its largest invasion of the occupied territories since 2002. (According to the Palestinian Ministry of Health, as of September 2024, Israel has killed nearly 700 Palestinians in the occupied West Bank since the beginning of the war on October 7, 2023.)

September 1, 2024—The bodies of six Israeli captives are retrieved in Gaza, leading to mass protests against Netanyahu.

September 2, 2024—Israel's largest trade union, the Histadrut, stages a general strike across Israel calling for a ceasefire agreement.

September 5, 2024—UN independent investigator on the right to food, Michael Fakhri, accuses Israel of carrying out a "starvation campaign" in Gaza. He says that "Palestinians in Gaza [make] up eighty percent of the people in the world experiencing famine or catastrophic hunger."

September 6, 2024—Twenty-six-year-old Ayşenur Ezgi Eygi, an American and Turkish dual citizen, is shot and killed by Israeli occupation forces during a protest against illegal Israeli settlements near Nablus in the occupied West Bank.

September 14, 2024—Netanyahu announces the expansion of Israel's military operation in Lebanon.

September 17-18, 2024—Thousands of pagers and hundreds of walkie-talkies explode simultaneously across Lebanon and Syria in what is described as an Israeli terror attack.

September 20, 2024—An Israeli airstrike on the southern Beirut suburb of Dahiyeh kills forty-five people, including Hezbollah's operations commander Ibrahim Aqil.

September 27, 2024—An Israeli airstrike on Hezbollah's central headquarters in Beirut kills the group's leader Hassan Nasrallah. Six other people are killed and at least 100 injured in the attack.

October 5, 2024—Israeli forces reenter Jabaliya in the northern Gaza Strip after their withdrawal in May. The army imposes a total siege on the area, initiating a process described by human rights organizations as the systematic extermination of Palestinians.

October 7, 2024—Marking the first anniversary of the war, Palestinian and Lebanese Resistance groups target Israel with barrages of rockets and missiles.

October 9, 2024—Dr. Soma Baroud, a prominent Gaza medical doctor, and the sister of the author of this book, is murdered in an Israeli strike on her car in the southern Gaza City of Khan Yunis.

October 17, 2024—Israel announces the killing of Hamas's political leader Yahya Sinwar during confrontations in the Tel Al-Sultan area, near Rafah, in the southern Gaza Strip.

October 19, 2024—A drone launched from Lebanon hits the residence of Israeli Prime Minister Benjamin Netanyahu in Caesarea.

October 20, 2024—The Al-Qassam Brigades kill Israeli Colonel Ihsan Daqsa, commander of the 401st Brigade, who was in charge of the military operation in Jabaliya. This marks the highest-ranking Israeli military official killed by the Palestinian Resistance in Gaza since the beginning of the war.

October 21, 2024—As the extermination of Palestinians in northern Gaza continues to gain momentum, Palestinian Resistance groups declare that they have carried out "complex ambushes" that killed and wounded many Israeli soldiers.

October 23, 2024—Spain's Defense Ministry announces that it is suspending all arms purchases from Israel, with the exception of maintenance contracts.

October 25, 2024—An Israeli airstrike targets a compound housing journalists in the Lebanese town of Hasbaiyya, killing three. Three others are injured.

October 28, 2024—The Israeli Knesset passes legislation designating the Palestinian refugee agency, UNRWA, a "terrorist organization."

November 6, 2024—Hezbollah fires over 150 rockets from Lebanon toward Israel. Israel continues its bombing campaign in Lebanon.

November 13, 2024—EU foreign policy chief Josep Borrell proposes suspending political dialogue with Israel due to its war on Gaza.

November 21, 2024—The International Criminal Court (ICC) issues arrest warrants for Israeli Prime Minister Benjamin Netanyahu, former Defense Minister Yoav Gallant, and Al-Qassam Brigades leader Mohammed Deif.

November 27, 2024—A ceasefire agreement between Israel and Hezbollah goes into effect at 4 a.m. local time. Despite initial agreement, Israel continues to bomb Lebanese targets.

November 29, 2024—The World Food Programme reports that all bakeries in central Gaza have been forced to shut down due to severe flour and water shortages.

December 5, 2024—Amnesty International accuses the Netanyahu government and the Israeli military of committing genocide in Gaza.

December 8, 2024—Following the collapse of the Bashar al-Assad government, Israeli forces seize full control of the UN buffer zone in the Golan Heights. They also take control of the Syrian side of Mount Hermon. In later days, Israel carried out intense bombing campaigns, which it claimed destroyed eighty percent of the full capabilities of the Syrian army. More incursions continued in following days and weeks.

December 19, 2024—Joining Amnesty International, Human Rights Watch accuses the Israeli government of genocide in Gaza.

December 27, 2024—Israeli forces raid Kamal Adwan Hospital in northern Gaza, after forcing most staff, patients, and their families to evacuate. The hospital's director, Dr. Hussam Abu Safiya, is detained and later reportedly tortured in an Israeli prison.

December 31, 2024—Yemen's Ansarallah targets Ben Gurion Airport and launches an attack on the American aircraft carrier USS Harry S. Truman, an act repeated many times in following weeks and months.

January 19, 2025—A ceasefire agreement between Israel and Hamas goes into effect at 11:15 a.m. local time. Several Israeli captives are released in exchange for hundreds of Palestinian prisoners. Israel continued to violate the ceasefire agreement

January 20, 2025—Donald Trump begins his second term as President of the United States. While Netanyahu welcomes Trump's inauguration as an opportunity to change the Middle East, Palestinians hope that Trump will bring a permanent end to the war.

January 30, 2025—Hamas confirms the killing of its military chief, Mohammed Deif, in an earlier Israeli airstrike.

February 4, 2025—During a joint press conference with Netanyahu, US President Donald Trump vows to "take over" Gaza, making it the "Riviera of the Middle East."

February 28, 2025—The Trump administration approves nearly $3 billion in weapons sales to Israel, scheduled for delivery between 2026 and 2028, bypassing standard congressional review.

March 5, 2025—Axios reports that the United States is holding direct talks with Hamas's chief negotiator Khalil al-Hayya in Doha.

March 8, 2025—Arrests of pro-Palestine students in the US continue with the detention of Columbia graduate and green card holder Mahmoud Khalil and, later, Turkish student Rumeysa Ozturk. Crackdowns on pro-Palestinian activities in major universities lead to mass arrests and punitive measures against students, including expulsions and denial of diplomas.

March 15, 2025—The United States launches Operation Rough Rider, carrying out airstrikes targeting dozens of locations in Yemen. Joint US-British attacks continue for weeks.

March 18, 2025—Israel resumes its war on Gaza with massive strikes on Rafah, tightening its siege on the entirety of the Gaza Strip.

March 19, 2025—The Al-Quds Brigades announce the killing of their military spokesperson, Haji Abu Seif (Abu Hamza), in an Israeli airstrike

March 24, 2025—An Israeli strike hits a car in eastern Beit Lahia, killing Palestinian journalist Hossam Shabat, who had previously been injured in another Israeli attack.

March 26, 2025—Ansarallah launches drone and missile attacks on US and Israeli targets. Military spokesperson Yahya Saree states that the operations aim to resist US-led aggression and support Palestinians under Israeli bombardment.

April 4, 2025—Ansarallah targets the USS Harry S. Truman and other US Navy vessels using cruise missiles.

May 1, 2025—Ansarallah announces it downed a US F-18 fighter during its attack on USS Harry Truman aircraft carrier in the Red Sea. A second F-18 was downed on May 7. According to a report published by the New York Times on May 12, Ansarallah's air defenses almost struck an F-35 fighter jet, "making real the possibility of American casualties."

May 2, 2025—As Israeli massacres continue across Gaza, Palestinian Resistance operations return to the scene, with the most effective in the Tel al-Sultan neighborhood in northern Gaza.

An Israeli drone targets the Freedom Flotilla Coalition's Gaza-bound aid ship off the coast of Malta, sparking a fire on board.

May 4, 2025—Ansrallah fires a ballistic missile at Tel Aviv, hitting the main terminal of Ben Gurion Airport, leaving a deep crater.

May 6, 2025—A truce is declared between Yemen and the US. President Trump announces a halt to US strikes, saying Ansarallah has pledged to stop attacking US ships in the Red Sea.

Ansarallah clarifies that the ceasefire does not in any way apply to Israel, and on May 9, resumes attacking Israeli targets.

May 19, 2025—While Israeli attacks and siege persist, the Al-Qassam Brigades launch a new operation in Beit Lahia, killing and injuring a number of Israeli soldiers. Beit Lahia is a short distance away from the Israeli border fence.

UNRWA states that ninety-two percent of Palestinian homes in Gaza have been destroyed by the Israeli war.

In a joint statement, the leaders of the United Kingdom, France and Canada threaten Israel with "concrete actions" over the genocide in Gaza, including targeted sanctions.

May 24, 2025—The World Food Programme warns that over 70,000 children in Gaza are suffering from acute malnutrition.

Israeli airstrikes kill eleven-year-old social media influencer Yaqeen Hammad in Gaza.

An Israeli airstrike kills the nine children of Palestinian pediatrician, Dr. Alaa al-Najjar, as she was working at the Nasser hospital in Khan Yunis. Her eleven-year-old son Adam and her husband are seriously injured.

May 25, 2025—Israel intensifies its targeting of displaced refugees sheltering inside schools and kindergartens, killing in a single strike over thirty Palestinians in a school in the Daraj neighborhood in Gaza.

May 27, 2025—The Ministry of Health in Gaza announced that the total number of casualties from the Israeli aggression has risen to 54,056 killed and 129,123 injured.

September 2025—During the United Nations General Assembly meeting, between September 21–23, several countries officially announce their recognition of the State of Palestine.They include France, the Untied Kingdom, Canada, and Australia, among others. The wave of recognition follows Israel's growing isolation on the international stage, with countries like Spain going as far as imposing direct sanctions on Tel Aviv.

September 2025—On September 23, Colombian President Gustavo Petro declares total solidarity with the Palestinian people in his UNGA address, calling for the implementation of the Uniting for Peace resolution to bypass Security Council paralysis, enforce international accountability and create a "powerful international army" to "liberate Palestine."

September 2025—Over forty boats, carrying nearly 500 activists from 44 countries, set sail to break the siege on Gaza. The flotilla includes prominent international figures such as Greta Thunberg and Mandla Mandela, the grandson of former South African President Nelson Mandela. The boats are illegally intercepted and raided in international waters by the Israeli navy. All activists are detained, subjected to abuse by Israeli prison authorities, and later deported.

September 2025—On September 29, US President Donald Trump announces the "Gaza Proposal," a 20-point plan intended to end the war in Gaza. Both Hamas and Israel acceptd the proposal, and a ceasefire follows on October 9, though Israel continues to violate the terms of the first phase of the agreement.

October 2025—On October 2, twenty-three-year-old Mohammed al-Badrasawi, the eldest of Ehab's children, is killed by the Israeli army. With his death, the only survivors of Ehab's family are his wife and teenage daughter. Two days earlier, Nasser's only surviving son, also named Mohammed, was killed in northern Gaza.

October 2025—As of October 9, 2025, the Gaza Ministry of Health announces that 67,194 Palestinians have been killed, while nearly 170,000 are wounded. The Ministry adds that 9,500 remain missing. However, independent estimates, including reputable international medical journals, indicate that the final death toll is expected to be significantly higher.

Notes

1. Alessandro Manzoni, *The Betrothed* (London: R. Bentley, 1834). Digitized by Harvard University, April 27, 2006.
2. "Longue durée." *Oxford Reference.* www.oxfordreference.com/view/10.1093/oi/authority.20110803100114325.
3. Palestine Chronicle TV. "Speaking to Professor Richard Falk: On Palestine, Israel and International Law." YouTube video. Posted September 22, 2020. https://www.youtube.com/watch?v=AMtVONP3_co.
4. Ofer Aderet, "'Israel Will Decline, and Jews Will Be a Persecuted Minority. Those Who Can Will Flee to America'," *Haaretz*, January 22, 2019, https://www.haaretz.com/us-news/2019-01-22/ty-article-magazine/.premium/israel-will-decline-and-jews-will-be-persecuted-those-who-can-will-flee/0000017f-e552-d9aa-afff-fd5a159f0000.
5. Antonio Gramsci, *Selections from the Prison Notebooks of Antonio Gramsci* (New York: International Publishers, 1971).
6. Tanya Reinhart, *Israel/Palestine: How to End the War of 1948* (New York: Seven Stories Press, 2002), 2.
7. *"A'oodhu billahi min ash-shaytaan-ir-rajeem."*
8. Walid Khalidi, *All That Remains: The Palestinian Villages Occupied and Depopulated by Israel in 1948* (Beirut: Institute for Palestine Studies, 1992), 87.
9. British Mandate village statistics show the Beit Daras population grew from 1,670 in 1922 to 1,804 in 1931, reaching 2,750 in 1945, and 3,190 in 1948.
   Beit Daras had 16,357 *dunums* in 1948. See "Bayt Daras," *Palestine Remembered*, n.d. https://www.palestineremembered.com/Gaza/Bayt-Daras/index.html.
10. The elementary school in Beit Daras was established in 1921. Ibid.
11. Bashir M. Nafi, "Shaykh 'Izz al-Din al-Qassam: A Reformist and a Rebel Leader" (Journal of Islamic Studies, 1997). https://www.academia.edu/87282132/Shaykh_Izz_Al_Din_Al_Qassam_A_Reformist_and_a_Rebel_Leader?utm_source=chatgpt.com.
12. Shurab, *Izz Al-Din Al-Qassam*, 251.
13. Ibid, 271–278.
14. Ibid, 251.

15. Abdul-Wahhab Kayyali, *Modern History of Palestine*, 10th ed. (Beirut: Arab Institute of Studies and Publications, 1977), 251; also see Ghassan Kanafani, *The Revolution of 1936–1939 in Palestine* (New York: 1804 Books, 2023), 41.

16. Haddad Al-Hussam, "Izz Al-Din Al-Qassam," *Bawabat Al-Harakat Al-Islamiyyah*, November 19, 2021, https://www.islamist-movements.com/10037.

17. Hamza Al-Aqrabawi, "Al-Wad Al-Ahmer: Tariq Al-Matbou'in Wa Al-Kharijin 'ala Al-Daula," *Babelwad.com*, n.d., https://tinyurl.com/yc4mh9n3.

18. Hama Al-Aqrabawi, "Al-Wad Al-Ahmer."

19. Kanafani, *The Revolution of 1936–1939*, 40.

20. Shurab, *Izz Al-Din Al-Qassam*, 35–56.

21. Ibid, 56–64.

22. Ibid.

23. Ibid.

24. Musbah Ghalawanji, "Al-Batal Al-Mujahid Al-Shahid Izz Al-Din Al-Qassam," *Al-Turath Al-Arabi* Magazine, no. 13 (1990).

25. Samih Hamouda. *Al-Wa'i al-Thouri.*

26. Shurab, *Izz Al-Din Al-Qassam*, 56–64.

27. Ibid., 105–110.

28. Even before the Mandate, the British Foreign Office actively promoted Jewish migration to Palestine, with Charles Henry Churchill appealing to Moses Montefiore, the leader of the British Jewish community, between 1841 and 1842. A lack of success did not detract from a more general belief that a significant Jewish presence in Palestine was strategically important, culminating in the (1917) Balfour Declaration, in which the British government formally expressed its support for establishing a "national home for the Jewish people" in Palestine. See Isaiah Friedman, *The Question of Palestine: British–Jewish–Arab Relations, 1914–1918* (London: Transaction Publishers, 1992).

29. The Histadrut is currently the largest workers' organization in Israel. After being established in 1920, it advocated Jewish labour rights, doing its utmost to exclude Arab workers. Already a powerful institution in its own right, it eventually became the hub of Labor Zionism, which bore primary responsibly for the ethnic cleansing of Palestinian laborers and the general population, along with the subsequent establishment of Israel on the ruins of Palestine. See Sawt El-Amel, "Separate and Unequal: The History of Arab Labor in Pre-1948 Palestine and Israel," *Laborers Voice*, February 19, 2007, http://www.labournet.net/world/0702/labvoice1.html.

30. Rogall observes: "Palestinian *fellahin* (peasants) viewed the land they cultivated as their birthright. They might not formally own it but that was somewhat beside the point. Landlordism had only really taken off in Palestine with the Ottoman Land Code of 1858. Many peasants failed to register their land under the new laws. The result was that many cultivators lost control of their land. The dispossessed ended up as sharecropping tenants on what had been their own land. When Zionist settlers purchased such land from the landlords, they evicted the *fellahin*. By 1930 some thirty percent of all Palestinian villagers were landless, while as many as seventy-five to eighty percent of the remainder didn't have sufficient land to meet their needs." Neil Rogall, "The Birth of Palestinian Resistance and the 1936 Uprising," *RS21*, September 12, 2014, https://tinyurl.com/3mdv7kpu.

31. Zionists subsequently made much of their "legal" purchases of Palestinian land, as part of the perpetuation of the associated myth that "Palestinians sold their land." Closer inspection instead reveals that, in the thirty years after the Balfour

Declaration, Jewish land ownership only increased from two to six percent of Palestinian land, the meagre return of decades of scheming, land confiscations and purchases. See Jonathan Kuttab, *Israel's Screen of Legality behind the Sheikh Jarrah Dispossession* (Washington, DC: Arab Center, 2021), https://arabcenterdc. org/resource/israels-screen-of-legality-behind-the-sheikh-jarrah-dispossession/.

32. Matthew Kelly, *The Crime of Nationalism: Britain, Palestine, and Nation-Building on the Fringe of Empire* (Berkeley: University of California Press, 2017).

33. In a significant about-face, the white paper proposed a single state of Palestine that would recognize Jewish citizenship rights. The Zionists rejected this outright, calling instead for partition.

34. For more on the struggles of Palestinian workers and peasants under the British mandate, see Ghassan Kanafani, *The 1936-1939 Revolt in Palestine* (New York: Committee for a Democratic Palestine, 1972).

35. Ilan Pappé, *The Ethnic Cleansing of Palestine* (Oxford: Oneworld, 2006), 51.

36. Around 5,000 Palestinians were killed, and 15,000 wounded. 108 rebels were executed. Khalidi, Walid, 1971/1987. From Haven to Conquest, IPS, Washington, 846-49.

37. Pappé, *The Ethnic Cleansing*, 217.

38. The Beit Daras woman fighter Latifa Abu Shanab was mentioned, though not by name, in Muhammad H. Al-Najjar, "al-Nās wa al-Turāth fī Isdūd (People and Heritage in Ashdod)," *AWRAD: Arab World for Research & Development*, 2015, 59–67. Details about Latifa were acquired through interviews conducted by one of Palestine's foremost historians, Dr. Salman Abu Sitta, who is considered one of the world's top authorities on the Nakba. The main interview from which the information above is taken was a phone interview conducted by Dr. Abu Sitta with Hussein Abu Shanab (Wadi), who was born in Beit Daras in 1940.

39. Hijazi, Yusuf. "No to the Culture of Forgetting: The Zionist Holocaust—The Massacre of Bayt Daras." OujdaCity, May 21, 2007, https://www.oujdacity.net/ regional-article-5150-ar/regional-article-5150-ar.html.

40. Pappé, *The Ethnic Cleansing of Palestine*, 150.

41. The city of Yafa was occupied by Zionist militias on May 13, 1948. *Palestine Remembered*, "District of Jaffa," n.d., https://www.palestineremembered.com/Jaffa/ Jaffa/index.html.

42. The American Friends Service Committee (AFSC) began working in Palestine in 1948, "setting up the refugee camp system for Palestinians in Gaza and providing assistance to people displaced inside the new Israeli state" under a UN mandate. See American Friends Service Committee, "History," n.d., https://afsc.org/history.

43. In 1951, Shati became an official camp with the same name when UNRWA became responsible for looking after the refugees. See Tayseer Muhaisen, "Palestinian Refugees in the Gaza Strip, 1948-1967," *Interactive Encyclopedia of the Palestine Question*, n.d. https://www.palquest.org/en/highlight/22188/palestinian-refugees-gaza-strip-1948-1967.

44. After World War I, Britain and France persuaded the League of Nations (the precursor to the United Nations) to grant them colonial authority over former Ottoman territories, with Britain obtaining a mandate for the West Bank, Gaza Strip, and Jordan. See University of Michigan, "The British Mandate in Palestine," https://lsa.umich.edu/content/dam/cmenas-assets/cmenas-documents/ unit-of-israel-palestine/Section1_BritishMandateInPalestine.pdf.

45. Al-Afranji observes: "The Bedouins in the Gaza Strip are a natural extension of the Bedouins living in southern Palestine, and part of the Bedouins in *al-badia*

(desert) of the Sinai Peninsula, Al-Naqab, and southern Jordan, and they traditionally used to move along its trails. " See Mahmoud Al-Afranji, "The Bedouins in The Gaza Strip," *This Week in Palestine*, February 28, 2023. https://thisweekinpalestine.com/the-bedouins-in-the-gaza-strip.

46. "Before 1948 Gaza had about 80,000 residents but the population almost tripled with an influx of more than 200,000 refugees mainly from the Jaffa and Beersheba districts." See Badil Resource Center for Palestinian Residency and Refugee Rights. "From the 1948 Nakba to the 1967 Naksa." Badil.org, June 2004. https://www.badil.org/phocadownloadpap/Badil_docs/bulletins-and-briefs/Bulletin-18.pdf.

47. See United Nations, *The Right of Return of the Palestinian People* (New York: United Nations, 1978), https://www.un.org/unispal/document/auto-insert-210170/.

48. See Badil, "From the 1948 Nakba."

49. Ahmed Hussein. "Fī dhikr an-nakbah: qiṣaṣ wa ḥikāyāt min mukhayyam ash-shāṭiʾ, yūthiquhā al-lājiʾ Maḥmūd Rūqt (On the Anniversary of the Nakba, Stories and Tales from the Beach Camp Documented by Refugee Mahmoud Rouqa)." *RefugeesPS.Net*. May 18, 2023. https://tinyurl.com/yrn669dz.

50. Al-Quds, "Abdel Nasser in the Palestine War," n.d, https://www.alquds.com/en/posts/71617.

51. On October 19, 1954, an Egyptian-British treaty established that British troops would completely withdraw from Egypt by June 1956. See Laurie Milner, "The Suez Crisis," BBC, March 3, 2011, https://www.bbc.co.uk/history/british/modern/suez_01.shtml.

52. Laub observes: "After a coup d'état that forced King Farouk out of power in July 1952, the military junta that took charge and the Brotherhood became rivals. [...] In 1954, a suspected Brotherhood member tried to assassinate Gamal Abdel Nasser, the leader of the Free Officers. See Zachary Laub. "Egypt's Muslim Brotherhood." Council on Foreign Relations. Last updated August 15, 2019. https://www.cfr.org/backgrounder/egypts-muslim-brotherhood.

53. See Avi Shlaim, *The Iron Wall: Israel and the Arab World* (London: Penguin Books, 2000), 83.

54. Nasser Youth Movement, "President Gamal Abdel Nasser's Visit to the Gaza Strip - March 29, 1955," August 8, 2022, https://nasseryouthmovement.net/Nasser-2703.

55. "The March 1955 Outburst in the Gaza Strip," *Interactive Encyclopedia of the Palestine Question*, https://www.palquest.org/en/highlight/21228/march-1955-outburst-gaza-strip.

56. Ibid.

57. On October 29, 1956, the Israelis invaded Gaza and Sinai, holding both areas for four months before. See Nur Masalha, "The 1956–57 Occupation of the Gaza Strip: Israeli Proposals to Resettle the Palestinian Refugees," *British Journal of Middle Eastern Studies* 23, no. 1 (1997): 55–68. https://tinyurl.com/vzuawsn5.

58. Ibid., 58.

59. Israeli forces killed at least forty-eight Palestinians in October, and, in the following month, at least 275 Palestinians in Khan Yunis and 110 Palestinians in Rafah. See Alex Winder, "1956 Warm," *Interactive Encyclopedia of the Palestine Question*, n.d., https://tinyurl.com/6b5e5rds.

60. Ibid.

61. Nasser annulled the All-Palestine Government in 1959 and, three years later, introduced a constitutional system of government in Gaza by dividing responsibility between legislative branch, mostly elected Palestinians, and the executive

branch, with appointed Egyptians and members of influential Gazan families. Two years later, he established a governing council in Gaza. See Joel Beinin, "How Egypt's Gamal Abdel Nasser Changed World Politics," *Jacobin*, February 11, 2021, https://jacobin.com/2021/11/Egypt-gamal-abdel-nasser-world-politics-arab-socialism-anti-imperialism-history.

62. See "Aḥmad Shuqayrī," Britannica, n.d., https://www.britannica.com/biography/Ahmad-Shuqayri.

63. Institute for Palestine Studies, "Palestine Liberation Organization: National Council Sessions: 1964–Present," May 28, 2021, https://www.palestine-studies.org/en/node/1651325.

64. John Laffin, *Arab Armies of the Middle East Wars 1948–73* (Oxford: Osprey Publishing, 1982).

65. Qur'an, Surah Āl ʿImrān, 3:160.

66. *"La hawla wala quwwata illa billah."*67. In June 1967, Israeli forces proclaimed a military government by issuing Military Order No. 2, which concentrated all powers and authorities in the hands of an Israeli military governor. See Tariq Mukhimer, *State Building Process: The Case of Palestine* (Ph.D. diss., Humboldt University, 2005).

68. Israel's transfer policies in Gaza intensified in the early 1970s, along with the dismantling of refugee camps. Anne Irfan observes: "Under the policies of military commander Ariel Sharon, 38,000 Nakba refugees were uprooted for the second time and resettled elsewhere in 1971." See Anne Irfan, "Israel's Policy toward Refugees in the Gaza Strip," *Interactive Encyclopedia of the Palestine Question*, n.d, https://www.palquest.org/en/highlight/21232/israel%E2%80%99s-policy-toward-refugees-gaza-strip.

69. The Israeli army regularly cracked down on Palestinian refugees, and starting in July 1971 Israeli bulldozers began dismantling and demolishing refugee camps, leaving tens of thousands homeless. See Joan Mandell, "Gaza: Israel's Soweto," *MERP* 136/137 (1985), https://merip.org/1985/10/gaza-israels-soweto/.

70. British documents revealed that "Israel devised a secret plan in 1971 to deport thousands of Palestinians from Gaza to Al-Arish, north of Sinai." See Gerard Deeb, "Egypt and its War on Secret Documents, *Middle East Monitor*, December 8, 2023, https://www.middleeastmonitor.com/20231208-egypt-and-its-war-on-secret-documents/.

71. In the 1970s and 1980s, Israel tried to establish "village leagues" by enlisting the services of collaborating local Palestinian leaders. See Rédaction Africanews and Associated Press, "Israel Working to 'Remove' Gaza Rule from Hamas and Choose an 'Alternative'," *Africanews*, June 8, 2024, https://www.africanews.com/2024/06/03/israel-working-to-remove-hamas-from-gaza-leadership-and-choose-an-alternative/.

72. Gisha observes that "since Israel's occupation of Gaza and the West Bank in 1967, it has exploited both Palestinian labor and natural resources in the territory." See Gisha - Legal Center for Freedom of Movement, "At All Costs," September 1, 2022, https://gisha.org/en/at-all-costs/.

73. The Israeli scholar Hillel Cohen claims that Israel's use of collaborators was extensive in the 1970s and 1980s. See Jonathan Cook, "Spotlight Shines on Palestinian Collaborators," *Al Jazeera*, February 17, 2014, https://www.aljazeera.com/features/2014/2/17/spotlight-shines-on-palestinian-collaborators. Regarding the Israeli police force, see Brynjar Lia, *A Police Force Without a State: A History of the Palestinian Security Forces in the West Bank and Gaza* (New York: Ithaca Press, 2006).

74. "Dalal al-Mughrabi, dubbed 'the Bride of Jaffa,' is considered one of the most prominent Palestinian freedom fighters and one of the most famous women among them." *Interactive Encyclopedia of the Palestine Question*, "Dalal Al-Mughrabi," n.d., https://www.palquest.org/en/biography/33687/dalal-al-mughrabi.

75. Shatila camp and the adjacent neighborhood of Sabra in Beirut were the scene of a massacre on 16-18 September 1982. See UNRWA, "Shatila Camp," n.d., https://www.unrwa.org/where-we-work/lebanon/shatila-camp.

76. https://www.facebook.com/fatehvoice/. 2018. "t kmāl ʿdwān." ʿmlīt kmāl ʿdwān", July 1, 2018. https://web.archive.org/web/20180701165018/http://www.fatehvoice.net:80/post/91069.

77. "*Biladi Biladi Biladi .. laki hubi wa fuadi ... Filstinu ya arda al-judud, iliki labuda an na'ud.*"

78. Local elections were held in the West Bank on April 12, 1976 on the order of Israeli military authorities, under the 1955 Jordanian municipal elections law.

79. Israel's invasion of southern Lebanon on March 14, 1978 is often referred to as Operation Litani. See Tom Ruys, Oliver Corten, and Alexandra Hofer, eds., *The Use of Force in International Law: A Case-Based Approach* (Oxford: Oxford University Press, 2018).

80. Gaza Central Prison, built in 1936 in the British Mandate period, was used by the Egyptians from 1948 to 1967 and by the Israelis until 1993. Following the Oslo Accords, the PA took over the prison, which was completely destroyed by Israeli F-16 fighter jets during the 2008–2009 war on Gaza. See "Gaza Central Prison Reopens as a Museum," *Middle East Monitor*, February 15, 2014, https://www.middleeastmonitor.com/20140215-gaza-central-prison-reopens-as-a-museum/.

81. Pappé, *The Ethnic Cleansing of Palestine*, 217.

82. In Gaza, Ahmed Yassin's family survived through weaving and fishing. See "Sheikh Ahmed Yassin," *Telegraph*, March 23, 2004, https://www.telegraph.co.uk/news/obituaries/1457499/Sheikh-Ahmed-Yassin.html.

83. Masalha, "The 1956–57 Occupation of the Gaza Strip."

84. "In 1954, a suspected member of the Brotherhood attempted to assassinate the leader of the Free Officers, Gamal Abdel Nasser. In response, thousands of suspected Brothers were imprisoned." Zachary Laub, "Egypt's Muslim Brotherhood," Council on Foreign Relations, last updated August 15, 2019, https://www.cfr.org/backgrounder/egypts-muslim-brotherhood.

85. *Interactive Encyclopedia of the Palestine Question*, "Ahmad Ismail Yasin," n.d., https://www.palquest.org/en/biography/9845/ahmad-ismail-yasin.

86. Nuwayhid Al Hoot Bayan, *Al Shaykh Al Mujahid Izz Al Din Al Qassam fi Tareekh Filasteen* (Beirut: Dar Al Istiqlal, 1987), 9. Al-Qassam was killed on November 20, 1935.

87. The accusation was made on October 26, 1954. The government radio station broadcast a report that a young man from the Brotherhood fired eight shots at Abdel Naser while he was giving a speech in Manshiya Maydan in Alexandria. He was unharmed.

88. Sheikh Yassin the man who lived despite Israeli missiles, The Palestinian Information Center, March 24, 2016. https://english.palinfo.com/o_post/Sheikh-Yassin-the-man-who-lived-despite-Israeli-missiles/

89. Ziad Abu-Amr, "Hamas: A Historical and Political Background," *Journal of Palestine Studies* 22, no. 4 (1993): 5–19, https://doi.org/10.2307/2538077.

90. *Interactive Encyclopedia of the Palestine Question*, "Ahmad Ismail Yasin," n.d., https://www.palquest.org/en/biography/9845/ahmad-ismail-yasin.

91. Ibid.
92. Matthew Bevan and Yasmin Parry, "Ahmed Yassin Was a Quadriplegic Refugee Who Ran a Charity. How Did He End up Founding Hamas?," *ABC*. October 20, 2023. https://www.abc.net.au/news/2023-10-21/the-disabled-refugee-who-founded-hamas/102993128.
93. The main function of this distinction is that refugee camps were managed, in terms of basic services such as food distribution, by UNRWA, while the larger city municipalities were governed by whatever authority that ruled over Gaza, including Israel.
94. International Middle East Media Center (IMEMC), "December 8, 1987 – The First Palestinian Uprising (Intifada)," December 9, 2019, https://imemc.org/article/december-8-1987-the-first-palestinian-uprising-intifada/.

    Amnesty International, "Israel and the Occupied Territories, Administrative Detention during the Palestinian Intifada," June 1989, https://www.amnesty.org/ar/wp-content/uploads/2021/06/mde150061989en.pdf.
95. Helena Cobban, "The PLO and the 'Intifada,'" *Middle East Journal* 44, no. 2 (1990): 207–33. http://www.jstor.org/stable/4328099.
96. Btselem, "Fatalities in the First Intifada,", n.d, https://www.btselem.org/statistics/first_intifada_tables.

    Yplus, "The First Intifada," n.d, https://yplus.ps/2023/12/26/the-first-intifada-2/.
97. Shatha Hammad, "Stories from the First Intifada: 'They Broke My Bones'," *Al Jazeera*, December 10, 2017, https://www.aljazeera.com/news/2017/12/10/stories-from-the-first-intifada-they-broke-my-bones.
98. "The Life and Death of Shaikh Yasin," *Al Jazeera*, March 24, 2004, https://www.aljazeera.com/news/2004/3/24/the-life-and-death-of-shaikh-yasin.
99. Hassan al-Banna founded the Muslim Brotherhood in March 1928, at twenty-one years old. Al-Banna offered to send volunteers to Palestine during the 1936-39 Palestinian rebellion. By October 1945, the movement opened a Palestine branch in Jerusalem, under the leadership of Sa'd Ramadan. The Gaza branch was established on November 25, 1946. See Jean-Pierre Filiu, "The Origins of Hamas: Militant Legacy or Israeli Tool?" *Journal of Palestine Studies* 41 (2012): 54-70, 10.1525/jps.2012.XLi.3.54.
100. "What is Hamas?," Council on Foreign Relations, April 18, 2024, https://www.cfr.org/backgrounder/what-hamas.
101. Ahmed Qasem Hussein, "The Evolution of the Military Action of the Izz Al-Din al-Qassam Brigades: How Hamas Established Its Army in Gaza," *Al Muntaqa* 4, no. 1 (2021): 78–97, https://www.jstor.org/stable/10.31430/almuntaqa.4.1.0078.
102. Alhdf, Bwābt, *Dhkr Mjzrt al-aḥd al-Asūd ' īūn qārt. bwābt l-hdf l-ikhbārīt*, May 20, 2019, https://tinyurl.com/8bb38mfn
103. Aion Qara, a historic Palestinian town, was one of the first Palestinian-Arab cities to be colonized by the Zionist movement, in 1882. In place of Aion Qara, the Israeli city of Rishon Lezion, south of Tel Aviv, was built. Palestinian Encyclopedia, "Rishon LeZion (City)," August 3, 2014, https://tinyurl.com/bdz28mmh.
104. Abdul Aziz al-Rantisi was one of the seven co-founders of the Hamas movement during the first *intifada*. Interactive Encyclopedia of the Palestine Question, "Abd al-Aziz Rantisi,", Interactive Encyclopedia of the Palestine Question, n.d., https://www.palquest.org/en/biography/14583/abd-al-aziz-rantisi.

    Mahmoud al-Zahar is a senior Hamas official. He was elected to the Palestinian Legislative Council (PLC) in 2006. Following Hamas's 2006 electoral victory, al-Zahar was appointed Palestinian foreign minister. See European Council on

Foreign Relations. "Mahmoud al-Zahar," n.d, https://ecfr.eu/special/mapping_
palestinian_politics/mahmoud_al_zahar_plc/.
Yunis al-Astal Hamas is a member of the Palestinian Legislative Council for
the area of Khan Yunis.

105. "Between October 30 and November 1, 1991, a so-called peace conference spon-
sored by the United States and the Soviet Union was held in Madrid to address
the Palestinian-Israeli conflict. In attendance were delegates from Israel, Palestine, Jordan, Lebanon, and Syria, as well as the two sponsors and the host, Spain.
It was the first time the Palestinians and Israelis would be involved in direct
negotiations." Yara Hawari, "Thirty Years of Sham 'Peace Process'," *Al Jazeera*,
November 1, 2021, https://www.aljazeera.com/opinions/2021/11/1/the-madrid-
conference-and-the-sham-peace-process.

106. The Oslo Accords was a set of agreements between Israel and the Palestine
Liberation Organization (PLO) that was supposedly aimed at establishing a
peace process through a two-state solution. Despite their early popularity among
Palestinians, increasing numbers have opposed the agreements throughout the
years. See Charmaine Seitz (2013). *Tracking Palestinian Public Support Over 20
Years of the Oslo Agreements* (Jerusalem: Jerusalem Media and Communications
Centre (JMCC), 2013), https://palestine.fes.de/fileadmin/user_upload/Publica-
tion_1/JMCC/JMCC_2013/Oslo_Agreements_English.pdf.

107. Following the Oslo Accords, the international donor community met in Washington to financially support the so-called peace-process.

108. "The [Gaza-Jericho] agreement addresses the withdrawal of Israeli forces from
Gaza and Jericho, a transfer of authority from the Israeli Civil Administration
to a Palestinian Authority, the structure and composition of the Palestinian
Authority and relations between Israel and the Palestinian Authority". See
"Agreement on the Gaza Strip and the Jericho Area (Cairo Agreement)," United
Nations Peacemaker, May 4, 1994, https://peacemaker.un.org/israelopt-cairoag-
reement94.
"[The Olso] agreement seeks to implement the Oslo I Agreement of 13
September 1993. It defines the security, electoral, public administration and
economic arrangements during the interim period of five years from the date of
the Agreement on the Gaza Strip and the Jericho Area of 4 May 1994 until per-
manent settlement in accordance with Security Council Resolution 242 and 338.
It also calls for Israeli-Palestinian cooperation and the release of Palestinian detainees." "Agreement on the Gaza Strip and the Jericho Area (Cairo Agreement),"
United Nations Peacemaker."Israeli-Palestinian Interim Agreement on the West
Bank and the Gaza Strip (Oslo II)," United Nations Peacemaker, September 28,
1995. https://peacemaker.un.org/israelopt-osloII95.

109. In July 1994 the Palestinian leader was allowed to return to the Gaza strip after
twenty-seven years in exile. *Yasser Arafat Arrives in Gaza* (1994: London: BBC
World Service), https://www.bbc.co.uk/programmes/p01bdmvm.

110. IMEU (Institute for Middle East Understanding), "Explainer: The Palestinian
Authority," July 2, 2021. https://imeu.org/article/fact-sheet-the-palestinian-au-
thority.

111. At the time of the signing of the Oslo Accords in 1993, there were approximately
128 settlements in the West Bank and 110,000 settlers. Thirty years later, there
are around 300 settlements and 465,000 settlers. See Peace Now, "30 Years after
Oslo," September 11, 2003, https://peacenow.org.il/en/30-years-after-oslo-the-
data-that-shows-how-the-settlements-proliferated-following-the-oslo-accords.

112. "Addameer and Al-Haq Address Israel's Torture of Palestinian Prisoners in a Joint Intervention at the Human Rights Council." *Al-Haq*, December 7, 2023. https://www.alhaq.org/advocacy/21351.html.
113. Qur'an, Surah al-Nisā', 4:135.
114. Qur'an, Surah al-Falaq, 113:1.
115. ālikhbārīt, smā. n.d. "*āljhād l-islāmī: sh-shīkh īāsīn trk irthan 'zīman jdīr bālāḥtrām wāltqdīr.*" sma l-ikhbārīt. https://tinyurl.com/36t6246c.
116. Ethan Bronner and Taghreed El-Khodary, "No Early End Seen to 'All-Out War' on Hamas in Gaza," *New York Times*, December 30, 2008, https://www.nytimes.com/2008/12/30/world/middleeast/30mideast.html.
117. In a hadith narrated by Ibn Umar (ra), our beloved Prophet said, "Teach your children swimming, archery and horse riding."
118. It is believed that Satia was a Pakistani ship—though other accounts claim that it was Greek—which was stranded off the Gaza coast for several days due to technical problems with its engine. Eventually the ship was caught in a storm and broke into two halves after it crashed into a large rock. Forty-seven sailors were rescued from Satia by the sheer efforts of Shati refugees, mostly fishermen. This event is believed to have taken place in 1973. See https://www.facebook.com/watch/?v=851697922917436.
119. Rantisi's family originated from the village of Rantis, northwest of Ramallah. "Abdel Aziz Al-Rantisi," All 4 Palestine, n.d., https://www.all4palestine.org/ModelDetails.aspx?gid=14&mid=78083&lang=en.
120. *Ṣaḥīfat al-Sabīl*. "Al-Awwal Marratan: Tafāṣīl Muḥāwalat Ightiyāl al-Shahīd ʿAbd al-ʿAzīz al-Rantīsī." April 16, 2022. https://tinyurl.com/zvm53jhj.
121. Adam Ali, "Palestinian Intifada: How Israel Orchestrated a Bloody Takeover," Al Jazeera English, September 28, 2020. https://www.aljazeera.com/news/2020/9/28/palestinian-intifada-20-years-later-israeli-occupation-continues.
122. OCHA, "The Humanitarian Impact of 20 Years of the Barrier – December 2022," December 30, 2022, https://www.ochaopt.org/content/humanitarian-impact-20-years-barrier-december-2022.
123. Tony Jones, "Hamas Leader Survives Assassination Attempt," ABC, June 10, 2003.
124. "Israel completed the removal of its military bases and Jewish settlements from the Gaza Strip. Many believe that with the implementation of the 'disengagement plan', Israel unburdened itself of Gaza and no longer bears responsibility for what happens there. The reality, however, is that Israel still controls many aspects of life in Gaza, and consequently the lives of Gaza's residents." Gisha, "The Illusion of Disengagement," September 12, 2019. https://gisha.org/en/the-illusion-of-disengagement/.
125. "Yasser Arafat 'May Have Been Poisoned with Polonium'," BBC, November 6, 2013. https://www.bbc.com/news/world-middle-east-24838061.
126. Btselem, "10 Years to the Second Intifada – Summary of Data," September 27, 2010. https://www.btselem.org/press_releases/20100927.
127. Yahya Sinwar, born in 1962 in Gaza, has been Hamas's leader in the Strip and a member of its Politburo since 2017. See "Yahya Sinwar." European Council for Foreign Relations (ECFR), n.d. https://ecfr.eu/special/mapping_palestinian_politics/yahya_sinwar/. Majdal Asqalan is a Palestinian village in Gaza district, depopulated during the Nakba, now part of Ashkelon in Israel.
128. Munaẓẓamat al-Jihād wa al-Daʿwah, which translates as "Organization for Jihad and Daʿwah (promotion of Islamic ideals)." See "Yahya Sinwar." Britannica, https://www.britannica.com/biography/Yahya-Sunwar.

129. See Peter Beaumont, "Election of New Hamas Gaza Strip Leader Increases Fears of Confrontation," *The Guardian*, February 13, 2017, https://www.theguardian.com/world/2017/feb/13/hamas-elects-hardliner-yahya-sinwar-as-its-gaza-strip-chief.

130. Mohamed Badereldin,"2000-2024: Timeline of Israeli Assassinations - World - Al-Ahram Weekly," Ahram Online, August 7, 2024, https://english.ahram.org.eg/NewsContentP/50/528690/AlAhram-Weekly/-Timeline-of-Israeli-assassinations-.aspx.

131. Salah Shehade was a Hamas member and Al-Qassam Brigades leader until he was assassinated by Israel on July 22, 2002. See "Shehade Was High on Israel Most-wanted List," CNN, July 23, 2002. https://edition.cnn.com/2002/WORLD/meast/07/23/shehade.profile/index.html.

    Emad Akel was a commander with the Al-Qassam Brigades, assassinated by Israel on November 24, 1993. See Robert Fisk, "Hamas mourns its greatest martyr," *Independent*, November 9, 1993.

    Mahmoud al-Mabhouh was the chief of logistics and weapons procurement for the Al-Qassam Brigades, who was assassinated by Mossad agents in Dubai on January 19, 2010. See Adrian Blomfield, "Ireland expels Israeli diplomat over Hamas assassination," *Telegraph*, June 15, 2010.

132. Israel carried out Operation Defensive Shield to dismantle the resistance infrastructure in the occupied West Bank. The focal point of the campaign was Jenin, where a ten-day battle in April 2002 killed dozens and destroyed hundreds of buildings. See "Jenin," Britannica, June 29, 2024. https://www.britannica.com/place/Jenin.

133. US Army General Keith Dayton commanded the Dayton Forces, a little-publicized American mission to build up security forces in the occupied West Bank that formally operated under the authority of the PA president Mahmoud Abbas. See Crisis Group, "Squaring the Circle: Palestinian Security Reform Under Occupation," September 7, 2010. http://www.crisisgroup.org/%7E/media/Files/Middle%20East%20North%20Africa/Israel%20Palestine/98%20Squaring%20the%20Circle%20—%20Palestinian%20Security%20Reform%20under%20Occupation.ashx.

134. Israel's Camp David proposal was widely publicized as a "generous offer" that Palestinians refused to accept. This was a self-serving myth. See Seth Ackerman, "The Myth of the Generous Offer." Fair.org, July 1, 2002, https://fair.org/home/the-myth-of-the-generous-offer/.

135. In April 2004, the-then Israeli Prime Minister Ariel Sharon directly threatened Yasser Arafat, saying he was "released from the pledge" of not harming him physically, and directly hinting he could be a target for assassination. See Conal Urquhart, "Sharon: 'We May Kill Arafat'," *The Guardian*, April 24, 2004, https://www.theguardian.com/world/2004/apr/24/israel.

136. "Yasser Arafat Dies in Paris Hospital," *The Guardian*, November 11, 2004, https://www.theguardian.com/world/2004/nov/11/israel.

137. After Lebanese Prime Minister Rafiq al-Hariri was assassinated in April 2005, Syria was forced to withdraw from Lebanon, making groups like Hezbollah, Hamas and Islamic Jihad, and, to an even greater extent, Iran more significant for its military and political strategy. See Hussein, "The Evolution of the Military Action."

138. See Ghaith al-Omari, "How the Palestinian Authority Failed Its People," *The Atlantic*, October 19, 2023.

139. See Democracy Now! "Jewish Settlers Receive Hundreds of Thousands in Compensation for Leaving Gaza," August 16, 2005.
140. See "Gaza Strip: Situation Report (7 June 2006) – OCHA report."
141. See IMEU, "Putting Palestinians "On a Diet": Israel'S Siege & Blockade of Gaza," n.d., https://imeu.org/article/putting-palestinians-on-a-diet-israels-siege-blockade-of-gaza.
142. Steve Niza, "Israel's 'Operation Mow the Lawn,'" Middle East Research and Information Project, December 7, 2012, https://merip.org/2012/12/israels-operation-mow-the-lawn/.
142. Hundreds of Hamas cadres received military training in Iran. "Al-Qassam Brigades: How Hamas Established Its Army in Gaza," *AlMuntaqa* 4, no. 1 (2021): 78–97, https://www.jstor.org/stable/10.31430/almuntaqa.4.1.0078, 15.
144. The "Gaza Envelope" includes settlements in Israel's southern district within seven kilometers (4.3 miles) of the Gaza Strip border. See Zeev Drory, Eyal Lewin, and Eyal Ben-Ari, "Kibbutz under Fire: Back to the Days of Sickle and Bayonet," *Israel Studies* 22, no. 2 (2017): 121–44.
145. See Hussein, "The Evolution of the Military Action."
146. Diwani script is a cursive style of Arabic calligraphy developed in the reign of the early Ottoman Turks. See "Dīwānī Script," Britannica, February 21, 2016, https://www.britannica.com/art/diwani-script.
147. The Omari Mosque—the Great Mosque of Gaza— was the largest mosque in the Strip before it was destroyed by Israel in 2023. See Rebecca Kulik, "Great Mosque of Gaza," Britannica, May 21, 2024, https://www.britannica.com/topic/Great-Mosque-of-Gaza.
148. Gilad Shalit is an Israeli soldier who was captured by Palestinian Resistance groups in Gaza, and who was held as a prisoner from 2006 to 2011. On October 18, 2011 he was released, under an agreement with Israel, in exchange for the release of more than 1,000 Palestinian prisoners. See "Gilad Shalit," Britannica, May 31, 2024, https://www.britannica.com/biography/Gilad-Shalit.
149. Of the 132 parliamentary seats, Hamas won seventy-six and Fatah forty-three. "Hamas Wins Huge Majority," *Al Jazeera English*, January 26, 2006, https://www.aljazeera.com/news/2006/1/26/hamas-wins-huge-majority.
150. A brief Fatah–Hamas civil war broke out in the Gaza Strip in June 10–15, 2007. See "Hamas Controls Gaza, Says It Will Stay in Power," CNN, June 14, 2007.
151. ʿĀmir ibn ʿAbd Allāh ibn al-Jarrāḥ, better known as Abu Obeida, was a Muslim commander and one of the Companions of the Prophet.
152. The Almohads, or al-Muwahhidun, was a Berber confederation that created an Islamic empire in North Africa and Spain, which was founded on the basis of the twelfth century religious teachings of Ibn Tumart. See "Almohads," Britannica, https://www.britannica.com/topic/Almohads.
153. Haddad, G. F. "Imam Shafi'i". spa.qibla.com.
154. "After twenty-two days of unrelenting aerial attacks and intensive ground incursions, 1,400 Palestinians had been killed, the majority civilians, including women and children. wounded." See "Operation Cast Lead and the Distortion of International Law," Al-Haq, n.d., https://www.alhaq.org/publications/8178.html.
155. In 2009, Judge Richard Goldstone, a South African Jewish jurist, agreed to head a mission to produce a UN fact-finding report on the 2008–09 war. After being vilified by Zionist lobbies, he retracted his report and said that the initial finding that Israel intentionally targeted civilians was wrong. See Conal Urquhart, "The Goldstone Report: A History," *The Guardian*, November 26, 2017, https://www.theguardian.com/world/2011/apr/14/goldstone-report-history.

156. Arrian of Nicomedia, *The Anabasis of Alexander*, trans. E. J. Chinnock (1884), Book 3, Chapter 26, https://www.gutenberg.org/ebooks/46976.

157. Ibid.

158. Due to the legendary steadfastness of the Gazans, the Romans decided to destroy the city following its fall in 103 BC. ālnāṣr, aḥmd ṭlb, *"ghzt.. l 'nt l-mkān ū 'qdt tārīkh s-sāst ūqwāfl l-'skr | tlfzīūn sūriā." tlfzīūn sūriā,"* May 9, 2023, https://tinyurl.com/bpa2r8tu.
Medievalists.net, "The Crusaders and Gaza," March 30, 2024, https://www.medievalists.net/2024/03/crusaders-gaza/.
"From Alexander to Napoleon, Gaza's Cycles of Death, Destruction and Revival," Economic Times, October 22, 2023, https://economictimes.indiatimes.com/news/international/world-news/from-alexander-to-napoleon-gazas-cycles-of-death-destruction-and-revival/articleshow/104623007.cms?from=mdr.

159. In 2006, the Hamas leader Ismail Haniyeh claimed his group had created twice the number of tunnels created by Vietnamese 'national liberation' forces in the Vietnam war. The 'Cu Chi' tunnels were seventy-five miles (around 121 km) long. See Rami Amichay and Nidal Al-Mughrabi, "Israelis Near Gaza Fear Hamas Is Tunnelling Beneath Them," Reuters, February 1, 2016, https://www.reuters.com/article/world/israelis-near-gaza-fear-hamas-is-tunnelling-beneath-them-idUSKCN0VA30V.

160. In March 1982, following the peace treaty between Israel and Egypt, Rafah was divided by a barbed-wire fence. Janet Hawley, "From the Archives, 1982: Rafah, a Town Divided," *The Sydney Morning Herald*, March 23, 2022, https://www.smh.com.au/world/middle-east/from-the-archives-1982-rafah-a-town-divided-20220111-p59nic.html.

161. In 2008, Israel allocated $23 million to training Egyptian officials, with the aim of stopping tunnel smuggling into Gaza. See Associated Press, "U.S.-Funded Program Fails to Stop Gaza Tunnels," *NBC News*, January 7, 2009, https://www.nbcnews.com/id/wbna28546053.

162. See UNCTAD, Report on Palestinian Assistance to the Palestinian People: Developments in the Economy of the Occupied Palestinian Territory (Geneva, n.d.), https://unctad.org/system/files/official-document/tdb62d3_en.pdf.

163. David Kirkpatrick, Anthony Shadid, and Alan Cowell, "Mubarak Steps Down, Ceding Power to Military," *New York Times*, February 11, 2011.164. "And He sent against them birds, in flocks. Striking them with stones of Sijjil (baked clay). And made them like an empty field of stalks (of which the corn has been eaten up by cattle." Qur'an, Surah Al-Fil 105:1-5.
Israel's "Operation Pillar of Defense" attack on the Gaza Strip last year killed 173 Palestinians and injured at least 1,221. See Al-Haq, "Voices from the Gaza Strip: A Year after Operation 'Pillar of Defense,'" n.d., https://www.alhaq.org/monitoring-documentation/6700.html.

165. During Israel's "Operation Pillar of Defense", on the Gaza Strip last year, 173 Palestinians were killed and at least 1,221 were injured. Ibid.

166. See Ban Ki-moon, UN Secretary-General, "Secretary-General's Remarks to the Security Council [as delivered]," November 21, 2012.

167. Yaakov Lappin, "Seven More IDF Soldiers and Officers Killed in Clashes With Hamas," *Jerusalem Post*, July 21, 2014, https://www.jpost.com/Operation-Protective-Edge/Four-IDF-soldiers-killed-by-terrorist-squad-that-infiltrated-Israel-from-Gaza-368343#google_vignette.

168. UNRWA, "2014 Gaza Conflict," n.d., https://www.unrwa.org/2014-gaza-conflict.

169. Interactive Encyclopedia of the Palestine Question, "The 2014 Gaza War," n.d., https://www.palquest.org/en/highlight/30097/2014-gaza-war.

170. The term the "Eaten Straw" is a direct reference to a formative event in Islamic history mentioned in the Quran, in a short chapter called Al-Fil, or The Elephant. The translation of the chapter is as follows: "Have you not considered, [O Muhammad], how your Lord dealt with the companions of the elephant? Did He not make their plan into misguidance? And He sent against them birds in flocks, Striking them with stones of hard clay, And He made them like eaten straw." Qur'an, Surah Al-Fil (105:1–5).

171. Interactive Encyclopedia of the Palestine Question, "The 2014 Gaza War," n.d., https://www.palquest.org/en/highlight/30097/2014-gaza-war.

172. Shujaiya, one of Gaza City's largest and most densely populated neighborhoods, had a population of 110,000 before Israel's 2023 war. In the east of the city, it is divided into a southern (Turkman) and northern (Jdeidah), with the latter being built in the twelfth century (Ayyubaid era). "Sons of Salah Al-Din: Shuja'iyya is Not Just a Neighbourhood, It's a Legacy," *Middle East Monitor*, December 14, 2023, https://www.middleeastmonitor.com/20231214-sons-of-salah-al-din-shujaiyya-is-not-just-a-neighbourhood-its-a-legacy//.

173. Interactive Encyclopedia of the Palestine Question, "The 2014 Gaza War," n.d., https://www.palquest.org/en/highlight/30097/2014-gaza-war.

174. Ibid.

175. Ibid.

176. "Senior US officers who had access to the 21 July Pentagon summary of Israeli operations were reportedly stunned to learn that eleven Israeli artillery battalions—a minimum of 258 artillery pieces—pumped at least 7,000 high-explosive shells into the Gaza neighborhood." Palquest, 'The 2014 Gaza War.'

177. Ibid.

178. Abeer Salman et al., "At Least 90 Palestinians Reported Killed in Israeli Strike Targeting Hamas Military Chief," *CNN*, July 15, 2024, https://edition.cnn.com/2024/07/13/middleeast/mawasi-deif-israel-hamas-gaza-intl/index.html.

179. "Who is Mohammed Deif, The Hamas Military Commander in Gaza?" *Al Jazeera*, July 14, 2024, https://www.aljazeera.com/news/2024/7/14/who-is-mohammed-deif-the-hamas-military-commander-in-gaza.

180. Ismail Mohammed Bakr (9), Zakaria Ahed Bakr (10), Ahed Atef Bakr (10), and Mohamed Ramez Bakr (11), were killed by Israeli naval fire on July 16, 2014 when playing on a beach. Robert Mackey, "Secret Israeli Report Reveals Armed Drone Killed Four Boys Playing on Gaza Beach in 2014." *The Intercept*, May 10, 2019, https://theintercept.com/2018/08/11/israel-palestine-drone-strike-operation-protective-edge/.

181. Palquest, "The 2014 Gaza War."

182. "Hudna is Hamas's offer of a long-term ceasefire with Israel. On close examination, the purpose and details of Hamas's hudna do not appear to differ substantially from the political positions of the PLO during the Camp David talks in 2000." Dag Henrik Tuastad, *The Hudna: Hamas's Concept of a Long-Term Ceasefire*, PRIO Policy Brief no. 9 (Oslo: PRIO, 2010).

183. Palquest, "The 2014 Gaza War."

184. "Israel Used 'Calorie Count' to Limit Gaza Food during Blockade, Critics Claim." *The Guardian*, October 17, 2012, https://www.theguardian.com/world/2012/oct/17/israeli-military-calorie-limit-gaza.

185. Ilan Pappé, *The Biggest Prison on Earth* (Oxford: Oneworld Publications, 2019).

186. OCHA. "Two Years On: People Injured and Traumatized During the 'Great March of Return' are Still Struggling", OCHA, 6 April 2020. https://www.un.org/unispal/document/two-years-on-people-injured-and-traumatized-during-the-great-march-of-return-are-still-struggling/.

187. Pietro Stefanini, "Militant Kites and Balloons: Anti-Colonial Resistance in Palestine's Great March of Return," *Partecipazione & Conflitto* 14, no. 2 (2021): 663–80, https://doi.org/10.1285/i20356609v14i2p6633.

188. A total of twenty-five Palestinians were killed and at least 154 wounded in Israeli airstrikes on Gaza between May 3–6, 2019. "Gaza Quiet After Israel, Hamas Agree to Cease-Fire." Associated Press, May 6, 2019, https://apnews.com/article/a22be-23bead74a34abbfba4661bd6f67.

The Unity Intifada of May 2021 was an eleven-day military offensive on the blockaded Gaza Strip that killed at least 260 and wounded more than 1,900. Maram Humaid, "In Gaza, Young Victims of Israeli Bombing Recount a Brutal 2021," *Al Jazeera*, December 31, 2021, https://www.aljazeera.com/news/2021/12/31/palestine-gaza-young-victims-israel-bombardment-may.

Between August 5–7, 2022, Israel launched at least 147 airstrikes on Gaza before Egypt mediated a deal, ending an Israel–Islamic Jihad war that killed forty-four Gazans. Gwen Ackerman and Saud Abu Ramadan, "Egypt Mediates Truce to End Israel-Islamic Jihad Fighting," Bloomberg, August 7, 2022.

189. Al-Jazeera, "Israeli Forces Raid Al-Aqsa Mosque, Over 40 Palestinians Injured." Al Jazeera, April 29, 2022. https://www.aljazeera.com/news/2022/4/29/dozens-injured-in-israeli-raid-on-al-aqsa-mosque-compound

190. In 2020, several Arab countries, including Bahrain, UAE and Morocco, signed bilateral normalization agreements with Israel. Adam Zeidan. "Abraham Accords." Encyclopedia Britannica, July 15, 2024. https://www.britannica.com/topic/Abraham-Accords.

191. Ilan Pappé, *The Biggest Prison on Earth* (Oxford: Oneworld Publications, 2019).

192. Al-Ribat College, formerly known as the police college, is a Palestinian educational institution located in Gaza City. It was established in 2009, with the mission of training the needed cadres for the ministries of interior and national security. Graduates from the college are slated to serve as officers. The college grants students a bachelor's degree in law, police science, and navy science.

193. "Israel's 169,500 active-duty personnel—maintained through conscription—have been boosted by 360,000 reserves. Hamas, on the other hand, is thought to have up to 40,000 fighters, although the exact strength and the composition of these forces is unclear. [...] The IDF is supported by a military budget of around $23.4 billion. Hamas is heavily dependent on foreign funding, and the extent of its military budget is not clear. The Times of Israel reported in 2016 that the group spent around $100 million on military infrastructure annually." David Brennan, "How Does Israel's Military Compare to Hamas Forces?," *Newsweek*, October 12, 2023, https://www.newsweek.com/how-israel-military-idf-compare-hamas-forces-gaza-strip-palestinians-offensive-1834142.

194. "What Happened in Israel? A Breakdown of How Hamas Attack Unfolded," *Al Jazeera*, October 9, 2023. https://www.aljazeera.com/news/2023/10/7/what-happened-in-israel-a-breakdown-of-how-the-hamas-attack-unfolded.

195. Several investigations have debunked Israeli claims about decapitated baby and mass rapes. See Assma Maad, William Audureau, and Samuel Forey, "'40 Beheaded Babies': Deconstructing the Rumor at the Heart of the Information Battle between Israel and Hamas," *Le Monde*, April 3, 2024, https://www.lemonde.fr/en/les-decodeurs/article/2024/04/03/40-beheaded-babies-the-itinerary-of-a-rumor-

at-the-heart-of-the-information-battle-between-israel-and-hamas_6667274_8. html.

196. Hamas Media Office, Our Narrative … Operation Al-Aqsa Flood, January 2024, https://archive.org/details/our-narrative-operation-al-aqsa-flood-web_202401/ mode/1up.

197. The reliability of Israel's anti-missile system Iron Dome has been repeatedly questioned, including by the prominent US scientist Theodore Postal, who rose to fame after the 1991 Gulf War by disputing the reliability of the US Patriot anti-missile system. He claims the Iron Dome is "even less reliable." Hiawatha Bray, "Israel's Iron Dome System Doesn't Work, Says Missile Defense Critic," *Boston Globe*, October 13, 2023. https://tinyurl.com/5fwu6kp9

198. Mohammed Deif declared in a televised speech on the morning of October 7 that the 'Al-Aqsa Flood Battle' had begun: "'We have decided to put an end to all of the occupation's crimes. The time is over for them (Israel) to (continue to) act without accountability. Thus, we announce the 'Al-Aqsa Flood' operation, and in the first strike within 20 minutes, more than 5,000 rockets were launched." [...] "'The era of (losing) bets has ended, and the occupation must be expelled." "'Today, the People Claim their Revolution': This is What Al-Qassam Commander Said in His Speech," *Palestine Chronicle*, October 7, 2023, https://www.palestinechronicle.com/today-the-people-claim-their-revolution-this-is-what-al-qassam-commander-said-in-his-speech/.

199. United Nations Economic and Social Commission for Western Asia (UN-ESCWA), The War on Gaza: 21st Century's Deadliest 100 Days (Beirut: UN-ESCWA, January 17, 2024), https://www.unescwa.org/news/escwa-war-gaza-21st-centurys-deadliest-100-days.

200. "Israel Announces 'Total' Blockade on Gaza," *Al Jazeera*, October 9, 2023, https://www.aljazeera.com/news/2023/10/9/israel-announces-total-blockade-on-gaza.

201. Emanuel Fabian, "Defense Minister Announces 'Complete Siege' of Gaza: No Power, Food or Fuel," *Times of Israel*, October 9, 2023, https://www.timesofisrael.com/liveblog_entry/defense-minister-announces-complete-siege-of-gaza-no-power-food-or-fuel/.

202. John Grady, "U.S. Carrier Moves to Mediterranean, Middle East Aim to Contain Conflict," USNI News, October 24, 2023, https://news.usni.org/2023/10/24/u-s-carrier-moves-to-mediterranean-middle-east-aim-to-contain-conflict-says-pentagon-official.

203. Humeyra Pamuk and Mike Stone, "US Has Sent Israel Thousands of 2,000-Pound Bombs since Oct. 7," Reuters, June 29, 2024, https://www.reuters.com/world/us-has-sent-israel-thousands-2000-pound-bombs-since-oct-7-2024-06-28/.

204. "The Mark 84 is a 2,000-pound (900 kg) US heavy unguided bomb that can create a crater 50 feet (15 m) wide and 36 ft (11 m) deep. Its development was kept under wraps for 14 years, but by 1991, the F-117 nighthawk had become a household word." Don Holloway, "Stealth Secrets of the F-117 Nighthawk," *Aviation History*, March 1996.

205. "Israel Has Destroyed 1,000 Mosques in Gaza since 7 October," New Arab, n.d., https://www.newarab.com/news/israel-has-destroyed-1000-mosques-gaza-7-october.

By May 9, Israel had destroyed at least three churches in Gaza. On 16 December, 2023, two Palestinian Christians, Nahida Anton and her daughter Samar Anton, were shot and killed by Israeli soldiers while walking inside the grounds of the Holy Family Church. Kiara Alfonseca, Kerem Inal, and Chris Looft, "Destruction in Gaza: Side-by-Side Aerial Look at the Israel–Hamas War's Devastating Damage," ABC News, May 9, 2024, https://abcnews.go.com/International/destruction-gaza-side-side-israel-hamas-wars-damage/story?id=1099584588.

206. By July 25, the Israeli military viewed eighty-three percent of the Gaza Strip as "unsafe" for Palestinian civilians. This also applied to areas not subject to evacuation orders, with the Israeli army launching several attacks on 'safe' areas soon after issuing "temporary" evacuation orders. "How Israel is shrinking Gaza's 'safe zones,'" *Al Jazeera*, July 25, 2024. https://www.aljazeera.com/news/2024/7/25/how-israel-is-shrinking-gazas-safe-zones.

207. "On 17 October 2023, a devastating explosion took place in the car park of the al-Ahli Hospital in Gaza City. The Gaza Health Ministry reported that 471 people were killed and 342 injured, with US intelligence agencies estimating between 100 and 300 casualties." Forensic Architecture, "Israeli disinformation: Al-Ahli Hospital," n.d., https://forensic-architecture.org/investigation/israeli-disinformation-al-ahli-hospital.

208. Pierre Emmanuel Ngendakumana, "Biden on Gaza Hospital Strike: Looks Like the 'Other Team' Did It," Politico, October 19, 2023, https://www.politico.eu/article/us-biden-on-gaza-hospital-strike-the-other-team-did-it/.

209. US President Joe Biden and US Secretary of State Antony Blinken visited Israel repeatedly. Other Western leaders also flocked to show their support including former British Prime Minister Rishi Sunak, French President Emmanuel Macron, Italian Prime Minister Giorgia Meloni, Canadian Foreign Minister Mélanie Jolie, German President Olaf Scholz, German Foreign Minister Annalena Baerbock, Dutch President Dick Schoof, and the EU leaders Ursula Von Der Leyen and Josep Borrell. "Israel–Hamas War Updates: Israel Reports Failed Incursion Near Gaza," *Wall Street Journal*, November 14, 2023, https://www.wsj.com/live-coverage/israel-hamas-war-news-gaza-palestinians/card/dignitaries-visits-to-israel-JbqAlbSX8QTXQppPewlV.

210. Warren Strobel and Nancy Youssef, "U.S. and Israel's 'Unprecedented' Intelligence Sharing Draws Criticism," *Wall Street Journal*, March 31, 2024, https://www.wsj.com/politics/national-security/u-s-and-israels-unprecedented-intelligence-sharing-draws-criticism-a85979b4.

211. Euro-Med Human Rights Monitor, "Israel Hits Gaza Strip with the Equivalent of Two Nuclear Bombs," November 2, 2023, https://euromedmonitor.org/en/article/5908/Israel-hits-Gaza-Strip-with-the-equivalent-of-two-nuclear-bombs.

212. "Thousands of Palestinians fled northern Gaza on Wednesday, traveling miles on foot through the battered enclave in a growing exodus as Israel intensifies its ground and air campaign." Abeer Salman, "'Nothing is left': Thousands of Palestinians flee south as Israel steps up Gaza City offensive," CNN, November 9, 2023, https://edition.cnn.com/2023/11/08/world/palestinians-fleeing-south-gaza-city-unbearable-situation/index.html.

213. Katie Polglase et al., "How Gaza's Hospitals Became Battlegrounds," CNN, January 12, 2024, https://edition.cnn.com/interactive/2024/01/middleeast/gaza-hospitals-destruction-investigation-intl-cmd/.

214. Nadeen Ebrahim et al., "Why Israeli Forces Are Raiding Gaza's Al-Shifa Hospital—Again," CNN, March 28, 2024, https://edition.cnn.com/2024/03/28/middleeast/gaza-shifa-hospital-raid-israel-war-explainer-intl/index.html.

215. "Prior to their capture of Dar al-Shifa hospital, the Israel Defense Forces went to great lengths to depict the medical complex as a headquarters for Hamas, from where its attacks on Israel were planned. The evidence produced so far falls well short of that." Julian Borger, "IDF Evidence So Far Falls Well Short of Al-Shifa

Hospital Being Hamas HQ," *The Guardian*, November 18, 2023, https://www.theguardian.com/world/2023/nov/17/idf-evidence-so-far-falls-well-short-of-al-shifa-hospital-being-hamas-hq.

216. "Israel acknowledged [...] that one of its ministries drafted a wartime proposal to transfer the Gaza Strip's 2.3 million people to Egypt's Sinai Peninsula, drawing condemnation from the Palestinians and worsening tensions with Cairo." "Intelligence Ministry 'Concept Paper' Proposes Transferring Gazans to Egypt's Sinai," *Times of Israel*, October 31, 2023, https://www.timesofisrael.com/intelligence-ministry-concept-paper-proposes-transferring-gazans-to-egypts-sinai/.

217. "Israel minister reprimanded over Gaza nuclear 'option' comment," *Le Monde* with AFP, November 5, 2023, https://www.lemonde.fr/en/international/article/2023/11/05/israel-minister-reprimanded-over-gaza-nuclear-option-comment_6229042_4.html.

218. The Rafah Crossing, the only way out of Gaza, was seized and closed by Israel in early May. Aaron Boxerman, "A Border Crossing Shuttered for Months Traps the Sick and Wounded in Gaza," *New York Times*, July 19, 2024, https://www.nytimes.com/2024/07/19/world/middleeast/rafah-palestinians-gaza-trapped.html.

219. United Nations, "*Genocide as Colonial Erasure – Report of Francesca Albanese, the UN Special Rapporteur on the Situation of Human Rights in the Palestinian Territories Occupied Since 1967*," October 1, 2024, www.un.org/unispal/document/genocide-as-colonial-erasure-report-francesca-albanese-01oct24/.

220. Aya Batrawy, "Survivors Recount Horrors of Israeli Siege on Gaza's Al-Shifa Hospital," NPR, April 2, 2024, https://www.npr.org/2024/04/02/1242328514/survivors-recount-horrors-of-israeli-siege-on-gazas-al-shifa-hospital.

221. "Palestinian Testimonies of Israeli 'Executions' at Al-Shifa Hospital," *Al Jazeera*, n.d., https://www.aljazeera.com/program/newsfeed/2024/3/25/palestinian-testimonies-of-israeli-executions-at-al-shifa-hospital.

222. United Nations Copenhagen, "Mass Graves in Gaza Show Victims' Hands Were Tied, Says UN Rights Office," April 23, 2024, https://un.dk/mass-graves-in-gaza-show-victims-hands-were-tied-says-un-rights-office/
   Muhammad Salmiya, "Stop the Gaza Genocide Immediately," The Lancet 403, 10441 (2024): 2286–2287, https://doi.org/10.1016/s0140-6736(24)00135-1

223. UN City Copenhagen, "Mass Graves in Gaza Show Victims' Hands Were Tied, Says UN Rights Office," UN, 23 April, 2024, https://un.dk/mass-graves-in-gaza-show-victims-hands-were-tied-says-un-rights-office/
   Muhammad Salmiya, "Stop the Gaza Genocide Immediately," *The Lancet* 403, no. 10441 (2024): 2286–87, https://doi.org/10.1016/s0140-6736(24)00135-1.

224. United Nations Human Rights Office. 2024. "Mass Graves in Gaza Show Victims' Hands Were Tied, Says UN Rights Office." UN Human Rights Office, April 23, 2024. https://un.dk/mass-graves-in-gaza-show-victims-hands-were-tied-says-un-rights-office/

225. United Nations, "*Genocide as Colonial Erasure – Report of Francesca Albanese, the UN Special Rapporteur on the Situation of Human Rights in the Palestinian Territories Occupied Since 1967*," October 1, 2024, www.un.org/unispal/document/genocide-as-colonial-erasure-report-francesca-albanese-01oct24/.

226. Muhammad Salmiya, "Stop the Gaza Genocide Immediately," *The Lancet* 403, no. 10441 (2024): 2286–87, https://doi.org/10.1016/s0140-6736(24)00135-1.
   International Criminal Court, Office of the Prosecutor, "Statement of ICC Prosecutor Karim A.A. Khan KC," May 20, 2024, https://www.icc-cpi.int/news/statement-icc-prosecutor-karim-aa-khan-kc-applications-arrest-warrants-situation-state.

227. *Qur'an*, Surah Al-Baqarah, 154.
228. *Qur'an*, Surah Luqman, 34.
229. "The Nakba of 1948 and today's Nakba in Gaza are not two separate events, the Chair of the United Nations Palestinian Rights Committee told a special event at UN Headquarters in New York today, stressing the need for an immediate ceasefire in the Strip and to achieve Statehood for Palestinians." United Nations, "Nakba of 1948 and Today Are Not Separate Events, But Ongoing Process of Palestinian Displacement, Replacement, Speakers Tell Panel, Urging Immediate Ceasefire in Gaza," May 17, 2024, https://press.un.org/en/2024/gapal1467.doc.htm.

   According to the UN, forty million tons of rubble covered Gaza on in mid-July 2024. Jason Burke, "Clearing Gaza of Almost 40m Tonnes of War Rubble Will Take Years, Says UN," *The Guardian*, July 15, 2024, https://www.theguardian.com/world/article/2024/jul/15/clearing-gaza-of-almost-40m-tonnes-of-war-rubble-will-take-years-says-un.
230. A Palestinian improvised anti-tank missile, named after the quadriplegic sheikh. "Origins of the Yasin 105, the Missile Destroying Israeli Tanks," *Jordan News*, November 5, 2023, https://www.jordannews.jo/Section-20/Middle-East/Origins-of-the-Yasin-105-the-missile-destroying-Israeli-tanks-32075.
231. According to a report by Euromed Monitor, "between 11 January and 23 March 2024, 256 people were killed in the Kuwait Roundabout area, in the southeast of Gaza City, 230 on Al-Rashid Street, in the southwest of the city, and 21 due to the targeting of aid distribution centers." Euro-Med Human Rights Monitor, "New Report: Killing Starving Palestinians, Targeting Aid Trucks Is a Deliberate Israeli Policy to Reinforce Famine in the Gaza Strip," April 3, 2024, https://euromed-monitor.org/en/article/6259/New-Report:-Killing-Starving-Palestinians,-Targeting-Aid-Trucks-is-a-Deliberate-Israeli-Policy-to-Reinforce-Famine-in-The-Gaza-Strip.
232. Rabiul Islam, "Scores Killed as Israel Bombs Al Mawasi 'Safe Zone' in Southern Gaza," *TRT World*, July 13, 2024, https://www.trtworld.com/middle-east/scores-killed-as-israel-bombs-al-mawasi-safe-zone-in-southern-gaza-18183425.
233. "Dozens of Palestinians Starved to Death under Israel's Blockade of Gaza," *Al Jazeera*, May 3, 2025, https://www.aljazeera.com/news/2025/5/3/57-palestinians-starved-to-death-under-israels-blockade-of-gaza.

Index

Abbas, Mahmoud, 148–49
Abbas Mosque, Sheikh Ahmed teachings on jihad, 102
Abdularahman. *See* al-Badrasawi, Abdularahman
Abdullah bin Omar Mosque, Diwani script on walls of, 152
Abdulnabi, Madallah
  Abdallah love of, 69–73
  Abdallah resentment for infertility of, 71–72
  Beit Daras massacre reaction, 54
  camping outside Saraya prison, 144–45
  death of, 150
  death of Mohammed reaction, 49–50
  dreams of, 18–19
  focus on her children, 144
  gift of transcending sphere of existence, 10
  Ibrahim infant born to, 73
  injuries during home raids, 145
  Jinn and companion of, 13–14, 20, 27–28, 69
  Mohammed kiss after death of, 49–50
  Mohammed prayers over, 20
  parents spoiling of, 16
Abdulnabi, Mahasin, 14–15
  anxiety and ailing health of, 27, 54–55
  death of children of, 10–11
  fleeing Beit Daras massacre, 53–55
Abdulnabi, Mohammed, 1, 27
  constant prayers of, 25–26
  Madallah kiss after death by, 49–50
  murder of, 29, 48
  as Qassamite rebel, 43, 44
  as true man of God embodiment, 25
  Zionists on agitator of, 46
Abdulnabi, Sumiya, 10–11
Abdulnabi family
  baraka of members, 9
  in Beit Daras community, 24
  from Idris bloodline, 24
  as members of *ashraf*, 25
Abu Shanab, Latifa, 243n38
  jihad dedication by, 51, 53
AFSC. *See* American Friends Service Committee
Ahl Al Bayt, 24–28
Al-Ahli Baptist Hospital massacre (October 17, 2023), 193, 223, 258n207
Ain Jalut battle, in southeastern Galilee in 1260, 211
Ain Jalut Brigades, 74
Akel, Emad, 145, 251n131

Alareer, Refaat, 224
Alexander the Great, Gaza conquered in 332 BCE by, 3, 162, 210
Allenby, Edmund, 212
American Friends Service Committee (AFSC), refugee camps set up by, 244n42
Amnesty International, on Israel genocide in Gaza, 234
Ansarallah group, Yemen, 224, 225
  attack on USS *Harry S. Truman*, 235, 237
  missile strike at Tel Aviv, 237
Apartheid Wall (June 23, 2002), of Palestine, 217
Al-Aqsa Flood (October 7, 2023) genocidal war, 5–6, 181, 183–85, 195–204, 220, 258n206. *See also* New Nakba, after Al-Aqsa Flood; war and genocide timeline
  al-Deif speech on, 189–90, 221, 257n198
  Ehab and Abdulrahman joining, 186
  Eretz Crossing attacked, 187
  Gallant on complete siege on Gaza, 192
  Gaza Envelope assault, 187
  Israel and US response to, 192–93
  Israeli hostages taken, 189
  Israel second phase ground invasion of October 27, 2023, 194
  Israel theory of military deterrence shattered by, 188
  November 24, 2023 temporary truce, 205
  ordinary Gazans joining operation of, 188
  Palestinians infiltration of Israel, 187
  Palestinians on offensive during, 187
  past, present and fate, 186–94
Al-Aqsa Mosque, Hamas 11-day war after April 2022 attack on, 179
Arab League
  countries joining Beit Daras battle, 52
  PLA establishment decision by, 74
  PNC, PLA, PLO established January-June 1964, 215
Arafat, Yasser, 214, 216
  arrival in July 1994, 122
  death of, 137, 217
  Hamas leaders arrested by, 124
  phased liberation and, 123
  Sharon direct threat to, 252n135
Al-Arish, Egyptian
  Israeli military occupation of, 83
  refugee camp removal to, 83, 246n70

259